Automotive Management

by
Jens Diehlmann
Ernst & Young Europe

Prof. Dr. Dr. Joachim Häcker
German Institute of Corporate Finance

2nd edition

Translation by
Prof. Dr. Mathias Moersch

Oldenbourg Verlag München

Bibliografische Information der Deutschen Nationalbibliothek

Die Deutsche Nationalbibliothek verzeichnet diese Publikation in der Deutschen
Nationalbibliografie; detaillierte bibliografische Daten sind im Internet über
http://dnb.d-nb.de abrufbar.

© 2013 Oldenbourg Wissenschaftsverlag GmbH
Rosenheimer Straße 143, D-81671 München
Telefon: (089) 45051-0
www.oldenbourg-verlag.de

Das Werk einschließlich aller Abbildungen ist urheberrechtlich geschützt. Jede Verwertung
außerhalb der Grenzen des Urheberrechtsgesetzes ist ohne Zustimmung des Verlages unzulässig
und strafbar. Das gilt insbesondere für Vervielfältigungen, Übersetzungen, Mikroverfilmungen
und die Einspeicherung und Bearbeitung in elektronischen Systemen.

Lektorat: Christiane Engel-Haas, M.A.
Herstellung: Tina Bonertz
Titelbild: Joachim Häcker
Einbandgestaltung: hauser lacour
Gesamtherstellung: Beltz Bad Langensalza GmbH, Bad Langensalza

Dieses Papier ist alterungsbeständig nach DIN/ISO 9706.

ISBN 978-3-11-048930-9
eISBN 978-3-486-73616-8

Preface

What is the current state of the automotive location Germany today, 125 years after the automobile was invented here and three years after the major crisis of 2009? What are the perspectives for German companies in a globalized world, characterized by high volatility, technological breakthroughs and the increasing scarcity of resources?

In a global comparison, the current positioning of the German automotive industry is as strong as it has rarely been before. Especially the past crisis has clearly demonstrated that the local companies are global leaders with regard to innovative power and flexibility – this is true both for products and processes. Quality and innovative strength, coupled with the force of strong and globally present brands (see Chapter 2); that is the current meaning of "Made in Germany." And apparently it is once again the premium segment which holds the key to sustainable success in the German automotive industry. Germany, respectively "Made in Germany" in itself can already be considered a premium brand. And experience shows that the buyers of automobiles all over the world are willing to pay appropriate prices for premium products (see Chapter 10).

But the enjoyment that comes with the exceptionally favorable business development witnessed by the German automotive industry in the years 2010 and 2011 should not mask the fact that the industry is facing major, if not monumental challenges in the years ahead – this is true for technological developments as well as for the self-image and business model of the industry.

For one thing, there is a clear trend towards electromobility, which is analyzed in detail in Chapter 4 of this book. This trend poses enormous technological challenges and is nothing less than an invitation to partially reinvent the automobile. Significant investments will become necessary and nobody can tell for certain where the journey will take us – whether and when these investments will be amortized. And even if the German automotive manufacturers have turned their full attention to the topic of electronic mobility with a slight delay, they are the global leaders when it comes to the development of alternative mobility concepts (see Chapter 7).

Closely linked to this topic is the transformation of the business model, away from the pure manufacturer of automobiles and towards a provider of mobility services more broadly. Here the companies suddenly compete with powerful companies from other industries – telecommunications, utilities or information technology – and at the same time are required to enter into new types of partnerships and strategic alliances (see Chapter 3). "Networked mobility" challenges the companies to newly define their role, without losing sight of their core competencies in the field of automotive technology. Establishing these new business fields and models could decisively change the face of the industry in the medium term. Particularly the automotive location Germany is characterized by a unique network of manufacturers, suppliers and researchers. When moving from the position of globally leading premium manufacturer towards supplier of premium mobility services, new forms of cooperation – including an open exchange of knowledge – are absolutely necessary.

Decisive for the changes is also the transformation of the needs of young consumers and their changed attitude towards the automobile: they want to remain mobile and will continue to use a vehicle. But that does not mean they also want to own it – they can also lease, rent or share it. What does that mean for the future of the automobile manufacturers? Will they lose their (brand-)loyal customers? Who "owns" the automobile customer of the future? Will the automobile manufacturers continue to dominate or will service and technology companies from other industries conquer some of that territory?

On balance, the financial and economic crisis has strengthened the automotive location Germany like no other location in this world. The topic of "finance" increasingly requires attention and the German automotive industry is well positioned in this regard. Be it in the field of financial services for the automobile (see Chapter 6), strategic currency management (see Chapter 8) or concerning a meaningful interpretation of the overarching goal of shareholder value (see Chapter 9).

What will be the positioning of the automotive location Germany in the year 2020 (see Chapter 10)? The perspectives appear bright, but only if we do not rest on past laurels, but instead continue to work on our strengths – a unique network and excellently trained minds – and are willing to increasingly leave the isolation of separate industries, and instead cooperate and innovate in the spirit of true partnership.

We hope you will enjoy this book,
Yours truly,

Claus-Peter Wagner
Country Lead Partner / Financial Services
Member of the Board of Directors Ernst & Young GmbH

and

Peter Fuß
Senior Advisory Partner Automotive
Germany, Switzerland, Austria (GSA)
Ernst & Young

Table of Contents

1	**The Automotive Value Chain**	**1**
2	**The Brand as a Central Value Component in the Automotive Industry**	**5**
2.1	Executive Summary	5
2.2	Definition of Terms and Framework	6
2.2.1	Definition of Terms: Brand and Brand Value	6
2.2.2	Aim of the Chapter	7
2.2.3	Structure and Approach	7
2.3	Functions and Uses of a Brand	7
2.3.1	Functions of a Brand in the Automotive Sector	7
2.3.2	Importance of a Brand in the Automotive Sector	9
2.4	Brand Perception	10
2.4.1	Brand Perception in the Automotive Sector	10
2.4.2	Brand from the Customer Perspective	12
2.4.3	Brand from the Employee Perspective	14
2.5	Brand Value and Brand Valuation	16
2.5.1	Introduction to Brand Valuation	16
2.5.2	Methods of Brand Valuation	17
2.5.2.1	Different Methods to Calculate a Brand Value – An Overview	17
2.5.2.2	Brand Census	18
2.5.2.3	Interbrand Method	23
2.5.3	Advantages and Disadvantages of the Valuation Methods Presented	29
2.5.3.1	Advantages	29
2.5.3.2	Disadvantages	29
2.5.4	Comparison of Market Capitalization and Brand Value	30
2.5.5	Development of Brand Values in the Automotive Sector	33
3	**Strategic Alliances in the Automotive Sector**	**35**
3.1	Executive Summary	35
3.2	Definition of Terms	35
3.2.1	Strategic Alliances or M&A	35
3.2.2	Proposition	37
3.3	Why Strategic Alliances and not M&A will Dominate the Automotive Industry in the Future	37
3.3.1	Volkswagen and Suzuki	38
3.3.2	BMW and SGL Carbon	39

3.3.3	Daimler and Renault/Nissan	40
3.3.4	BMW and MyCityWay	40
3.3.5	BMW and Sixt	41
3.3.6	Assessment of the Joint Approaches	41

4 Strategic Development Potential of the Automotive Industry – The Example of Electric Vehicles   43

4.1	Executive Summary	43
4.2	Definition of Terms and Scope	44
4.3	Drivers of Future Developments in the Automotive Industry	44
4.3.1	Environmental Drivers	44
4.3.2	Competition	48
4.3.3	Challenges	52
4.4	Electric Vehicles	53
4.4.1	Technological Developments	53
4.4.1.1	Alternative Drive Technologies	53
4.4.1.2	Technology of the Electric Vehicle	54
4.4.1.3	Competing Products and Developments	56
4.4.1.4	Strengths and Weaknesses of Electric Vehicles	60
4.4.2	Sales Markets and their Future Development	66
4.4.2.1	Criteria for Selection and Analysis	66
4.4.2.2	USA	67
4.4.2.3	Europe	70
4.4.2.4	Japan	76
4.4.3	China	79
4.4.3.1	India	82

5 Product Policies in the BRIC Countries   87

5.1	Executive Summary	87
5.2	Scope of the Analysis	87
5.2.1	Status Quo of Automobile Distribution in the BRIC Countries	87
5.2.2	The Four P's – Product as the Crucial Success Factor	90
5.2.3	Standardization or Integration and Adaptation or Differentiation	91
5.2.4	Importance of Product Adaptation for Automobile Manufacturers	92
5.3	Relevance of the BRIC Countries for the Automotive Industry	92
5.3.1	Brazil	92
5.3.2	Russia	93
5.3.3	India	95
5.3.4	China	96
5.4	Customer Demands and Requirements in the BRIC Countries	97
5.4.1	Brazil	97
5.4.2	Russia	99

5.4.3	India	101
5.4.4	China	103
5.5	Recommendations for Action	105

6 The Changing Business Field of the Automotive Financial Service Providers — 109

6.1	Executive Summary	109
6.2	Basic Terms and Scope	109
6.3	Classification of the Market for Automobile Financial Services	110
6.3.1	Captive and Independent Financial Service Providers	110
6.3.2	Financing of the Own Brand Versus Financing of Other Brands by the CFCs	111
6.3.3	Corporate Affiliation and Legal Separation of the CFCs	112
6.3.4	The Classical Product Areas of the CFCs	113
6.3.4.1	Retail Leasing	113
6.3.4.2	Retail Finance	114
6.3.4.3	Wholesale Finance	114
6.3.4.4	Fleet Business	114
6.3.5	Strategic Relevance of the CFCs	115
6.4	Leasing and Financing Today – An Overview of the Market for Leasing and Financing	117
6.5	What are the Current Business Approaches of the CFCs?	119
6.5.1	The Classical Captive Finance Approach	119
6.5.2	Advanced Automotive Banking Approach	119
6.5.2.1	Services Related to Mobility	120
6.5.2.2	Services Unrelated to Mobility	121
6.5.3	Cross-selling and Crossover in the Automobile Financial Services Sector	122
6.6	CFC – Quo Vadis?	124
6.6.1	The Strategic Options of the CFCs	124
6.6.2	The Fields of Action for the Developed Automobile Markets in the Triad	125
6.6.2.1	Accelerate Financing of Used Vehicles	125
6.6.2.2	Develop or Expand the Business with Fleet Customers	125
6.6.2.3	Introduce or Expand the Offering of Products with Risk Adjusted Pricing	126
6.6.2.4	Establish Bank Branches	126
6.6.2.5	Convert to a Bank Holding Company	128
6.6.2.6	Rework Governance Structures and Operating Concepts	129
6.6.2.7	Optimize the Areas Refinancing, Liquidity Management and Risk Management Jointly with the Automobile Manufacturers	130
6.6.3	Recommendations for Action in the New Growth Markets	131
6.6.3.1	Establish Financing Companies in Brazil, Russia, India and China	131
6.6.3.2	New Operating Strategies for the Growth Markets	131
6.6.4	Promising Answers to New Mobility Trends	132
6.6.4.1	User-based Mobility via Car Sharing	132
6.6.4.2	Location Based Services – Participation in Mobility Services that are Not Linked to the Vehicle	134

6.6.4.3	The Expansion of Fleet Management – Corporate Car Sharing: The Model of Siemens	135
6.6.5	New Leasing Models in the Area of Electronic Vehicles	136
6.6.5.1	Splitting Battery and Vehicle Leasing	136
6.6.5.2	Chances and Risks in the Area of Electromobility	138

7 Mobility Needs and Mobility Concepts — 141

7.1	Executive Summary	141
7.2	Definition of Terms	142
7.3	Determinants of Future Mobility Needs	143
7.3.1	Societal Developments	143
7.3.2	Moral Developments	144
7.3.3	Economic Developments	146
7.3.4	Demographic Developments	148
7.3.5	Urban Developments	152
7.3.6	Ecological Developments	154
7.3.7	Technological Developments	155
7.4	Concepts in the Mobility Area	157
7.4.1	Mobility Concept – Mu by Peugeot	157
7.4.2	Mobility Concept – "Better Place"	159
7.4.3	Mobility Concept – PRT 2getthere	160
7.5	Outlook – Novel Mobility Concepts	162
7.5.1	"Car Packaging and Pooling" – a Mobile Usage Concept	162
7.5.2	Combination of "Better Place" & "PRT" – a Novel Mobility Concept	165
7.5.3	Future Potential Competitors of the Automobile Manufacturers	169

8 Strategic Currency Management for Automotive Manufacturers — 171

8.1	Executive Summary	171
8.2	Fundamentals	172
8.2.1	Definition of Terms	172
8.2.1.1	Currency	172
8.2.1.2	Currency Management	172
8.2.2	Chapter Focus	173
8.3	Currency Management: Reasons and Current Challenges	174
8.3.1	Uses of Currency Management	174
8.3.2	Current Challenges in Currency Management of Automobile Manufacturers	175
8.4	Setup and Execution of Currency Management	176
8.4.1	Setup of Currency Management at an Automobile Manufacturer	176
8.4.2	Operational Structure of Currency Management at an Automobile Manufacturer	177
8.4.3	Banking Policy	179
8.5	Instruments Used in Currency Management by Automobile Manufacturers	179
8.5.1	Overview of Available Financial Instruments	179

8.5.2	Forwards and Futures	180
8.5.3	Options	181
8.5.3.1	An Overview of Options	181
8.5.3.2	Range Options	182
8.5.4	Swaps	182
8.6	International Strategies for Automobile Manufacturers	182
8.6.1	Natural Hedging	183
8.6.2	International Cash Management	184
8.6.2.1	Techniques to Optimize Cash Flows	185
8.6.2.2	Investing Excessive Cash Levels	185
8.6.3	International Investment Planning of Automobile Manufacturers	187
8.6.3.1	Investment Planning from Different Perspectives	187
8.6.3.2	Parameters for the Investment Planning of Automobile Manufacturers	188
8.6.4	Financial Hedging	189
8.6.4.1	Exchange Rate Forecasting	189
8.6.4.2	Calculating the Exposure	189
8.6.4.3	Exposure Management	190

9 Maximizing Shareholder Value in the Automotive Sector — 193

9.1	Executive Summary	193
9.2	Definition of Terms	193
9.2.1	Shareholder Value and Stakeholder Value	193
9.2.2	Automobile Manufacturers and Automotive Industry	194
9.2.3	Strategic Financial Management	195
9.2.4	Sustainability and Sustainable Development	195
9.2.5	Expectations	197
9.3	Maximizing Shareholder Value in the Automotive Industry to Date	197
9.3.1	Capital Markets	198
9.3.1.1	Stock Market Listing	198
9.3.1.2	Availability of Information	200
9.3.1.3	Securities Transactions	201
9.3.2	Accounting Standards	202
9.3.2.1	National Accounting Standards – The Example HGB	203
9.3.2.2	International Accounting Standards – The Example IFRS	203
9.3.3	Company Strategy	204
9.3.3.1	Company Goals	204
9.3.3.2	Growth Strategy	206
9.3.3.3	Management Remuneration	207
9.3.3.4	Corporate Social Responsibility	208
9.4	Maximizing Shareholder Value in the Automotive Industry in the Year 2020	209
9.4.1	Capital Markets	209
9.4.1.1	Stock Market Listing	210
9.4.1.2	Information Management	210
9.4.1.3	Securities Transactions	211
9.4.2	Accounting Standards	211

9.4.3	Company Strategy	211
9.4.3.1	Company Targets	211
9.4.3.2	Growth Strategy	214
9.4.3.3	Management Remuneration	215
9.4.3.4	Corporate Social Responsibility	216
10	**Automotive Industry or Mobility Industry in the Year 2020**	**217**
10.1	Traditional Brands will Disappear – Local Brands will be Established	218
10.2	Regulations in Support of Ecology and Sustainability Provide the Framework Conditions	218
10.3	New Mobility Demands of the Customers Gain in Importance	218
10.4	New Mobility Providers are Successful on the Market	219
10.5	The Networked Vehicle will Become an Information and Communication Instrument	219
10.6	Strategic Alliances are Key to Obtaining a Competitive Advantage	219
10.7	Triad was Yesterday, BRIC is Today and Emerging Markets will be Tomorrow	220
10.8	Tier-2 and Tier-3 Automotive Suppliers will Look for a New Orientation	220
10.9	Electromobility – There is More than One Way Forward	220
10.10	The Automobile Manufacturers Create a Global Brand Image	221
11	**Bibliography**	**223**

List of Figures

Figure 1:	The automotive value chain and company leadership pyramid	2
Figure 2:	Importance of brand loyalty	8
Figure 3:	Importance of a brand from the company perspective	9
Figure 4:	Multi brand strategy of the VW Group	11
Figure 5:	The brand architecture of BMW	12
Figure 6:	German automobile manufacturers dominate – fans of the Facebook page in million	13
Figure 7:	Process of cognitive mapping	13
Figure 8:	Reasons for open positions in companies	15
Figure 9:	Typical process of preference formation when selecting an employer	15
Figure 10:	Employer ranking among engineers	16
Figure 11:	Brand decision funnel	19
Figure 12:	Index of brand strength of German premium automobile brands	20
Figure 13:	Transfer in the premium segment	21
Figure 14:	Transfer in the volume segment	21
Figure 15:	Calculating brand strength shares	22
Figure 16:	Evaluating the potential of brand profitability	22
Figure 17:	Brand values according to Brand Census	23
Figure 18:	Steps in the methodology of brand valuation according to Interbrand	24
Figure 19:	Determination of economic profit	25
Figure 20:	Importance of the brand relative to company assets for selected industries	26
Figure 21:	Importance of automobile brand among relevant demand factors in the roadster segment	27
Figure 22:	Steps to calculate the brand value (in € million) according to the Interbrand Method	28
Figure 23:	Comparison of brand value and market capitalization on 16. September 2010	32
Figure 24:	Brand value in the Interbrand ranking of the automobile manufacturers (2001–2010)	33
Figure 25:	Types of strategic alliances	35
Figure 26:	Environmental drivers	45
Figure 27:	Vehicle density – Comparison of industrial countries and developing countries	45
Figure 28:	Percentage share of the population living in cities by regions from 1950–2030	46
Figure 29:	CO_2 emissions by region 2005–2030	47
Figure 30:	Competitive forces according to Porter's Five Forces Model	49
Figure 31:	Market leaders and potential new competitors by countries in 2010	50
Figure 32:	Developments in drive technology	54
Figure 33:	Advantages and disadvantages of various batteries	55
Figure 34:	Bio fuels	58
Figure 35:	Overview of CO_{2eq} balance of alternative fuels for 2010	58
Figure 36:	Strengths and weaknesses of the EVs	61
Figure 37:	Overview of CO_2 balance in the year 2008	64
Figure 38:	Examples of current or future EV models	65
Figure 39:	Overview of the criteria analyzed by region	66
Figure 40:	Sales development in the USA 2005–2010	67
Figure 41:	Market shares in the USA in 2010	68
Figure 42:	Sales by segments – USA 2010	69
Figure 43:	Market shares by drive technology 2025 in Northern America	69
Figure 44:	Sales development in Western Europe 2005–2020	71
Figure 45:	Sales development in selected EU countries 2005–2010	72
Figure 46:	Sales development in Central and Eastern Europe 2006–2020	72
Figure 47:	Market shares in Europe in 2010	73
Figure 48:	Sales by segment – Europe – Jan.–Nov. 2010	74
Figure 49:	Market shares by drive technology 2025 in Europe	74
Figure 50:	Sales development in Japan 2005–2020	77
Figure 51:	Market shares in Japan in 2010	77

Figure 52:	Sales by segment – Japan 2010	78
Figure 53:	Market shares by drive technology 2025 in Japan and Korea	78
Figure 54:	Sales development in China 2005–2020	80
Figure 55:	Market shares in China Jan.–Sept. 2010	80
Figure 56:	Sales by segment – China 2010	81
Figure 57:	Market shares by drive technology 2025 in China	81
Figure 58:	Sales development in India 2005–2020	83
Figure 59:	Market shares in India – April 2010–March 2011	83
Figure 60:	Passenger car density (per 1,000 inhabitants) as of 2008	84
Figure 61:	Sales by segment – India 2010	84
Figure 62:	International car sales outlook	88
Figure 63:	International activities of the BMW Group	88
Figure 64:	International activity of the VW Group	89
Figure 65:	The four P's of marketing	90
Figure 66:	Types of international marketing	91
Figure 67:	Vehicle sales and production – 1990 until 2009	93
Figure 68:	Development for ULCC 2007–2020	95
Figure 69:	Regional change in importance in the automobile industry	96
Figure 70:	Customer demands in the BRIC countries and implications for the automotive industry	107
Figure 71:	Overview of the twelve captive financial service providers and their brands	111
Figure 72:	Group structure of Volkswagen AG, Daimler AG and BMW AG (as of 2010)	113
Figure 73:	Overview – Different tasks of fleet management	115
Figure 74:	Summary of the strategic relevance of the CFCs	116
Figure 75:	Additions of new vehicles 2008–2010 (in Euro million)	117
Figure 76:	Additions of new vehicles 2008–2010 (by volume)	118
Figure 77:	Top 5 leasing markets in Europe (in Euro billion)	118
Figure 78:	Product range of the CFCs	119
Figure 79:	Stylized setup of full service leasing and fleet management	121
Figure 80:	Possibilities for expansion of the CFCs	122
Figure 81:	Stylized presentation of cross-selling and crossover	123
Figure 82:	Trend towards more valuable vehicles	123
Figure 83:	Purchasing behavior in the new vehicle business	124
Figure 84:	Presentation of a typical company structure of an automobile company	127
Figure 85:	Example of a CFC bank holding	128
Figure 86:	Development of Credit Default Swaps (CDS) in the automotive industry	130
Figure 87:	Selected societal fields of development	144
Figure 88:	Population development in Germany	148
Figure 89:	Population development and age structure	149
Figure 90:	Population by age group	150
Figure 91:	Vehicle ownership by group of owner	151
Figure 92:	Mobility aspects and derived needs	162
Figure 93:	Car Package to combine several classes of automobiles as needed	165
Figure 94:	Switching station of "Better Place" for quick switching of batteries	167
Figure 95:	The link between financial derivatives and instruments of currency management	173
Figure 96:	Organizational structure of currency management	176
Figure 97:	Coverage in months	178
Figure 98:	Advantages of the most important financial instruments for currency management	180
Figure 99:	Possibilities for natural hedging	184
Figure 100:	Automobile manufacturers of the triad & Tata as examples for newcomers in the emerging markets	195
Figure 101:	Integrated sustainability triangle	196
Figure 102:	Stock market listing and free float of the automobile manufacturers	199
Figure 103:	Share price development of the automobile manufacturers since 1990	199
Figure 104:	Open Xetra order book for BMW ordinary shares (ISIN DE0005190003) on June 27, 2011, at 01:29 pm	200
Figure 105:	Central differences in the valuation of assets according to HGB and IFRS	202
Figure 106:	Goal of self preservation	205
Figure 107:	Economic and social goals of the automobile manufacturers	206
Figure 108:	Product market matrix	206
Figure 109:	Volume strategy	207

List of Figures

Figure 110: Annual reports of VW AG following the regulation of management remuneration 208
Figure 111: Examples of specific CSR projects 209
Figure 112: Comparison of the company goals with a focus on the sustainability dimensions 214

1 The Automotive Value Chain

The Volkswagen Golf is the most popular automobile in Germany. According to a sales ranking which was published by the Handelsblatt, 258,000 customers have purchased the VW Golf in the year 2011. In second to last place in this ranking is the Lexus LS with 33 new registrations. It became clear that neither the extensive features, the outstanding manufacturing and reliability nor the innovative hybrid engine of the Japanese luxury car were able to support sales.

The poor performance of the Lexus clearly demonstrates that we are currently witnessing a paradigm change with regard to the use of passenger cars. Efficiency and brand image increasingly dominate. Product quality continues to be important, but users modify their decision criteria.

In the first edition of the book, we have laid out the value chain in the automotive industry. It starts with research & development. In the following, the activities of the automotive suppliers, integrated logistics of distribution and production management dominate. Once the vehicle is completely assembled, it is sold. Now the three milestones in the finance area follow: financing and leasing, insurance and services as well as mobility services. The next step focuses on after sales, repairs and maintenance as well as on remarketing. The value chain is completed with the disposal of the vehicle.

At current numerous challenges are present in the automotive industry. We have dealt with four important and current changes in the automotive value chain.[1]

In the area of research & development, the automobile manufacturers are faced with interesting strategic development opportunities. Electric vehicles in particular deserve to be mentioned here. Furthermore, very interesting opportunities to increase sales are presented in the BRIC countries. Third, the financial service providers in the automotive industry are required to significantly modify their service range if they want to continue with their sizeable contributions to the automotive manufacturers. Finally – and we consider this to be a central consideration – both the demand for mobility and mobility concepts are undergoing dramatic change.[2]

In addition to changes in the value chain, new strategic challenges must be met at the company level. Against this backdrop, the value chain in Figure 1 is superseded by a pyramid which addresses company leadership (strategy). At the third strategic level, financial strategy, globally active automotive companies must optimize their currency management. While activities such as natural hedging are in the domain of the company leadership, the finance area will focus on elements of currency management such as financial hedging. The question of which alliances to establish is of primary importance and needs to be answered along the entire automotive value chain. At the second level of the company management pyramid,

---

[1] We would like to thank the company Ernst & Young for the numerous research activities and for funding the book. In particular, Christopher Ley and Michelle Lo deserve to be mentioned in this regard. We also want to stress the role of Nikolaj de Lousanoff, whose analytical way of thinking decisively shaped the structure of this book. We also thank the publisher Oldenbourg Verlag and its staff, especially Miss Engel-Haas, for their cooperation which was always pleasant, competent and constructive.

[2] On page 169 of the first edition, a detailed breakdown of the value chain by value contributions is presented.

management needs to anticipate future trends in the automotive sector and to position the brand accordingly. The primary goal is the optimization of shareholder value. Efficient operations along the automotive value chain must be assured at the level of the COO and the CTO in particular. The levels 1 through 3 of the company management pyramid are primarily in the domain of the CEO and CFO.

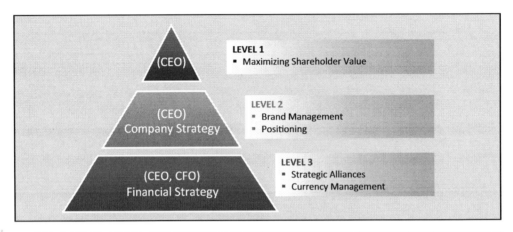

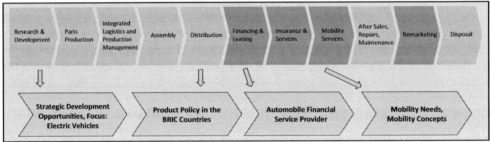

Figure 1: The automotive value chain and company leadership pyramid
Source: Authors' presentation

From Figure 1 follows the structure of the book:

Chapter 1:   The Automotive Value Chain
Chapter 2:   The Brand as Central Value Component in the Automotive Industry
Chapter 3:   Strategic Alliances in the Automotive Sector
Chapter 4:   Strategic Development Potential of the Automotive Industry – The Example of Electric Vehicles
Chapter 5:   Product Policies in the BRIC Countries
Chapter 6:   The Changing Business Field of the Automotive Financial Service Providers
Chapter 7:   Mobility Needs and Mobility Concepts
Chapter 8:   Strategic Currency Management for Automotive Manufacturers
Chapter 9:   Maximizing Shareholder Value in the Automotive Sector
Chapter 10: Automotive Industry or Mobility Industry in the Year 2020

With these extensions, our book "Automotive Management" becomes a textbook which simultaneously maintains its high practical relevance. Why an additional book or textbook about the automotive industry? All the books we scrutinized so far are very good at analyzing individual economic aspects of the automotive value chain. But all aspects, including a strategy for leading a company, have not yet been presented in their totality. In our opinion, the current global challenges faced by the automotive industry necessitate a unified perspective.

Additionally, the recent turbulences on the global capital and currency markets with their massive ramifications for the real economy have made it clear that the topic of "finance" plays an increasingly larger role also and especially in the automotive industry. The financial crisis has led to fundamental change in the entire automotive industry and has made it clear that the demands on automobile manufacturers have undergone noticeable change not only with regard to technology. Obviously, technology remains dominant in the automotive value chain. The implementation of technological innovation in the vehicle in order to successfully satisfy client preferences in the market place continues to be paramount. And quite apparently it is also important to successfully position the brand (see Chapter 2) and to satisfy new mobility needs with the help of appropriate mobility concepts (see Chapter 7). At the end of the day, automobile manufacturers are companies that must compete for the patronage of their shareholders against numerous companies from many different sectors. They need to create shareholder value; otherwise the share price will suffer.

Especially the crisis in the banking sector in the year 2008, which turned into a global financial and economic crisis, highlighted the real economic risks to which the automotive industry is exposed. This is true for production (for example layoffs, short-time work and so forth), for marketing (for example budget cuts) as well as for quality management (cost pressures versus quality standards). Meanwhile, the recent example of the VW group shows the strategic opportunities provided by an increase in shareholder value. The concept of "shareholder value," which at present appears almost almighty is the subject of a critical assessment in Chapter 9. Regardless of the conclusions reached in the shareholder value discussion, it is quite apparent that in recent years the global economy and global politics have moved in the direction of "finance." While 20 years ago the process chain was defined as "purchasing – production – sales" and financing was merely mentioned as a lubricant, today the lubricant dominates the process. This tendency is reflected in the setup of the book as displayed in Figure 1.

We have made an effort to write the book in a way that is accessible to readers who have a general interest in business, economics and politics. At the same time, it also addresses experts in the field. This includes managers in finance departments of companies, controlling and strategy departments, auditors, financial service providers and management consultants. Academic research and business practice are merged in this volume. With this publication in the English language, we look forward to the global reception – and hopefully use – of our "holistic view of automotive management" at the leading automobile manufacturers, automotive suppliers and automotive financial service providers. Following the leitmotiv of the German Institute of Corporate Finance "to combine academic research and business practice," we are happy to make a contribution to the still young academic field of "automotive business," "automotive" or "automotive management" (see: www.dicf.de).

2 The Brand as a Central Value Component in the Automotive Industry

2.1 Executive Summary

This chapter demonstrates how the financial valuation of brands can be accomplished and points out the link between brand value of a company and its market capitalization.[3]

> Main chapter insights:
>
> 1. A **comparison** of **brand value** and **market capitalization** of the companies included in the study shows that the brand value across industries of the 30 most valuable global brands according to Interbrand makes up a share of about 25% of market capitalization.
>
> 2. In contrast to other industries, the **average percentage** of the brand value **in the market capitalization of the automobile manufacturers** (here: Toyota, Mercedes Benz, BMW and Honda), which are among the most valuable brands stands at approximately **40%**.
>
> 3. Mercedes Benz, BMW, Honda, Porsche, Audi and Hyundai have experienced a **positive development** of their **brand values** over the last ten years. In contrast, the image of **Toyota** and **Ford** suffered strongly. This was reflected in **declining brand values**.
>
> 4. New engine types result in an increasing similarity of the technical product specifications of individual models. As a consequence, the customers' purchase decisions will depend more and more on the brand image.
>
> 5. An **efficient brand management** and **increasing investments in the brand** are of high importance, especially for automotive manufacturers. Examples include **sponsorship** activities or the opening of **automotive museums**.

---

[3] We thank Nathalie Dirian and Corina Schwarz for their support in the topic area of "brand and brand valuation." Their work has made the success of this book possible.

2.2 Definition of Terms and Framework

2.2.1 Definition of Terms: Brand and Brand Value

The term "brand" can be looked at from different perspectives and defined in various ways. There are also differing valuation methods that can be used to assess the brand value. In the context of this chapter and particularly against the background of the central importance for the entire automotive value chain, the following definition of "brand," which is provided by Pepels is most suitable:

> "In general, a **brand** is the formal labeling of products and services or companies, which signifies to interested buyers the origin in order to achieve an identification or profile and to differentiate from products that have a different origin/come from a different company. A brand at the same time constitutes the personality ('the face') of a product/company and possibly reflects the values of their users."[4]

This definition includes all aspects which characterize a brand, respectively the term brand, in the context of competition, competitors and product recognition of a company, particularly also with regard to the automotive sector. Accordingly, the brand to a large degree determines how a product or service is perceived and even more, whether or not the product is bought or the service is used.

How does a brand create value? To answer this question, the term "brand value" must be defined first.

The term **brand value** is frequently replaced by the term brand equity and it defines the monetary value of a brand. In order to determine the strength or value of a brand, different quantitative as well as qualitative methods are employed. But the methods to measure brand value are subject to severe criticism. Oftentimes important factors, which are used for the calculations cannot be determined with precision. Examples are expenses that are directly linked to sales or other mostly subjective values.[5]

Automobile manufacturers, which are also referred to as **Original Equipment Manufacturers** (OEM), receive some of their components from different suppliers and integrate these into their own products. Marketing and sales is also done by the OEM.

A **premium manufacturer** is an OEM that is active in the upper price segment and differentiates itself from its competitors by technology and quality of its vehicles as well as by its customer service. The cars produced by the premium manufacturers are mostly positioned in the upper middle segment all the way to the luxury segment.

The counterparts are the **volume manufacturers**, which tend to be positioned in the lower price segment. Since their margins are low, they require high volumes of deliveries or sales. The automobiles which are produced by volume manufacturers are usually found in the segment of small and medium sized cars.

---

[4] See Pepels, W. (2008), p. 136.
[5] See Pepels, W. (2008), pp. 136ff.

2.2.2 Aim of the Chapter

The aim of the chapter follows from the above stated problem of providing a precise determination of the brand value. How can the brand be considered a central value component in the automotive sector if it is not possible to give a precise definition, calculation or determination of the strength or value of the brand? This chapter aims at answering this question, at least as far as this is possible. The calculation of a brand value in general and for the automotive sector in particular is explained using different methods. Furthermore, the importance of a brand and the brand value is discussed in detail. In closing, the brand value is compared to the market value of equity, in other words the market capitalization.

2.2.3 Structure and Approach

The outcome of this chapter is the ability to calculate or determine the value of a brand, which is needed to demonstrate the relevance of the brand, specifically in the automotive sector. In addition to the calculation of the brand value, the value of a brand in the automotive sector is also determined by other factors, which are analyzed as well. These factors are subsumed under the term brand perception. They include the brand architecture in the automotive sector, the client perspective and the perspective of the employees (employer branding) concerning the brand. In the following Section 2.3, the functions and uses of a brand will be defined broadly in order to set the scene. But the key element of the chapter is the explanation of two methods for calculating the brand value. A comparison of the values from the Interbrand method with the corresponding market capitalizations and the presentation of the development of brand values in the automotive sector conclude this chapter.

2.3 Functions and Uses of a Brand

2.3.1 Functions of a Brand in the Automotive Sector

Considering the wide range of products and services available in the twenty first century, a strong brand increasingly plays an important role for a company. Particularly in the automotive sector, the brand is a key consideration. Since the automobile is considered a status symbol in many countries, particularly the ability to **differentiate** is of enormous importance.[6] A major concern of many buyers is the differentiation from others with the help of their automobile. Thus the brand constitutes a status symbol.[7] Due to similar technology and equipment in the automotive sector, the brand in addition to design is one of the last possibilities for the manufacturers to achieve differentiation from the competition.[8]

In this context, the brand also serves to facilitate buying decisions of the customers. With the purchase of an automobile, the buyer aligns himself with a specific social category. Put differently, the brand provides orientation during the purchasing process. This is also called the

---

[6] See Göttgens, O., Böhme, T. (2005), p. 44 and p. 49.
[7] See Göttgens, O., Böhme, T. (2005), p. 49.
[8] See Häusler, J., Stucky, N. (2003), p. 13.

lighthouse function of a brand. The brand informs the customer what to expect from a specific automobile.⁹ Especially since the automobile is among the highly priced goods, a customer must feel trust in order to make a purchase. He must be sure that he can rely on the attributes which are promised by the brand.¹⁰

Such a state of trust can particularly be established if the customer has personally experienced the brand. A strong tie to a brand is frequently associated with a specific product experience. This arouses emotions in the conscience of the customer, which in the future will be associated with the brand. But due to the large amount of impressions that consumers are exposed to on a daily basis, it is increasingly difficult to create a specific event which catches the attention of a (potential) customer. For that reason, the automobile manufacturers face the challenge of presenting their products to customers in new and innovative ways. Automobile manufacturers accomplish this primarily through the interaction of the (potential) customer with the brand. In the auto city of VW or the BMW world, for example, the brand is showcased and a lasting customer impression is created. The interaction of brand and products creates **customer loyalty**.

Studies demonstrate that consumers unconsciously forge a bond with a brand already during childhood. If the parents or other reference persons have used products of a specific brand, the consumer feels an emotional attachment to that brand. He is trusting and more willing to rely on that brand compared to brands that he became aware of only recently. This is demonstrated by Figure 2.

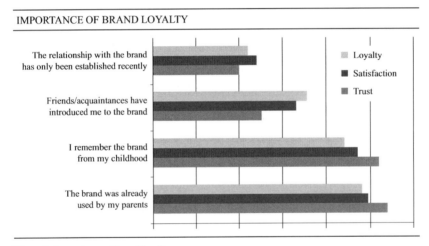

Figure 2: Importance of brand loyalty
Source: Diehl et al., (2009), p. 40

Furthermore, these customers show heightened loyalty as well as increased satisfaction. Thus customer loyalty plays a large role for companies.¹¹ In order to utilize the effects of customer loyalty, automobile manufacturers must assure that children, as potential future customers,

---

⁹ See Esch, F.-R., Knörle, C. (2008), p. 96.
¹⁰ See Göttgens, O., Böhme, T. (2005), p. 49.
¹¹ See Diehl, S., et al. (2009), p. 40.

2.3 Functions and Uses of a Brand

are already in contact with the automotive brand. This requirement is met by the automobile manufacturers, such as BMW or Audi among others in the form of toy cars.[12]

Strong brand loyalty ultimately results in the identification of customer with the company brand. This **identification function** is particularly important in a poor economic environment. In such a situation, customers especially rely on known quality and look for safety in a brand. Thus a strong brand is not as vulnerable during times of crisis as a company with no-name-products, thanks to its customers' need for identification.[13]

2.3.2 Importance of a Brand in the Automotive Sector

The functions of a brand already give a first indication of the enormous benefits of a fully established company brand. The loyalty of the customers to the brand and therefore the products of the company establish barriers to entry for potential rivals. If customers are already tied to a specific brand, it is very difficult for new providers to get a foothold in the market. This is particularly true for the automotive sector, where status and prestige play a dominant role and are symbolized largely by the brand. But not only potential rivals are held back. A strong brand management also gives a company a **competitive advantage** over existing competitors. An overview of the advantages of a brand from the company perspective is provided in Figure 3.

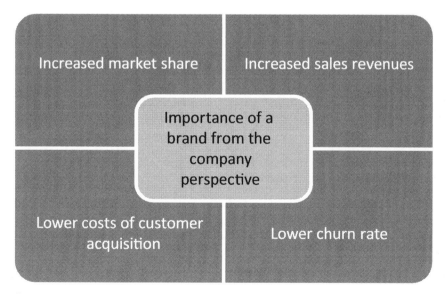

Figure 3: Importance of a brand from the company perspective
Source: Authors' presentation

---

[12] See Diehl, S., et al. (2009), p. 41.
[13] See Häusler, J., Stucky, N. (2003), p. 13.

Since customers have usually committed to a specific brand ahead of time when purchasing a vehicle, the probability to lose clients to a competitor goes down for automobile manufacturers.[14] The churn rate is thus reduced.

The low churn rate and the high probability of further purchases contribute to the fact that a brand manufacturer in the automotive sector can achieve a higher **market share** than a supplier with a weak brand. Furthermore, the market share can be increased even more by winning over new customers. Since a strong brand helps to establish trust among potential buyers, the acquisition of new customers is facilitated.[15]

Additionally, a strong brand management also has a positive influence on the **sales** of a company. Automobiles that are associated with a positive brand image can be sold at a premium.[16] Customers accept a higher price because of the brand. Furthermore, the automobile manufacturer can offer additional products from the same brand which allows efficient cross-selling.[17] BMW for example secures additional business by offering financing and leasing products through BMW Bank for the automobiles sold.[18] Financing and leasing products also provide an opportunity to realize up-selling potential. In the automotive sector, the term up-selling refers to the sale of a more valuable vehicle or equipment version as the result of targeted sales support employing financial products.[19] As examples, the automobile manufacturer in addition to the product in question can sell high-quality supplementary equipment or a stronger engine system. On top of that, BMW can also utilize the advantage that longtime customers switch from a less expensive model to a higher priced model within the company, for example from the BMW 1 Series to the BMW 3 Series.

While it initially requires significant amounts of time and financial resources to develop and introduce a brand, it can actually lead to **cost reductions** in the long run. As an example, it is easier, and thus less expensive, for a company with a strong brand to acquire new customers or to maintain its competitive position.[20]

2.4 Brand Perception

2.4.1 Brand Perception in the Automotive Sector

Important for the brand architecture in the automotive sector is the choice of an appropriate brand strategy, which must accommodate a growth process that provides both breadth and depth. The aim must be to address specific customer preferences with the brand strategy.

One possibility for structuring the brand architecture is the multi brand strategy. In that case, the automotive company or the automobile group consists of an umbrella brand and several sub-brands. An advantage of that strategy lies in the fact that it provides the potential customer with a broad choice among different sub-brands which are united under the umbrella brand. He is

---

[14] See Häusler, J., Stucky, N. (2003), p. 13.
[15] See Göttgens, O., Böhme, T. (2005), p. 44.
[16] See Bamert, T. (2004), p. 51.
[17] See Göttgens, O. Böhme, T. (2005), p. 44.
[18] See BMW Bank (2011).
[19] See Ueno, S. (2006), p. 5.
[20] See Göttgens, O., Böhme, T. (2005), p. 44.

2.4 Brand Perception

thus not forced to choose a vehicle or product from a competing brand. Customers who are unable to find a suitable product within one sub-brand are not forced to switch to the competition, but can move to another sub-brand under the umbrella brand to find a model of their choice.[21]

The globally leading example for such a multi brand strategy is the VW Group. In Figure 4 the setup of the VW Group with its sub-brands is displayed. The commercial vehicles operation of VW is also part of the group, but will not be considered here. Within the various sub-brands, there are different classes of vehicles.

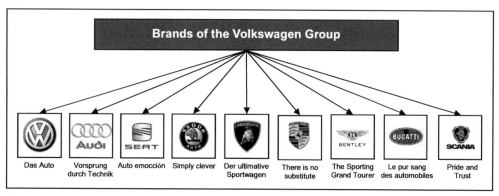

Figure 4: Multi brand strategy of the VW Group
Source: Volkswagen AG, (2009)

It is the aim of the Volkswagen Group to offer products for all consumer groups. This approach, in addition to being a multi brand strategy is also called a full range strategy. This means that the Volkswagen Group covers all product categories from small car (for example VW Vox) via SUV (Sport Utility Vehicle) and class (for example Audi Q 7) all the way to sports cars (for example Porsche, Bugatti Veyron) or heavy trucks.

A differentiated form of the multi brand strategy is utilized for example by the BMW AG, where the company itself constitutes the umbrella brand. Next to the brands Mini and Rolls-Royce as well as the BMW motorcycle brand, the BMW brand with its sub-brands takes center stage. Sub-brands are the individual types of automobiles such as the BMW 3 Series or BMW 5 Series.

The setup of this multi brand strategy is illustrated in Figure 5.

This strategy is different from the one used by VW, since BMW considers the different types of vehicles as sub-brands and consequently marketing is conducted individually and differently for each type. Establishing a new sub-brand also serves the purpose of targeting a new circle of customers for BMW. This allows the future establishment of independent "brands" such as the BMW 1 Series as youth car or the X Class such as the BMW X1 to X6 Series as SUV.

---

[21] See Esch, F.-R. (2010), p. 12.

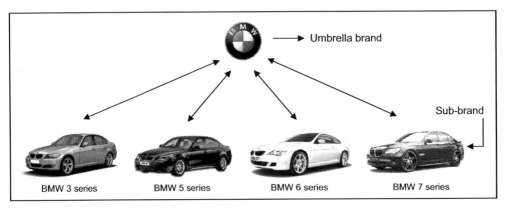

Figure 5: The brand architecture of BMW
Source: Esch, F.-R., (2010), p. 518

2.4.2 Brand from the Customer Perspective

When defining the value of a brand, the customer perspective is important. Their subjective assessment of the brand value is of utmost importance, since the customers decide whether or not to purchase the product or the service. In the case of the automotive industry, the image of a manufacturer is a decisive factor when customers choose an automobile.

A recent study of the journal *WuV – Werben und Verkaufen* shows that the German automobile manufacturers and their brands, based on the number of members of their company pages on Facebook, are in a leading position when it comes to recognition by potential customers. The study shows that viral marketing has already become very important and is still gaining in importance for companies and their brands. Life, especially of young people, is taking place to a large degree in the virtual space and this fact should be considered in marketing and in brand management. The membership numbers of the respective Facebook pages for the automobile manufacturers according to a statistic which was published in April 2011 are displayed in Figure 6.

Even though this ranking does not directly make a statement about purchasing decisions, the statistic can still be considered as an indication of the subjective assessment of potential customers.

In the following, one method for the presentation of the perspective of the customer on the brand will be described in detail.

This method is called cognitive mapping and stands for the determination of positive and negative attributes associated with the brand from the perspective of the customer.[22] The process of cognitive mapping is displayed graphically in Figure 7.

The process consists of five steps. In a first step, free associations with the brand are collected which are then handled in a second step with the help of a triad test. The triad test can also be understood as a comparison of similarities. The similarities of associations and their structures are determined and a list of triads is constructed.[23]

---

[22] See Franzen, O., Burkhardt, A. (2006), p. 62.
[23] See Grunwald, T. (2007), pp. 33–34.

2.4 Brand Perception

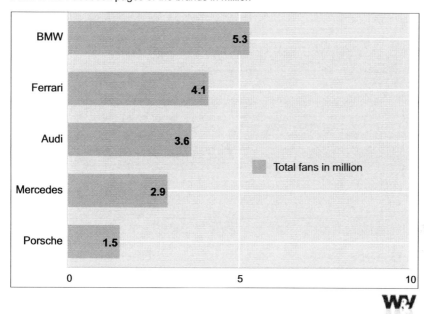

Figure 6: German automobile manufacturers dominate – fans of the Facebook page in million
Source: Werben und Verkaufen (2011)[24]

From the comparison of similarities, a distance matrix is developed in a third step. It shows all congruities and the structure of the associations.

In the fifth and final step, a correspondence analysis is used to develop the brand molecule from the distance matrix. During the correspondence analysis, identical or similar associations in a specific area are identified and presented in the brand molecule.[25]

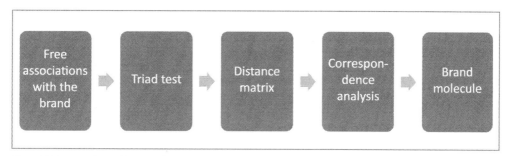

Figure 7: Process of cognitive mapping
Source: Authors' presentation based on Franzen, O., Burkhardt, A., (2006), p. 62

---

[24] See Werben und Verkaufen (2011): Facebook-Ranking: Deutsche Automarken belegen Spitzenplätze. 29.April 2011. [online].
[25] See Grunwald, T. (2007), p. 35.

This method can be clarified by displaying the subjective feelings – specifically of customers – with the help of an example, in this case BMW.

The core associations with BMW according to the cognitive mapping are both *sheer driving pleasure* as well as *good engines*. These two associations are also identified as the core attributes of the brand BMW by the cognitive mapping. Additional positive attributes that are evoked by customer associations are *dynamism, speed* and *elegance of the automobiles* as well as *technology, safety, reliability* and *comfort as a result of quality*. In addition to the positive associations, there are also negative ones when it comes to the BMW brand. Among others, these include *arrogant drivers* and *overly expensive products*. This may even imply that BMW drivers are considered to be "braggarts." But on balance the associations with BMW are positive and are even transferred to the federal state of Bavaria in general. According to the cognitive mapping, many customers associated the federal state of Bavaria with the attributes engines, quality and technology.[26]

The example shows how cognitive mapping can be used to display spontaneous associations with a brand. In the best case – BWM is an example – cognitive mapping supports a targeted management of brand associations. In the case of BMW, the success can be measured by the fact that the core association exactly corresponds to the current advertising slogan – sheer driving pleasure.[27]

2.4.3 Brand from the Employee Perspective

Next to the perception of the brand or the company from the perspective of the customers, the perception of potential or current employees plays an increasingly important role. While such a perspective on the brand is not the focus of the chapter, this important aspect is nonetheless not ignored either.

The brand is gaining in importance from the perspective of employees especially against the backdrop of an increasing shortage of qualified personnel in Germany and in Europe. Already in 2010 there was a shortage of about 1.9 million specialists in German medium sized companies and this trend will worsen in the years to come.[28] Specifically in the fields of engineering and electrical engineering, there are not enough qualified applicants to fill all open positions, as is shown clearly in Figure 8.

The report shows that the attitudes of potential employees, especially of specialists, can have a lasting effect on companies. If the brand is not valued by employees, potential new hires will be less inclined to apply for an open position. Therefore the employee's perception of the brand or the company can already be a decisive factor in the struggle for committed and qualified specialists and thus the future success or failure of a company.[29]

In order to provide theoretical support for this hypothesis, the process of preference formation in choosing an employer according to Petkovic will be discussed briefly in the following section. Figure 9 provides a graphical illustration of this process.

---

[26] See Franzen, O., Burkhardt, A. (2006), p. 62.
[27] See Franzen, O., Burkhardt, A. (2006), p. 62.
[28] See BIBB Report 10/09 (2009).
[29] See BIBB Report 10/09 (2009).

2.4 Brand Perception

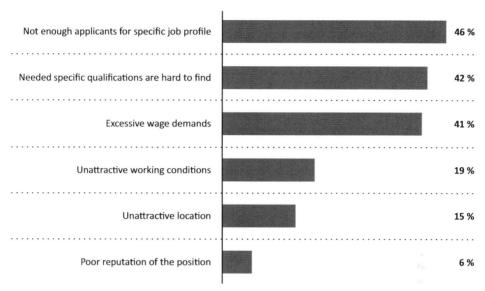

Figure 8: Reasons for open positions in companies
Source: BIBB Report 10/09 (2009)

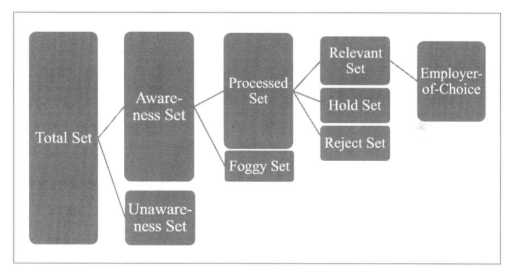

Figure 9: Typical process of preference formation when selecting an employer
Source: Authors' presentation based on Petkovic, M., (2008), p. 15

As can be seen from Figure 9, the decision against a company and its brand can be reached very early. Both the first step, the identification of the awareness set and the second step, the reduction to the processed set, imply the elimination of many companies. In order to prevent this, especially companies in the automotive industry, which are rather dependent on qualified specialists, should assure that their company brand is represented in a positive fashion in this area as well. Ways to achieve this are the increased provision of internships for students and the participation in job fairs at universities. This form of brand assessment is frequently called employer branding.[30]

The question that comes to mind against the background of this chapter is the following: how are the automotive companies (manufacturers and suppliers) rated as employers by current and potential employees?

In order to provide an answer to this question, a study from the year 2011 is used, in which different groups of employees were asked to state their favorite employer. Especially in the case of engineers it becomes obvious that they most frequently pick automobile manufacturers and their suppliers, as is clearly shown by Figure 10. Other groups of employees that were asked during the study were students of business and informatics as well as natural scientists. These groups considered the automotive sector to be less attractive as an employer than the engineers.[31]

Rank	Company	Percent of Persons Interviewed
1	BMW	17.0
2	Audi	16.3
3	Porsche	13.2
4	Siemens	12.9
5	Robert Bosch	10.9
6	Daimler	9.2

Figure 10: Employer ranking among engineers
Source: Authors' presentation based on Wirtschaftswoche (2011)

2.5 Brand Value and Brand Valuation

2.5.1 Introduction to Brand Valuation

This chapter deals primarily with the value of a brand. But initially it must be understood why a brand valuation should be conducted. In the past decades the value of a brand has gained significantly in importance and played a major role particularly during M&A transactions, where it contributed to an increased goodwill. While in 1981 the acquisition price of a company was still covered to 82% by the value of tangible assets, this share had declined to 56% by 1988. This development clearly shows that purchasers are willing to pay more for intangible assets such as a brand name.[32] This trend is also clearly visible in the automotive sector and will be illustrated with reference to the acquisition of Rolls Royce by BMW. Following a long series of negotiations between BMW AG, Volkswagen AG and Rolls Royce in the year 1998, the following result was achieved: VW acquired Rolls Royce Motor Cars for

---

[30] See Petkovic, M. (2008), pp. 15ff.
[31] See Wirtschaftswoche (2011).
[32] See Häusler, J., Stucky, N. (2003), p. 6.

£ 430 million, but left certain parts, such as the brand name to BMW. The brand Rolls Royce cost BMW £ 40 million. In the context of a complex deal between VW and BMW, in 2003 BMW finally also obtained the right to produce Rolls Royce automobiles, while VW was awarded the manufacturing site in England and the brand name of the Bentley models.[33] The transaction shows the enormous appreciation for a luxury brand such as Rolls Royce in the automotive sector. One goal of the valuation of a brand is thus the determination of an appropriate purchase price in a transaction, which also incorporates the brand value. A further goal of brand valuation is optimization of the brand management. The determination of the brand value gives valuable information to a company which can be used, for example, to reach internal decisions concerning the future communications strategy.[34]

Here again, a differentiation must be made regarding the various submarkets in which the brand is represented. While the brand Mercedes Benz is very strong, for example, in the automobile segment and customers base their buying decision on the trust in the brand, the brand name Mercedes Benz in the truck sector primarily plays an important role with regard to the identification with quality. But a corporate customer will base his decision in this segment primarily on the price and particular product specifications.[35]

2.5.2 Methods of Brand Valuation

2.5.2.1 Different Methods to Calculate a Brand Value – An Overview

Over time, a large number of methods for the valuation of a brand have been developed.[36]

In particular, the following brand valuation methods deserve to be highlighted. The companies which use these approaches are in brackets:

- 360 Degree Brand Stewardship (Ogilvy & Mather)
- Advanced Brand Valuation (PricewaterhouseCoopers Corporate Finance)
- BBDO Brand Equity Evaluator (BBDO)
- Brand Ambassador Approach (Brand Consultants)
- Brand Assessment System (Gesellschaft für Konsumforschung)
- Brand Census (Konzept & Markt)
- Brand Performance System (Konzept & Markt)
- BrandStock
- Brand-Value-Creation Approach (Boston Consulting Group)
- Brand Wheel (Bates)
- BrandZ
- CAPO (&Equity)
- Conversion Model (TNS Emnid)
- facit (facit-Marketingforschung)
- Genetic Code of the Brand (Institut für Markentechnik)
- Grey Tools (Grey)

---

[33] See Buerkle, T. (1998).
[34] See Häusler, J., Stucky, N. (2003), p. 8.
[35] See Häusler, J., Stucky, N. (2003), p. 12.
[36] See Schimansky, A., et al. (2008), pp. 28ff.

- icon Brand Navigator (icon Brand Navigation Group)
- Implied System (TNS Worldwide)
- Interbrand Approach (Interbrand Zintzmeyer & Lux)
- Ipsos*Builder (Ipsos)
- Brand Monopoly Approach (McKinsey & Company)
- Brand Essence Model (Publicis Sasserath Brand Consultancy)
- Market Router (Sturm und Drang)
- Morphological Analysis (rheingold Institut für qualitative Markt- und Medienanalysen)
- Promicheck (Promikativ)
- res$^+$ (we do communication)
- Strategic Brand Management (Roland Berger Strategy Consultants)
- Semion brand€valuation Approach (semion brand-broker)
- The Big Picture (McCann-Erickson)
- WISA (Technische Universität Berlin)
- Y&R Brand Asset Valuator (Young & Rubicam)

The above list makes clear that "the one brand valuation method" does not exist. The numerous approaches yield different brand values and for that reason the published results cannot be interpreted as objective figures. The fact that in most cases the methodology is not fully revealed supports the subjective character of the brand values obtained by the various methods. In one case, the company is "ranked as number one" – in another study it does not even make the top ten.

To illustrate the calculation of the brand value in the automotive sector, the Brand Census and the Interbrand approach are selected. The Interbrand method is the best-known procedure internationally and has been established in the marketplace for the past ten years. Since 2001, the company publishes the 100 most valuable brands in a ranking. Since its inception, this Top-100 of brands has always included a large number of automobile manufacturers. While the Interbrand method draws heavily on sales that are relevant to the brand, the Brand Census focuses on the strength of a brand and on gains in market share. In order to capture the brand value adequately from a completely different perspective, the Brand Census, as an additional well known approach, is also included in this chapter.

2.5.2.2 Brand Census

The index of brand strength as basis

Brand valuation with the help of the Brand Census is based on the perception of the brand by the customer. Thus the model is strongly tied to the demand side.

Since the brand value depends mainly on the customers' perception, the relationship of the customer to the brand is initially measured in the context of the Brand Census. Thus this step measures the *Customer Based Brand Equity*. The following variables are of particular relevance in this context:[37]

- Brand awareness
- Brand image

---

[37] See Franzen, O., Burkhardt, A. (2006), p. 59.

2.5 Brand Value and Brand Valuation

- Purchase of the brand
- Brand satisfaction
- Brand loyalty

These five points show the intensity of anchoring of the brand in the minds of the people. The determination of the brand strength follows these variables. With the help of the Brand Decision Funnel, the brand strength is ultimately measured. A representative survey is conducted, in which the aided awareness, familiarity, the relevant set as well as purchase, satisfaction and loyalty are checked.[38]

Based on the Brand Decision Funnel, each step of the funnel is assigned percentage shares which follow from the survey. After that, a weighting of the different steps of the brand funnel is conducted. Specific calculations are used to determine the importance of an individual step for the overall strength of the brand. In a next step, the percentage shares of the individual steps of the funnel from the survey are multiplied with their percentage weightings. Finally, the values calculated in that fashion are added up over the steps of the funnel in order to arrive at a value for the brand strength. This procedure is displayed in Figure 11. Brand strength of 100 would thus imply that a brand is always known, preferred and purchased by 100% of those surveyed. The brand would have to reach the highest possible value of 100% at all levels of the funnel – but this is not realistic. This fact is also taken into consideration and index values that are too low are avoided when determining the index of brand strength. Initially the brand strength of a best practice brand is determined. It gives an indication of the maximum value that can be obtained in a specific industry. The brand strength which is obtained for the other brands considered is then stated relative to the best practice brand. This leads to standardization.[39]

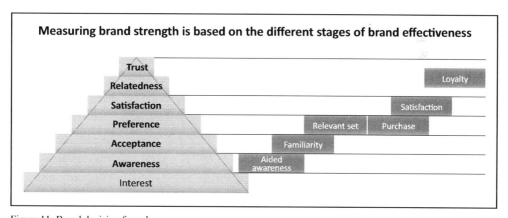

Figure 11: Brand decision funnel
Source: Franzen, O., Burkhardt, A., (2006), p. 59

The determination of brand strength for the German premium automobile manufacturers Mercedes Benz, BMW as well as Audi which is displayed in Figure 12 was compiled with the help of a CATI survey (Computer Aided Telephone Interviewing). The CATI survey is a

---

[38] See Franzen, O., Burkhardt, A. (2006), p. 59.
[39] See Franzen, O., Burkhardt, A. (2006), p. 60.

computer-based survey of the respondents which is conducted by telephone. In the year 2006, 1000 drivers in Germany participated in the survey. With regard to the index of brand strengths, Audi had a lead over the two other brands. With 91 points, Audi was thus the strongest of the automotive brands listed in this study.[40]

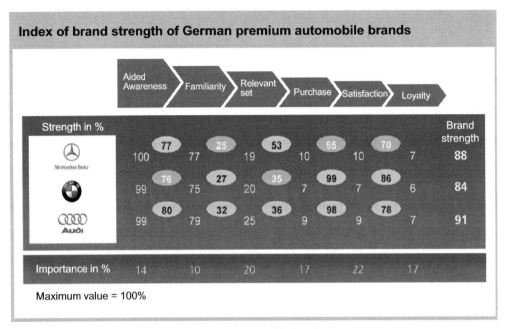

Figure 12: Index of brand strength of German premium automobile brands
Source: Franzen, O., Burkhardt, A., (2006), p. 61

The values in the gray and yellow fields are transfer rates. They show the percentage of respondents that continue to be present with a positive value in the next step of the funnel. As an example, the transfer rate from satisfaction to loyalty provides the share of those respondents that are happy with the brand and are also loyal. The example makes it clear that BMW has the highest transfer rates between purchase and satisfaction as well as between satisfaction and loyalty. This shows that customers who purchase an automobile from BMW are for the most part very satisfied and would again choose the same brand for their next purchase. However, BMW shows the lowest transfer rate between the relevant set and a purchase. This value means that fewer customers who have BMW on their shortlist will actually purchase a vehicle of the BMW brand, than customers who prefer Mercedes Benz. The transfer rates for Mercedes Benz, meanwhile, allow the opposite conclusion. Here the bigger problem seems satisfying the customers following the purchase and convincing them to become loyal to the brand.[41]

---

[40] See Franzen, O., Burkhardt, A. (2006), p. 60.
[41] See Franzen, O., Burkhardt, A. (2006), p. 60.

2.5 Brand Value and Brand Valuation

A study by BBDO Consulting demonstrates that the manufacturers of highly respected automotive brands in the premium segment have difficulties to ultimately convince their customers to make a purchase despite the positive image.[42] Figure 13 makes this point.

Figure 14 shows the situation of the automobile brands in the volume segment. They mostly suffer from the problem that they only obtain low image values despite their high levels of prominence.[43]

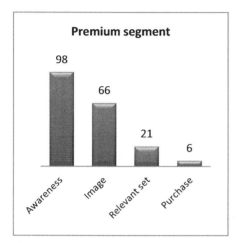 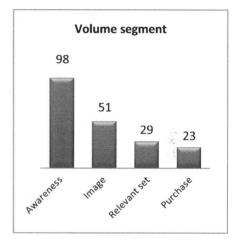

Figure 13: Transfer in the premium segment
Source: Authors' presentation based on
Göttgens, O., Böhme, T., (2005), p. 48

Figure 14: Transfer in the volume segment
Source: Authors' presentation based on
Göttgens, O., Böhme, T., (2005), p. 48

Thus the calculation of an index of brand strength does not only serve to calculate a monetary brand value, but also serves as the starting point for an efficient brand management.

Determination of brand value

In the following, a monetary brand value can be determined on the basis of the calculated index of brand strength. To do that, the index of brand strength for a specific brand is taken as a fraction of the sum of the brand indexes for all brands relevant for the industry. This gives a percentage share, which provides information about the contribution of an individual brand to the strength of all relevant brands in a segment.[44] Figure 15 clarifies this approach for the example of the automotive industry.

In a next step, the profit potential of the market is allocated among the respective brands. To do this, the market volume of the selected relevant brands needs to be ascertained. For the example of the automotive industry, this value was € 75 billion for the year 2006 according to Franzen and Burkhardt. Starting from this amount, the potential market profit is calculated. To do this, the average profitability, taken as a percentage figure is considered. Franzen and Burkhardt utilize the average EBIT, which stood at about 7% during the year 2006 for the selected relevant brands in the automotive industry. This leads to an estimated market

---

[42] See BBDO Consulting (2002).
[43] See Göttgens, O., Böhme, T. (2005), p. 48.
[44] See Franzen, O., Burkhardt, A., (2006), p. 62.

profit of € 5.25 billion. Finally the market profit is distributed according to the shares of the brand strength among the brands considered as shown in Figure 16.[45]

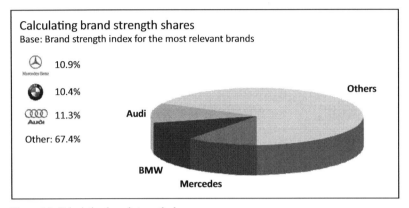

Figure 15: Calculating brand strength shares
Source: Franzen, O., Burkhardt, A., (2006), p. 62

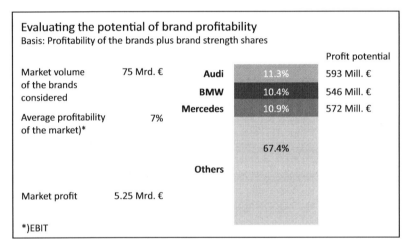

Figure 16: Evaluating the potential of brand profitability
Source: Franzen, O., Burkhardt, A., (2006), p. 62

According to this approach, the brand Audi had a profit potential of € 593 million. In order to arrive at an actual monetary value of the brand, the profit potential which is determined is discounted. The simplifying assumptions are that the brand will continue to exist forever and that the riskless rate of interest is 5%. Discounting is done with the help of the following formula:[46]

$$Brand\ value = \frac{Profit\ potential * 100}{Interest\ rate}$$

---

[45] See Franzen, O., Burkhardt, A. (2006), p. 62.
[46] See Franzen, O., Burkhardt, A. (2006), p. 62.

2.5 Brand Value and Brand Valuation

This leads to the following brand values for the year 2006:

	Profit potential	Brand value
Audi	€ 593 million	€ 11.9 billion
BMW	€ 546 million	€ 10.9 billion
Mercedes	€ 572 million	€ 11.4 billion

Figure 17: Brand values according to Brand Census
Source: Authors' presentation based on Franzen, O., Burkhardt, A., (2006), p. 62

As can be seen in Figure 17, Audi has a brand value of € 11.9 billion according to the Brand Census. Audi thus obtains the best result according to this method. For Mercedes Benz the value was € 11.4 billion, while BMW was in last place among the three automotive brands considered with a brand value of € 10.9 billion.

2.5.2.3 Interbrand Method

In the eighties a lot of merger and acquisition processes were characterized by transaction prices that frequently exceeded the asset value of the company. As a consequence of this development, it became increasingly clear that another variable in addition to the asset value must have a decisive influence on the value of a company.[47]

The issue of calculating the value of a brand was taken up again by the company Interbrand in cooperation with the London Business School in 1988 and especially the case of *Rank Hovis McDougalls* in England influenced the analysis. *Rank Hovis McDougalls* is an English producer of baked goods known for its high quality of goods and a widely respected brand. In 1988, it was looking for an effective method to seek protection against a takeover by *Goodman Fielder Watthie*. With the help of the newly developed Interbrand method, it was possible to determine the value of the brand of *Rank Hovis McDougalls* in a traceable way. It served as the basis for the balance sheet treatment of the internally generated brand value as an immaterial asset. This reform of the Accounting Standards, which was introduced officially in England in 1989, helped the company to improve its key figures, to obtain cheaper financing, and ultimately to successfully defend against a hostile takeover.[48]

The Interbrand method led to a new definition of brand management. An efficient brand management must fulfill two main goals. First of all, the sustainable management of the brand must serve to achieve a potential selling or purchase price in an M&A process. Questions concerning accounting and financing must be resolved reliably by management. This means that the optimization of the brand value will lead to efficient financing and an optimized balance sheet structure.

The second goal is to optimize investments in the brand and to obtain a sustainable increase of the brand value via brand management.[49]

---

[47] See Schimansky, A., Stucky, N. (2004), p. 434.
[48] See Schimansky, A., Stucky, N. (2004), pp. 435ff.
[49] See Schimansky, A., Stucky, N. (2004), p. 435.

In the Interbrand method, the brand value is defined as an asset value which serves the function of assuring customer loyalty. But the basis of the Interbrand method is the earnings value of the brand; put differently, the earnings generated by the brand. Its determination is at the core of the Interbrand method. Schimansky and Stucky describe the usefulness of a brand in the following way:

> "In order to capture the usefulness of a brand for their owners, the brand value is defined as the net present value of those future earnings that can be traced exclusively to the existence of the brand."[50]

This means that the earnings of a company must always be broken down into sales which are attributable to the brand and those that are not.

The process of the Interbrand method for the determination of the brand value

Fundamentally, the approach can be broken down into three main phases as well as a preliminary and a final procedural step, as displayed in Figure 18.

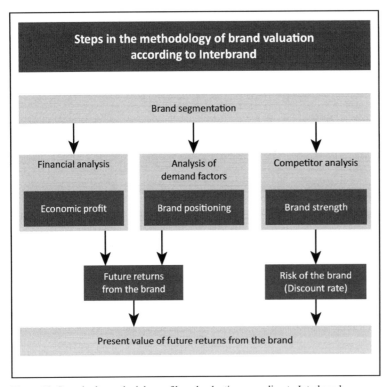

Figure 18: Steps in the methodology of brand valuation according to Interbrand
Source: Schimansky, A., Stucky, N., (2004), p. 438

Before the three main steps of the analysis can be conducted, a very important step is the classification of the products of a brand or a company by individual segment. This step particularly

---

[50] See Schimansky, A., Stucky, N. (2004), p. 435.

serves to enhance the transparency of the brand value calculation. Especially in the automotive sector, many buying decisions are determined by emotions which can be different for different vehicle models or sub-brands. This can be true even within the same brand, for example in the case of BMW. Following the core part of the Interbrand method, the appreciation for the brand by the customers is made explicit and a monetary brand value is determined.

First process step: segmentation

Segmentation mostly serves the purpose of categorizing the products of a company into homogeneous subgroups. For these subgroups all following process steps are conducted individually. The segmentation is important because the different products of a brand differ in the status that they have with customers. For that reason, they can be assigned to so-called sub-brands. Since these trigger different emotions with potential customers, a different valuation for the individual sub-brands or subgroups follows.[51]

Second process step: financial analysis to isolate the economic profit

The second process step can be described with reference to Figure 19.

	Sales / earnings of pro-forma profit and loss statement
−	Sales that are not attributable to the brand
=	Sales attributable to the brand
−	Operative costs (personnel, marketing & administrative costs)
−	Goodwill write-offs & special effects
=	EBIT (Earnings before Interest and Tax)
−	Taxes & Cost of capital (determined using WACC[52])
=	Economic profit

Figure 19: Determination of economic profit
Source: Authors' presentation based on Schimansky, A., Stucky, N., (2004), pp. 439–440

It is important at this step that the financial analysis is based on the values from a pro forma profit and loss statement. In most cases these planning values cover five years. The most important factor in this process step is the determination of sales that are attributable to the brand. However, this factor cannot be discussed in more detail at this point, since Interbrand does not publish any poignant information about this process step. But in general it can be inferred that the economic profit which is determined by the financial analysis expresses the ability of a brand to create economic value.[53]

Third process step: determination of the share of the brand in the company assets

While the second step dealt with calculating the contribution of the brand to the sales of the company, this step serves to determine the share of the brand in the assets of the company. It

---

[51] See Schimansky, A., Stucky, N. (2004), p. 438.
[52] WACC = Weighted Average Cost of Capital.
[53] See Schimansky, A., Stucky, N. (2004), pp. 439–440.

requires the determination of demand factors and the demand behavior of the customers for the individual products in the segments is analyzed. "The demand for the output of the company, concretely the product or the service, arises through factors that always have their base in the assets of the company."[54] Among them are quality, design, price and additional factors which are influenced decisively by the company assets. That the brand value should not be neglected when a company makes internal decisions is illustrated in Figure 20. The table shows that in the automotive industry, the brand had a share of 40% of the economic profit in the year 2008. In comparison, this value was only 10% in the chemical industry.[55]

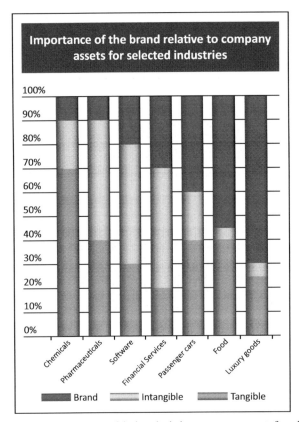

Figure 20: Importance of the brand relative to company assets for selected industries
Source: Schimansky, A., Stucky, N., (2004), p. 440

The determination of the degree of influence that the brand has on the assets of a company is guided by two analytical steps: first, by an analysis of market research data, a so-called secondary analysis and second, by interviews with company representatives and major buyers or users of the product. These interviews are conducted based on demand factors. Figure 21 provides an overview of substantial demand factors in the automotive industry, which are used to determine the share of the brand in company assets.

---

[54] See Schimansky, A., Stucky, N. (2004), p. 440.
[55] See Schimansky, A., Stucky, N. (2004), p. 440.

2.5 Brand Value and Brand Valuation

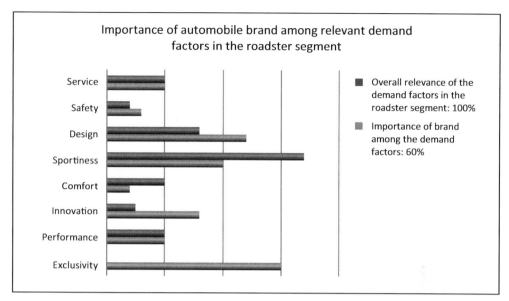

Figure 21: Importance of automobile brand among relevant demand factors in the roadster segment
Source: Authors' presentation based on Schimansky, A., Stucky, N., (2004), p. 442

Once the factors are determined, they are quantified with the help of the two steps of the analysis and combined to yield a fraction of the company assets.

With the quantitative determination of the economic profit and the share of the brand in the company assets, all factors that can provide insights concerning the financial status quo of the brand have now been included in the analysis.[56]

Fourth process step: determination of the risk of the brand and the discount rate

In this step an analysis of the competitive situation is used to determine the strength of the brand. This helps to determine the risk of the brand and ultimately the rate used to discount the economic profit and the share of the brand in the company assets.

In order to determine the strength of the brand, surveys are conducted among market participants. The first factor to be determined is the dynamism of the relevant sales market of the product. This includes growth forecasts for the market, the general competitive structure and the market volume. These factors are combined to arrive at a value for the overall market dynamic. A second factor is the stability of the brand or the reaction of the brand to past market changes. Here it is important to obtain empirical data which shows the degree of broad uninterrupted success of the brand in the marketplace. Additional factors are market leadership, in other words the influence of the brand on the market, the trend of the brand, the development of the brand in the past and the support for the brand by the company. With the advance of globalization, the degree of internationalization of the brand is increasingly relevant. This factor determines the degree of risk diversification across different regional markets. A final factor is brand protection, which refers to the legal protection of the brand.[57]

---

[56] See Schimansky, A., Stucky, N. (2004), p. 443.
[57] See Schimansky, A., Stucky, N. (2004), pp. 443–444.

Fifth process step: determination of the monetary brand value

Once all factors are determined, a quantitative method is used to aggregate them in a brand risk premium. This is used to calculate the discount rate as a combination of the risk-free rate of return and the specific brand risk premium. This discount rate is used in the following step to discount the economic profit and the share of the brand in company assets in order to arrive at the monetary value of the brand.[58]

With the help of the following example in Figure 22, the entire monetary approach is briefly presented.[59]

	2001	2002	2003	2004	2005	2006	2007
Sales in the brand segment	440	480	500	520	550	580	620
Minus operative costs	(374)	(408)	(425)	(442)	(468)	(493)	(527)
EBIT	66	72	75	78	82	87	93
Minus taxes 33%	(22)	(24)	(25)	(26)	(27)	(29)	(31)
NOPAT	44	48	50	52	55	58	62

	2001	2002	2003	2004	2005	2006	2007
Operative assets	220	240	250	260	275	290	310
Minus cost of capital 5%	(11)	(12)	(13)	(13)	(14)	(15)	(16)

	2001	2002	2003	2004	2005	2006	2007
Economic profit	33	36	37	39	41	43	46
Brand returns (for relevance of 45%)	15	16	17	18	18	19	21

	2001	2002	2003	2004	2005	2006	2007
Discount rate 15%							
Discount factor		1.0	1.15	1.32	1.52	1.75	2.01
Discounted brand earnings			15	14	12	11	10

	2001	2002	2003	2004	2005	2006	2007
Values up to 2007		62					
Perpetuity (Growth = 2%)		16					
Present value of the brand segment		78					

Figure 22: Steps to calculate the brand value (in € million) according to the Interbrand Method
Source: Authors' presentation based on Schimansky, A., Stucky, N., (2004), p. 447

---

[58] See Schimansky, A., Stucky, N. (2004), p. 446.
[59] EBIT = Earnings before Interest and Taxes; NOPAT = Net Operating Profit after Taxes.

The brand values which are calculated with the Interbrand method are published annually and are publicly available.

2.5.3 Advantages and Disadvantages of the Valuation Methods Presented

2.5.3.1 Advantages

Both methods enable companies to assign a monetary value to their brand. This value can be used to assess the brand value relative to that of competing brands and to reach internal management decisions, for example concerning marketing activities. At the same time, the brand value can also be relevant for external parties, such as prospective buyers. In a company transaction this may lead to a sales price that significantly exceeds the asset value.

The process of calculating the brand value can furthermore be used to identify problematic areas. The transfer rates from one stage of the funnel to the next which are calculated by Brand Census can be used to identify major weaknesses of the brand. If, for example, the transfer rate from *familiarity* to *relevant set* is very low, this informs management about possible fields of action. The Interbrand method and the results from the assessment of brand strength also allow conclusions about problematic areas of the brand.

And finally, the Interbrand method is one of the few methods which has gained global acceptance over the past ten years.[60] This bestows credibility and trust upon a brand value that was calculated with the Interbrand method.

2.5.3.2 Disadvantages

One of the main disadvantages of the brand valuation procedures is the lack of publicly available information. This problem is especially severe with regard to the quantitative methods to calculate sales that are attributable to the brand. For external observers it is hard to assess how Interbrand and other valuation companies have determined the precise value of sales that are attributable to the brand. The Interbrand method suffers from the same weakness when the share of the brand in company assets is calculated.

In order to calculate brand values according to the Brand Census, the indexes of brand strength of all relevant brands in the industry are assessed. This also leaves considerable room for interpretation, especially concerning the question of relevant brands.

Due to the lack of publicly available information it is not possible to reproduce with precision how the qualitative factors are translated into monetary values.

---

[60] See Schimansky, A., Stucky, N. (2004), p. 456.

An additional disadvantage of the Brand Census follows from the attribution of the market profit to the individual brands. It is assumed that the future profit potential will remain unchanged and that the strength of the brands will not vary. Especially the automotive sector is subject to constant innovation and change. It is therefore not realistic to assume that market profit and brand strength are unchanged in the future.

In closing it can be stated that each method for calculating the brand value has its own advantages and weaknesses. But the plurality of methods frequently leads to a critical stance concerning brand valuation, especially since each method arrives at a different brand value. The two methods presented in this chapter can lead to results that differ significantly. As an example, Interbrand values the BMW brand at approximately € 16 billion. According to Brand Census, the value is only € 11 billion.[61] No generally accepted brand value follows from the use of the different methods.

2.5.4 Comparison of Market Capitalization and Brand Value

Even though the numerous methods used for brand valuation suffer from the disadvantages listed above, they still offer an opportunity to arrive at an approximate estimate of the value of a brand. The aim of this chapter is to determine whether the brand value corresponds to the market value of equity of a company as represented by the market capitalization. In order to analyze which fraction of the market capitalization can be explained by brand value, the 30 most valuable brands are related to the market capitalization of the respective company. The brand values – based on the Interbrand ranking from 16 September 2010 – are compared to the corresponding market capitalization on the same day.

It must be mentioned that some brands belong to companies that hold several other very strong brands in their product portfolio. This is the case for Gillette, for example. This well-known brand must be assigned to the company Procter & Gamble. When the brand value of Gillette is compared to the market capitalization of Procter & Gamble, it must be taken into consideration that additional strong brands, such as Wella, Ariel or Pringles influence the company value. A similar picture emerges when comparing the value of the brand Nescafé and the market capitalization of the company Nestlé. The market value of equity of Nestlé is also in part determined by other well-known brands such as S. Pellegrino, Nestea or Häagen-Dazs. This helps to explain why the two brands mentioned, Gillette and Nescafé only hold a share of 14% and 7% in the market capitalization of the corresponding company.

On average the monetary value of the most valuable 30 brands according to Interbrand amounted to 25.76% of the market capitalization of the respective companies. Put differently, the value of the top-30 brands accounted for about one fourth of the market value of equity.

---

[61] See Franzen, O., Burkhardt, A. (2006), p. 62.

2.5 Brand Value and Brand Valuation

It can also be observed that the percentage share of the brand value in market capitalization declines with lower brand value. While the ratio for the ten most valuable brands was 32%, the brands on positions 21–30 only accounted for 23% of the market value of equity. This fact also makes it clear that a high brand value does not necessarily imply a high market capitalization. Even though Disney is ranked number 9 among the most valuable brands, the company only has a market capitalization of US$ 64 billion. J.P. Morgan on the other hand has a value at the stock exchange of close to US$ 162 billion, but its brand is only ranked in position 29 among most valuable brands.

A focus on the automobile manufacturers reveals that three of the four automotive brands that are among the 30 most valuable brands have an above average value. The 21% calculated for Toyota is the lowest share when comparing brand value and market capitalization. This is explained by the high market capitalization. BMW with a figure of 61% is significantly above average. A plausible explanation is the low market capitalization compared to the other automobile manufacturers. On the other hand, the high percentage value is also an indication of the strength of the brand. The high brand value of BMW compared to its market capitalization indicates that brand management is of major importance. Investments in the brand, such as building the BMW world, can quite possibly contribute to an increased market capitalization and should not be underestimated.

Additional representatives from the automotive sector which are among the 100 most valuable brands according to Interbrand are for example Ford and Volkswagen. Ford with a brand value of US$ 7.2 billion is in position 50 of the ranking. This is equivalent to 16% of the market capitalization. Volkswagen has a brand value of US$ 6.9 billion and obtained position 53. Relative to the market capitalization, the brand value accounts for 23%. The lower percentage values compared to the Top-30 brands confirm that the share in the market value of equity declines with lower placements in the ranking. In addition, the Volkswagen Group, just as Nestlé and Procter & Gamble, is made up of several strong brands. Audi (position 63) and Porsche (position 72) are also among the 100 most valuable brands according to Interbrand, but were valued independently. However, the market capitalization of the Volkswagen Group also includes these brands.

In summary, it can be concluded that the value of a brand plays an important role in the automotive industry. The brand values of Toyota, Mercedes Benz, BMW and Honda on average account for 39% of their market capitalization. This stresses the importance of an efficient brand management for automobile manufacturers. The results described are summarized in Figure 23.

Rank	Brand	Brand Value according to Interbrand in $m	Market capitalization in $m	Brand value relative to market capitalization
1	Coca Cola	70,452	128,877.22	54.67%
2	IBM	64,727	155,051.40	41.75%
3	Microsoft	60,895	822,532.10	7.40%
4	Google	43,557	121,704.80	35.79%
5	General Electric	42,808	168,222.54	25.45%
6	McDonald's	33,578	75,818.14	44.29%
7	Intel	32,015	98,189.33	32.61%
8	Nokia	29,495	144,368.05	20.43%
9	Disney	28,731	63,887.77	44.97%
10	Hewlett-Peckard	26,867	339,643.00	7.91%
11	Toyota	26,192	121,900.52	21.49%
12	Mercedes Benz	25,179	59,049.80	42.64%
13	Gillette	23,298	166,648.07	13.98%
14	Cisco	23,219	120,198.30	19.32%
15	BMW	22,322	36,440.50	61.26%
16	Louis Vuitton	21,860	64,128.80	34.09%
17	Apple	21,143	255,759.50	8.27%
18	Marlboro	19,961	93,994.43	21.24%
19	Samsung	19,491	73,649.75	26.46%
20	Honda	18,506	62,304.10	29.70%
21	H&M	16,136	355,352.30	4.54%
22	Oracle	14,881	127,664.70	11.66%
23	Pepsi	14,061	210,574.72	6.68%
24	American Express	13,944	48,614.51	28.68%
25	Nike	13,706	29,123.07	47.06%
26	SAP	12,756	58,232.75	21.91%
27	Nescafé	12,753	175,007.50	7.29%
28	IKEA	12,487	Not publicly listed	
29	J.P. Morgan	12,314	161,608.60	7.62%
30	Budweiser	12,252	68,053.80	18.00%

Figure 23: Comparison of brand value and market capitalization on 16. September 2010
Source: Authors' presentation based on Interbrand (2010) and Bloomberg (2010)[62]

---

[62] Note: The market capitalization of BMW AG was calculated using an exchange rate of 1.3075$/€ (as of 16. September 2010).

2.5.5 Development of Brand Values in the Automotive Sector

As can be seen clearly from Figure 24, numerous automobile manufacturers are represented in the Top-100 of the Interbrand ranking, which is published annually. Some of them, such as Toyota or Mercedes Benz, have already appeared among the 100 most valuable brands globally since 2001.

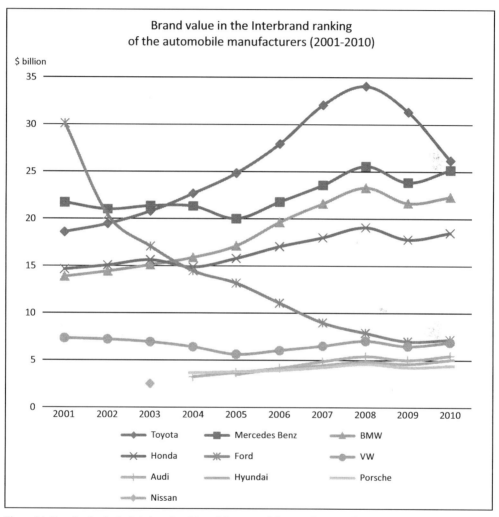

Figure 24: Brand value in the Interbrand ranking of the automobile manufacturers (2001–2010)
Source: Authors' presentation based on Interbrand (2010), as of: 16. September 2010

It is apparent that both Toyota and Ford have witnessed major reductions in the value of their brand over time. The value of Ford declined from about US$ 30 billion in 2001 to only about US$ 7.5 billion in 2010. Factors that may influence the continuous decline of the brand value can be poor brand management, declines in product quality or other negative news.

An additional negative example in the industry is Toyota. Since the product recall campaign in 2008, which lasted until 2010 and affected about 1.53 million vehicles, particularly in the US, Japan and Europe, the brand value is in continuous decline. This shows how massively a loss in quality in combination with negative press reports can affect the image of a company brand.[63]

A negative trend such as the one which is observable in the case of Toyota can fatally affect the future of the company. In light of newer forms of propulsion, such as electric drives, the differences in the various engines of the automobile manufacturers will continue to decline. It can be expected that the purchasing decision of the customer will increasingly depend on the image of the brand and will no longer be determined by technical product specifications.

Figure 23 shows that in the automotive industry the share of the brand value, as calculated using the Interbrand method, is higher on average than in other sectors. BMW for example shows a brand value in excess of 60% of its market capitalization. This means that more than half of the market capitalization can be explained by the brand value. Figure 24 demonstrates that the brand value of BMW has witnessed an increase from about US$ 20 billion to close to US$ 25 billion specifically between 2006 and 2008. This improvement can also be linked to the BMW world, which opened at the end of 2007. With this instrument of customer retention and brand management, the brand experience of potential customers is expanded and internalized.

Despite a share in the market capitalization that is high on average, the automobile manufacturers are also characterized by a large volatility in these percentage shares. The company Honda, for example, which is active in the volume segment, only has a share of the brand value of about 29% of the market capitalization. In comparison, BMW – a company which is active in the high-price segment – shows a value in excess of 61%. This relation supports the hypothesis that especially in the high-price segment of the automotive industry, the importance of the brand is already elevated and can be expected to go up further in the future.

A comparison of the brand values in the automotive sector thus highlights the increasing future relevance of efficient brand management and targeted marketing.

---

[63] See Weltonline (2010).

3 Strategic Alliances in the Automotive Sector

3.1 Executive Summary

Strategic alliances in the automotive sector will become increasingly important in the future. In contrast to mergers and acquisitions, their relevance will go up markedly. The number of strategic alliances that were initiated has gone up strongly since the year 2009. This is due in particular to the advanced stage of the consolidation process in the industry. In addition to the classical alliances within the industry, the trend towards alliances across industries will intensify, as the example of BMW and MyCityWay illustrates. The term strategic alliance includes equity capital stakes of up to 20% and contractually agreed forms of cooperation in defined areas, but also separately established companies such as joint ventures.[64]

3.2 Definition of Terms

3.2.1 Strategic Alliances or M&A

Since the automotive industry has already reached a high degree of consolidation, strategic alliances are increasingly gaining in importance. Figure 25 provides an overview of all types of strategic alliances. The analysis in Section 3.2.1 is based on De Pumphilis (2005).

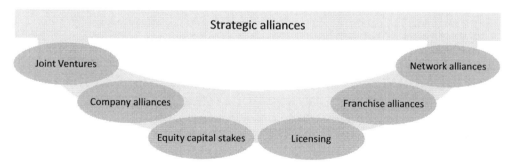

Figure 25: Types of strategic alliances
Source: following De Pamphilis (2005)

---

[64] We thank Benjamin Müller for his suport in the topic area of "strategic alliances." His activities have greatly contributed to the success of this book.

> The most important types of strategic alliances are:
> - Joint Ventures
> - Company alliances
> - Equity capital stakes
> - Licensing
> - Franchise alliances
> - Network alliances.
>
> Depending on the type, different effects concerning control, exit options, resource use, as well as the sharing of risks and profits must be considered.[65]

Joint Ventures: These are cooperating companies which were founded by two or more independent companies in order to achieve common strategic or financial goals. Joint ventures are separate legal entities, in which each partner retains his own identity and independence.

Company alliances: In comparison to joint ventures, these are not legally separate companies. Company alliances in the automotive industry are formed predominantly for the purpose of joint use of knowledge in the following areas:

- Research & development
- Marketing
- Technology
- Purchasing & procurement

However, company alliances can turn into joint ventures over time.

Participations: In this type of strategic alliance, one company acquires a minority stake (normally 5–20%) in another company. In some cases the minority investor possesses a call option which enables him to increase his stake.

Licensing: Two types of licensing exist:

- Licensing of a specific technology, a product or a process in order to seize opportunities
- Trade licenses in which one company grants a manufacturer of, for example, consumer goods the right of use

A licensing agreement normally specifies which rights of use are granted, how and where they can be utilized and for how long the license holder has the right of use. In contrast to joint ventures and company alliances as sub-categories of the major category of strategic alliances, no sharing of risk and return takes place. Licensing can thus be considered a rather riskless form of a strategic alliance, which requires an initial investment.

Franchise alliances: These are networks in which companies are connected via several licensing contracts. The licensing agreements usually grant rights for the use of goods and services.

Network alliances: These are alliances of companies that frequently cross international borders. Such agreements can lead to a situation where two companies are cooperating in one market while they are competitors in another one. Alliances of this kind are mostly used to

---

[65] See Ernst, D., Häcker, J. (2006), pp. 6ff.

get access to abilities in related, but still different industries (for example computer and multimedia industry).[66]

All of these types of strategic alliances imply that a maximum of 20% of the shares is acquired.

> In addition to this group of strategic alliances, cooperation in the form of mergers & acquisitions is also possible. §271 HGB talks about a participation or acquisition if the buyer acquires at least 20% of the nominal value of the target company. In the case of a merger, two companies join forces or are combined in a newly founded company.

Synergies were overestimated or cultural differences underestimated in the past. In the times of globalization numerous takeovers and mergers took place in the automotive sector as well. One of the largest mergers in this context was between Daimler Benz AG and Chrysler Motor Corporation. The two companies merged in the year 1998 to form Daimler Chrysler, but separated again several years later due to significant problems.

3.2.2 Proposition

Numerous takeovers in the past have resulted in a group of approximately 15 large automobile manufacturers, which are responsible for close to 100% of global automotive production. This makes it seem unlikely that there will be a lot more major takeovers in the years to come.

Since the automotive manufacturers will continue to discover weaknesses in the automotive value chain which offer the potential to increase competitiveness, the search will be on for potential partners that can provide this knowledge in exchange. This necessity also follows directly from the heterogeneity of the industry. In the future, these types of cooperation agreements will involve mainly strategic alliances. Ultimately there will be a few very large automotive manufacturers left on the global market. These will on occasion provide support to each other via strategic alliances in relevant areas. In addition, there will also be a significant number of strategic alliances across industries.

3.3 Why Strategic Alliances and not M&A will Dominate the Automotive Industry in the Future

Following strong sales declines in the wake of the financial crisis in 2008 and 2009, the automotive industry again witnessed strong sales growth in 2010. Global production of 70 million units even surpassed the pre-crisis level and advanced by 21% compared to 2009. More than half of the growth is generated by the booming regions in Asia-Pacific, particularly China and India. In order to pursue a sustainable growth strategy, the presence in these markets by the automobile producers is thus an absolute necessity.[67]

---

[66] See Ernst, D., Häcker, J. (2011), pp. 6ff.
[67] See Kuhnert, F., Niederdrenk, R., Maser, J.C. (2011), pp. 10–11.

In some cases, strategic alliances and not M&A is the only possibility to get access to a market. As an example, the Chinese government until recently only gave foreign manufacturers access to the home market via a joint venture with a Chinese producer.

In addition to strategic development opportunities in the existing product portfolio in new markets, it is above all important to open up new product segments. As an example, there is a trend in Germany, but also in other important markets, towards the low cost segment.[68] Especially the German automobile manufacturers, however, have their strengths mostly in the premium segment. They are therefore dependent on strategic alliances with automobile manufacturers that are successfully represented with their product portfolio in the segment of small vehicles.

Furthermore, the automotive industry may be at a juncture. It is certain that the automobile in its current form is not fit for the future. The most important raw material used by today's combustion engine will become scarce and therefore more expensive in the near future. Additionally, the companies are under pressure to produce fleets that are low in emissions in order to make a meaningful contribution towards environmental protection. At this point it is not obvious which drive technology will dominate in the future. From the perspective of the companies, strategic alliances offer a convincing option to obtain the necessary knowledge about the technologies of the future or to distribute the required investments among several parties. Especially the German automobile manufacturers lack the necessary knowledge in the major technology areas of electric drive, batteries and carbon fiber.[69] The only choice for those companies is to enter into strategic partnerships in order to quickly acquire the necessary expert knowledge.[70] In addition, the automobile manufacturers aim to distribute the risks inherent in developing such technologies among a number of partners.

Some of the most interesting strategic alliances across industries and within the sector – including the underlying strategic considerations – are shown in the following sections as illustrations: Volkswagen and Suzuki, BMW and SGL Carbon, Daimler and Renault/Nissan as well as BMW with MyCityWay and Sixt.

3.3.1 Volkswagen and Suzuki

In the fall of 2009, the largest German automobile manufacturer Volkswagen entered into a strategic partnership in the form of a cross holding with the Japanese automobile manufacturer Suzuki Motor Corporation. In this context, VW acquired 19.9% in the Japanese manufacturer for € 1.7 billion.[71] Suzuki meanwhile used half of the proceeds to establish a position of 2.5% in the Wolfsburg-based company.[72]

The stated aim of VW was to profit from the leading role of Suzuki in the segment of small cars and mini cars. Important components were to be developed jointly and used both in the brands of Volkswagen and Suzuki. Suzuki meanwhile was interested predominantly in the knowledge of the Wolfsburg-based company in the area of fuel-efficient diesel engines as

---

[68] See PricewaterhouseCoopers (2011).
[69] See Reuter, W. (2011), p. 1.
[70] See Reuter, W. (2011), p. 1.
[71] See Hucko, M. (2010).
[72] See Manager Magazin online (2010).

well as alternative drive technologies, such as the hybrid or electric engine. In addition, the strategic partnership served as compensation for geographical weaknesses. While VW has a tradition of strength in the regions Europe and South America, Suzuki holds a particularly strong market position in Asia. Especially in the market segment of small cars and mini cars, it holds a high market share.[73] With a market share of 37.2% in the year 2011 in the Japanese segment of small cars, Suzuki has a particularly strong position and was also able to record strong growth in other important Asian markets such as China (+44%) and India (+21%).[74] Even though Volkswagen has a high market share in China, they are lagging behind especially in India and other important Asian automobile markets. However, there have recently been frictions in the cooperation between the two producers. Both parties accuse the other side of contract violations. Suzuki was dissatisfied that it did not get the anticipated advantages in the transfer of knowledge, while VW felt ignored, when the Japanese ordered diesel engines from Fiat. Suzuki even demanded that the VW Group should dispose of its Suzuki shares. It remains to be seen how the conflict develops in the future.

3.3.2 BMW and SGL Carbon

With an eye on the growing relevance of CO_2 emissions for reaching the global climate protection targets and the currently still very low range of electric vehicles, the total weight of the automobile is gaining quickly in importance. With the goal to increasingly replace steel and aluminum components with carbon, BMW entered into a strategic partnership with SGL Carbon, the global leader in the production of carbon products. The Bavarian automobile manufacturer and SGL Carbon in 2009 founded a joint venture for the manufacturing of carbon fibers and semi-finished textile products. BMW holds 49% and the SGL Group 51% in the joint venture.[75] In the spring of 2011, the ultra-modern carbon fiber plant of the joint venture with an investment volume of US$ 100 million was completed in Moses Lake, Washington State (USA). The parts which are developed there are to be used in the Mega City Vehicle or in the BMW i3.[76,77]

In March 2011 Volkswagen, in an unexpected move, took an 8% share (as of October 2011 the share stood at about 9.9%[78]) in the carbon fiber specialist and surprised the automobile manufacturer from Munich. This made Volkswagen the second largest shareholder after the major owner Susanne Klatten, who holds 22.25% through her investment company Skion and is also a major shareholder of the VW-rival BMW.[79] Following the acquisition by VW, Susanne Klatten increased her holding to close to 27%, assuring her a blocking minority. With its participation in SGL Carbon, Volkswagen pursues the same goal as BMW. It considers the topic of lightweight construction to be of major importance in reducing emissions and gasoline use.[80]

---

[73] See Ziesche, B. (2010).
[74] See Suzuki Motor Corporation (2010), pp. 6–7.
[75] See ATZ online (2009).
[76] See SGL Group (2010).
[77] See SGL Group (2011).
[78] See FTD (2011).
[79] See Manager Magazin online (2011).
[80] See Telebörse (2011).

3.3.3 Daimler and Renault/Nissan

In the spring of 2010, Daimler AG and the Renault/Nissan alliance agreed on a strategic partnership in the form of a cross holding.[81] The equity stakes were limited to 3.1% of the shares. The Japanese/French alliance received a share of 3.1% in Daimler AG; the Stuttgart-based company meanwhile took a 3.1% stake in both Renault and Nissan.

The cooperation focuses primarily on a joint architecture in the segment of small cars, the powertrain, as well as cooperation in the area of light commercial vehicles.[82] The new Smart fortwo, the four-seater of the brand with the same name, as well as the new model of the Renault Twingo are to be based on a platform that is developed jointly. In the field of the joint powertrain, the focus is on fuel efficient diesel and gasoline engines. Renault will provide smaller three and four cylinder aggregates to Daimler, which can then serve as the base for smaller Mercedes models. In exchange, the Stuttgart-based company will deliver larger four and six cylinder engines to the Nissan subsidiary for premium vehicles of the Infinity brand. In the area of light commercial vehicles, Daimler plans to add one model to its portfolio in 2012. The new entry-level model is to be developed on the basis of Renault models and manufactured at a French Renault plant.

The generation of additional sales volumes, a better utilization of the Daimler and Renault/Nissan manufacturing sites and the sharing of investment costs are expected to lead to significant cost savings for all parties involved. Both Daimler and Renault/Nissan hope to realize a savings potential of € 2 billion over the next five years, which could be the result of synergies alone.[83] In addition, Daimler AG expects to benefit from the knowledge of Renault in the segment of small cars. Just like VW, Daimler urgently needs to catch up in that area and depends on strategic partnerships. Renault on the other hand hopes to gain in reputation as a consequence of the collaboration with the Stuttgart-based manufacturer of premium automobiles.

3.3.4 BMW and MyCityWay

In complete contrast to the classical strategic partnerships within the automotive sector, BMW in February 2011 formed a partnership with the software developer MyCityWay from the United States. This participation in the amount of US$ 5 million[84] exemplifies technology-driven alliances across industries. The equity capital was provided by the venture capital company BMW i Ventures, which was founded shortly before the transaction in New York. With this partnership, the BMW Group hopes to get access to promising concepts in the area of novel mobility services.[85] The newly developed application MyCityWay can be used to display useful information about a number of cities on a smartphone such as the iPhone by Apple. This allows the user to find the quickest way to a specific destination or to locate different businesses or restaurants in the vicinity. With this application, BMW wants to react

---

[81] See Daimler AG (2010).
[82] See Daimler AG (2010).
[83] See Spiegel online (2010).
[84] See Wauters, R. (2011).
[85] See Börse Express (2011).

to the changing mobility needs in the so-called megacities and address new areas in the field of vehicle-independent mobility services.[86]

With MyCityWay, BMW pursues the aim of winning over new customer groups for the brand by offering alternative mobility services and to be well positioned in the emerging field of vehicle-independent mobility services.

3.3.5 BMW and Sixt

An additional and far reaching change for the automotive sector is already taking shape in the minds of the younger generation. According to a study by Zipcar, the automobile is increasingly losing in importance among the age group from 18 to 34 years. As an example, 35% of those interviewed agreed with the statement that today an automobile requires substantial maintenance costs. 45% stated that they will occasionally leave the car in the garage and for ecological reasons utilize alternative means of transportation.[87] To participate profitably in this development, some automobile manufacturers increasingly rely on the concept of car sharing. As an example, Daimler AG in the year 2008 started the car sharing project "Car2Go" in Ulm and shortly after expanded this offering in the US in Austin, Texas. Meanwhile the City-Smarts can also be utilized in Hamburg and Dusseldorf, Amsterdam, Vienna and Lyon as well as in Vancouver, Washington D.C. and San Diego.[88]

The largest offensive to date by a manufacturer with regard to the topic of car sharing was started by BMW AG in the spring of 2011. Jointly with the car rental company Sixt, BMW is offering 800 Minis and BMW Series 1 in Munich and Berlin for car sharing since April 2011. Both companies hold 50% in the joint venture "DriveNow." BMW provides the automobiles as well as the technology in the cars. Sixt provides its knowledge in the areas of service and rental, the IT-infrastructure and a comprehensive network for the registration of customers. The automobiles can be rented for 29 Eurocents per minute including gasoline and insurance.[89] Neither fixed rental stations nor car keys are required.[90] Available automobiles can be located and booked via the internet or a smartphone. They can be started using a driver's license and an integrated chip. With this partnership, BMW targets the growing number of drivers that do not own their own vehicle and wants to familiarize them with its own brand of vehicles.

3.3.6 Assessment of the Joint Approaches

In the past years, strategic alliances have increasingly gained in importance, a trend that will continue in the future as well. One reason for this development is the fact that the consolidation process in the automotive industry appears largely completed. In addition, especially the German premium manufacturers depend on partnerships, since they have always held a weak position in the segment of smaller vehicles. Without a global presence in this segment, Volkswagen, for example will not be able to reach the ambitious goal of becoming the glob-

---

[86] See Bimmer Today (2011).
[87] See Zipcar (2011).
[88] See Car2Go (2012).
[89] See DriveNow (2011).
[90] See Krix P. (2011).

ally largest automotive group. Furthermore, it is important to adjust to the evolving customer demands in a mobility environment that is constantly changing. Especially with regard to expensive batteries for electronic vehicles, most automobile manufacturers simply lack the knowledge needed for their development. Thus a strategic alliance offers the opportunity to benefit from the expert knowledge of the partner and to spread the development costs among a number of parties, without having to enter into a permanent relationship as is the case with M&A activities. Additionally, a strategic partnership is frequently less expensive.[91]

On the other hand, strategic alliances are also risky for the partners involved. Disagreement about the use of earnings or about the respective areas of competency may develop as the cooperation evolves. In some cases the result can be a long and wearing struggle, which puts a significant strain on the partnership and can even threaten its continuation.[92] As an example, Suzuki already admitted problems in the partnership with Volkswagen after slightly more than one year. The companies had not yet agreed on a common approach and only a "harmonization of cultures is happening at the moment."[93]

The automotive industry is currently undergoing monumental change and will continue to witness grave shifts. Since the consolidation process has already advanced significantly, the automobile manufacturers will increasingly resort to strategic alliances in the most important technological fields. Besides traditional alliances within the industry, alliances across industries will increasingly gain in importance. Even though this form of cooperation offers many advantages, the automobile manufacturers should not lose sight of the disadvantages and seek contractual security early on.

---

[91] See Spiegel online (2010).
[92] See Reuter, W. (2011), p. 2.
[93] See Hucko, M. (2010).

4 Strategic Development Potential of the Automotive Industry – The Example of Electric Vehicles

4.1 Executive Summary

This chapter deals with an analysis of the strengths and weaknesses of electric vehicles and the potential for substituting conventional automobiles with electric vehicles in various markets by 2020. It is quite likely that electronic mobility will succeed as an alternative to the conventional combustion engine in the long run. However, the timing of the breakthrough is not yet known.

- One reason for the market penetration of the electric vehicles is the increasing environmental awareness of both the population and most states and governments. The increasing scarcity of crude oil and the related price increases of gasoline are major drivers for the development efforts in the field of electric drives.
- The major obstacles at present are the limited range, the lack of infrastructure, and the high purchase prices for electric vehicles. The establishment of an infrastructure is moved forward with the help of a number of governmental measures and support programs. Customers expect an extended range and prices that are competitive compared to conventional vehicles.
- Automobile manufacturers and suppliers increasingly cooperate in order to meet the challenges and problems involved in achieving market penetration for electric vehicles. These relate mostly to the areas of material development and production as well as to joint activities with regard to specific hybrid or electric vehicle components (batteries).
- The share of electric vehicles in overall automobile sales in the year 2025 is forecast between 40% and 50% in the regions USA, Europe and Japan. Since all of these are saturated automobile markets, substitution between vehicles with conventional combustion engines and electric vehicles will take place.
- The still relatively low motorization rates both in China and in India continue to facilitate high growth rates. According to the forecast, the share of electric vehicles in total automobile sales in 2025 will be around 33%.
- It is likely that electric vehicles will only play a subordinate role in India. This is due to the high purchase price, relative to a low per-capita income, the lack of an adequate infrastructure and the absence of government incentives.
- In Russia and Brazil electric vehicles will most likely also be of little relevance, since these countries are endowed with large amounts of domestic raw materials and also lack the necessary infrastructure.

In parallel to the development of electric vehicles, research and development on alternative drive systems and fuels will continue as well.[94]

4.2 Definition of Terms and Scope

The changing framework conditions in the global automotive industry such as tighter environmental regulations or urbanization require adequate strategic reactions of the automobile manufacturers in order to assure continued market success. Strategy is defined as the long-term focus on the company goals and the use of corresponding measures and resources.[95]

Among the strategic development opportunities of the automotive industry are changes in product markets served, improvement or development of products, as well as the adaptation of the business model.

The automotive industry comprises both automobile manufacturers and automotive suppliers. The automobile manufacturers are in direct contact with the customers, whose perspective is reflected here. For that reason, the strategic development opportunities considered only relate to the automobile manufacturers.

Due to the substantial linkages between automobile manufacturers and their suppliers, especially with regard to electromobility, the strategic developments require a joint approach to be successful.

In this chapter, the electric vehicle (short EV) and its potential as a strategic development opportunity will be considered. Since the focus is on the final consumer, at this point an EV is a passenger car. This passenger car is powered at least partly with the help of electric energy stored in batteries. Electric motorcycles and commercial vehicles are not considered in this chapter. The focus of the study is exclusively on the mass market for electromobility. Hybrid technology is taken into consideration, since it is seen as an interim solution until the full-fledged electric vehicle is ready.

In addition to the purely technical development of EVs and the attendant strengths and weaknesses, a number of markets and their development are also studied. Among them are the triad markets, consisting of the US, Europe and Japan as well as two BRIC countries, China and India.

In closing, two cooperations of BMW are presented. They illustrate strategic development opportunities that are already implemented by a premium manufacturer.

4.3 Drivers of Future Developments in the Automotive Industry

4.3.1 Environmental Drivers

In the future, the global automotive industry will face severe societal, ecological and economic challenges. It is essential for the automobile manufacturers to identify the future driv-

---

[94] We thank Katharina Hubele and Amna Musemic for their support in the topic area of "electronic vehicles." Their work has made the success of this book possible.
[95] See Johnson, G., Scholes, K., Whittington, R. (2006), p. 9.

4.3 Drivers of Future Developments in the Automotive Industry

ers of consumer trends or societal change early on and to align their strategic orientation. Of particular relevance for strategic developments in the field of electronic mobility are future mobility trends, technologies, environmental policies, growth markets and urbanization. Figure 26 provides a graphical summary of the environmental drivers.

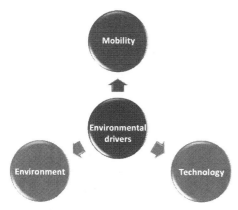

Figure 26: Environmental drivers
Source: Authors' presentation

Mobility

Future mobility developments will be of major importance for the global automotive industry. The automobile manufacturers must face the challenges posed by changes in mobility requirements and the increased demand for mobility services.

The constantly increasing global population implies a significant increase in traffic and a higher motorization rate. More than 7 billion people live on this planet[96] at current and especially in industrialized countries the passenger car density is high. In the OECD countries there are on average 558 passenger cars per 1000 inhabitants (see Figure 27).

Region	2000 Vehicles/ 1,000 P	2010 Vehicles/ 1,000 P	2020 Vehicles/ 1,000 P	2030 Vehicles/ 1,000 P	Growth 2000–2020 Vehicles/ 1,000 P
Industrialized countries					
OECD	520	558	633	724	39.2%
Non-OECD	190	241	326	436	129.5%
Developing countries					
BRIC & Indonesia	29	42	88	146	403.4%
Others	50	54	67	83	66%
Global	131	144	180	225	71.8%

Figure 27: Vehicle density – Comparison of industrial countries and developing countries
Source: Authors' presentation, based on Leschus, L., Stiller, S., Vöpel, H. (2009), p. 13; P = Persons

---

[96] See United Nations – Department of Economic and Social Affairs (2011).

According to an assessment of the United Nations, population growth will continue at a rapid rate. The global population in the year 2030 is estimated at 8.3 billion.[97] Disposable income will go up markedly in numerous regions of the world and especially in the BRIC countries.[98] In a recent study, the "Food and Agriculture Organization of the United Nations" (FAO) assumes annual growth of per-capita income in the Asian countries of 5%.[99] With an increasing global population and the advances in disposable income, the corresponding increase in the motorization rate will be strong. As Figure 30 shows, an increase in the number of passenger cars by 403.4% between the year 2000 and the year 2030 is expected for the BRIC countries and Indonesia alone.[100] This dynamic development would mean that in China alone the passenger car density would go up by a factor of ten by the year 2030.[101]

Next to the quantitative increase in motorization, alternative forms and concepts of mobility will gain in popularity. Particularly in the triad markets, customers will change their attitude towards automobiles in light of steadily increasing gasoline prices and a rising awareness for environmental causes. The automobile will continue to be highly relevant for daily mobility, but steadily lose importance as a status symbol. Looking forward, customers will increasingly demand individual mobility solutions that are tailored to their personal situation. Not ownership, but instead the use of an automobile will dominate.[102] Looking forward, there will be increasing customer demand for alternative forms and concepts of mobility such as rental cars, car sharing or linkages to the train system or other means of public transportation.

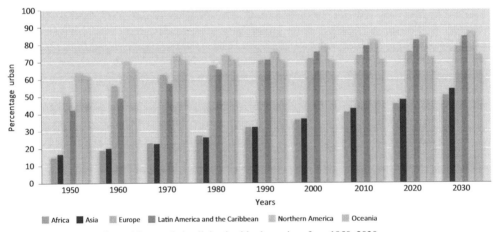

Figure 28: Percentage share of the population living in cities by regions from 1950–2030
Source: United Nations Population Fund (2007), p. 11

---

[97] See United Nations – Department of Economic and Social Affairs (2011).
[98] See Leschus, L., Stiller, S., Vöpel, H. (2009), p. 8.
[99] See United Nations – Department of Economic and Social Affairs (2011).
[100] See Leschus, L., Stiller, S., Vöpel, H. (2009), p. 13.
[101] See Leschus, L., Stiller, S., Vöpel, H. (2009), p. 7.
[102] See Winterhoff, M., et al. (2009), p. 33; Roland Berger Strategy Consultants, Amrop (2011), pp. 3, 18–19.

4.3 Drivers of Future Developments in the Automotive Industry

This trend is further reinforced by the increasing urbanization of the world population. According to forecasts by the "United Nations – Department of Economic and Social Affairs" (UNDESA), about 70%[103] of the total world population will live in cities by the year 2050 (see Figure 28).

The size of cities or the population density will therefore be highly relevant for future traffic patterns and the automobile.[104] In rural areas the passenger car density will continue to be higher than in the cities, because of the weaker offering of the public transportation system.[105]

These different trends allow the deduction of evolving new mobility concepts, which in some cases coincide with fundamentally new mobility demands.[106]

Environmental protection

The increasing motorization rate not only results in a doubling of global energy demand by the year 2050[107] but also in a strong increase of carbon dioxide emissions.

The future CO_2 emissions of the BRIC countries and the European OECD countries are displayed in Figure 29. It becomes apparent that the CO_2 emissions in China will go up drastically. With a share of about 30%, China will be responsible for the biggest share of CO_2 emissions by the year 2030.[108] This is caused by increases in prosperity and an enormous demand for energy.

A reduction of CO_2 emissions by 50% is needed in order to reach the goal of limiting global warming to two degrees. The European Union is pursuing the ambitious goal of an 80%[109] reduction of emissions by 2050 compared to 1990.

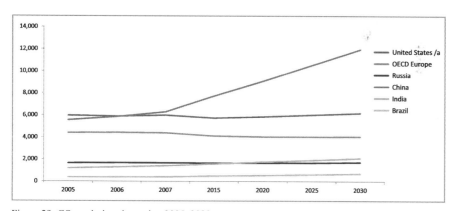

Figure 29: CO_2 emissions by region 2005–2030
Source: Authors' presentation based on Butler, R. A. (2005)

---

[103] See United Nations – Department of Economic and Social Affairs (2009).
[104] See Leschus, L., Stiller, S., Vöpel, H. (2009), p. 12.
[105] See Bundesinstitut für Bau-, Stadt- und Raumforschung (2011).
[106] See Winterhoff, M., et al. (2009), pp. 7ff.
[107] See Leschus, L., Stiller, S., Vöpel, H. (2009), p. 7.
[108] See Butler, R.A. (2005).
[109] See Der Natur-Blog (2011).

A substantial contribution towards the achievement of these climate goals must be made by the transportation sector. Already in 2008, the global share of transportation in total CO_2 emissions amounted to 22%.[110] Next to the energy sector it was the major cause of the harmful greenhouse gases.

The depletion of crude oil is hastened by the increasing motorization. Even if there continue to be discoveries of new oil fields, a supply shortage of crude oil is possible in the medium term, according to an assessment of the International Energy Agency (IEA).

Public policy measures and international climate agreements are used by governments to counter the advancing global warming. These measures provide incentives for research and development on alternative technologies as well as the conception of new mobility solutions.[111] One of the most important environmental agreements is the Kyoto Protocol which was signed in 1997 and came into force in 2005. 141 countries made a commitment to reduce greenhouse gases until 2012 by 5% compared to the level reached in the year 1990.

Technology

In order to provide sustainable mobility solutions that advance technological progress and allow the use of alternative fuels and new drive technologies, innovation is urgently needed.[112]

Technological advances in the information and communications industry are particularly relevant for the automotive industry. Research and development in the field of computer-based support systems will increasingly aid drivers. Sensors for example will give comprehensive and timely information about traffic conditions and relate a comprehensive picture of the overall situation in real time. Driver assistance and navigation systems already help to make driving more secure and comfortable. The demand for comprehensive services and support such as media integration or online connectivity will go up strongly. Online connections among vehicles will help to identify potential sources of accidents and to avoid accidents.[113]

4.3.2 Competition

Competition is the second important influencing factor for strategic developments in the area of electromobility. The analysis of the competitive forces that affect the automobile manufacturers follows the five forces model of Porter. The five forces model analyses the underlying competitive forces and in that way makes predictions about the future development of the industry and the market.[114]

The five forces are interrelated as is shown in Figure 30.[115]

---

[110] See International Energy Agency (2010), p. 9.
[111] See Winterhoff, M., et al. (2009), p. 7.
[112] See Winterhoff, M., et al. (2009), p. 7.
[113] See Verein Deutscher Automobilindustrie (2011), p. 19.
[114] See Porter, M. E. (1999), pp. 9ff.
[115] See Porter, M.E. (2008).

4.3 Drivers of Future Developments in the Automotive Industry

Figure 30: Competitive forces according to Porter's Five Forces Model
Source: Authors' presentation based on Porter, M.E. (2008)

Rivalry among existing competitors

The global automobile market is characterized by intense competition between manufacturers of similar products. All market participants fight for increases in their market share.[116]

The automobile market in the triad countries is in a mature or saturated stage. In this phase, growth is only possible at the expense of other competitors. This frequently results in price wars and correspondingly low margins. In contrast, the automotive industry in the BRIC countries is in the growth phase, where rapid expansion is still possible.[117]

The degree of product differentiation among the automobile manufacturers influences the intensity of the competition. Design, quality, equipment and brand consciousness are means to achieve product differentiation for automobiles. The strategy which is pursued by the automobile manufacturers – volume or premium manufacturer – plays a decisive role. Companies which pursue the same strategic approach can be seen as direct competitors.

Due to the high capital and investment intensity, market exit barriers are high in the automotive industry. These high market exit barriers and the enormous importance of the automotive sectors for the economic strength of many industrial nations prevent the reduction of excess capacities. This leads to increasing rivalry among the competitors.[118]

Threat of new entrants

New competitors in a market generate additional capacity and new products. The increased capacity will normally lead to an overall decline in prices, which in turn leads to cost pressures and reduced profitability. Whether new competitors constitute a threat depends on the existence of barriers to market access and on the reactions of established competitors. The biggest barriers to market access for new competitors in the automotive sector are distribu-

---

[116] See Johnson, G., Scholes, K., Whittington, R. (2006), p. 85.
[117] See Johnson, G., Scholes, K., Whittington, R. (2006), pp. 85ff.
[118] See Johnson, G., Scholes, K., Whittington, R. (2006), p. 85.

tion channels, capital needed to enter the market, lack of cost advantages via scale effects, product differentiation and a lack of experience with the needed technologies.[119]

No new competitors can be expected from Russia and Brazil. In 2010 AvtoWAZ (Lada) had a market share of about 27%[120] in Russia. This makes the company the market leader in that country. In 2010 Fiat SpA with a market share of 23.1% was ahead of Volkswagen with a market share of 22.7% in Brazil.[121] Figure 31 provides an overview of the current market leaders as well as possible new competitors in the BRIC countries.

Country	Market leader	Potential new competitors
Brazil	Fiat SpA, about 23.1%	No potential new competitors
Russia	AvtoWAZ (Lada), about 27%	No potential new competitors
India	Maruti Suzuki, about 49%	Tata Motors
China	VW, about 10.2%	Geely, Chery, BYD

Figure 31: Market leaders and potential new competitors by countries in 2010
Source: Authors' presentation, based on Eichner, S. (2011); Caradvice (2010); Japan Automobile Manufacturer Association (JAMA) (2011); German Trade & Invest (2011c), pp. 2–3; German Trade & Invest (2011e)

The Indian automobile market is characterized predominantly by traditional manufacturers and joint ventures. Maruti Suzuki is the market leader with a market share of about 49% in 2010[122]. The next largest market participant, Hyundai Motor, follows at a distance with a market share of approximately 14%.[123] Tata Motors is considered to be a new potential competitor. It had a market share in 2010 of 14%.[124] Tata Motors was also able to obtain access to the Triad markets with its acquisition of the brands Rover and Jaguar.

In China the automotive sector continues to be regulated by the government. For foreign automobile manufacturers, joint ventures were the only possibility to get access to the market. Nonetheless, the market leader in 2010 was a European company – VW with 10.2%.[125] The market is made up of numerous Chinese automobile manufacturers with low market shares. The consolidation planned by the Chinese government is likely to reduce the number of Chinese automobile manufacturers to five.

Potential new competitors are Chery, BYD and Geely. Especially Geely deserves to be mentioned among these competitors. The company is the first automobile manufacturer that is independent of the government and that has accomplished access to the triad markets with its acquisition of Volvo. Both local competitors possess sufficient capital, especially provided via government support programs, to play an important role on the Chinese market in the medium term. With regard to product differentiation, quality and equipment as well as the brand awareness of the customers are of particular importance for the manufacturers from

---

[119] See Johnson, G., Scholes, K., Whittington, R. (2006), pp. 81–82.
[120] See Eichner, S. (2011).
[121] See Caradvice (2010).
[122] See Japan Automobile Manufacturer Association (JAMA) (2011).
[123] See German Trade & Invest (2011c), pp. 2–3.
[124] See German Trade & Invest (2011c), pp. 2–3 – from 01.04.2010 until 31.03.2011.
[125] See German Trade & Invest (2011e) – 01.01.2010 until 30.09.2010.

4.3 Drivers of Future Developments in the Automotive Industry

China. The quality demands of the customers may make market entry more difficult. However, existing weaknesses can be compensated by the new entrants via cheaper prices. It is possible to win over customers for their products in that way.

Threat of new substitutes

The demand for the original good is reduced if equivalent substitutes are available. For the automobile, the public transportation system with its busses, trains or the subway can be a substitute. In combination with the upcoming increase in urbanization, the passenger car density in the cities will tend to go down.

The currently dominant petrol and diesel engines will be replaced by alternative drive technologies in the long run. This shift towards alternative drive technologies and fuels will affect the BRIC countries and the triad markets to the same degree.

Bargaining power of customers

The competitive behavior of customers is typically characterized by the following features: the buyers attempt to pay lower prices and want higher quality and more service for the same price. The future demand for mobility and the customer requirements will develop differently in the various markets. It can be expected that automobile sales will tend to be stagnant in traditional markets, while increasing demand for individual mobility is more likely in the BRIC countries. For the year 2025 it is expected that about 31%[126] of global automobile production will be sold in the Chinese market.

The changes in mobility demand in the individual sales markets are also characterized by different buyer preferences and customer demands. Demographic developments, among others, play an important role in the triad markets. An ageing society has specific mobility needs, which are relevant also for the design of passenger cars. For this specific customer segment, safety, comfort and the equipment of the vehicle with driver assistance and navigation systems are relevant.[127]

Specific customer demands in the BRIC countries relate to financing solutions, functionality and robustness of the vehicles.

The biggest growth potential until 2025 is expected for the segment of small vehicles.[128] The reasons are that the small cars are equipped with the most current technological innovations and that their size allows an efficient use of fuel. But in the future, price pressures from the consumers can be expected in the small vehicles segment in the BRIC countries as well.

Bargaining power of suppliers

Suppliers have a decisive influence on prices and quality of the final product. They are powerful if the automotive industry is not an important customer, the product of the supplier makes an important contribution to the product of the buyer or the buying industry, the products of the supplier are differentiated or high costs are incurred when switching suppliers and forward integration appears possible.[129]

---

[126] See Roland Berger Strategy Consultants, Amrop (2011), p. 10.
[127] See Newsclick (2009).
[128] See Roland Berger Strategy Consultants, Amrop (2011), p. 16.
[129] See Porter, M. E. (1999), pp. 35–36.

However, in most cases, the suppliers to the automotive industry are dependent on the manufacturers. The automobile manufacturers frequently account for a large share of total sales and demand large quantities.

The dependency of the automobile manufacturers on their suppliers increases with a differentiated product offering. The suppliers are increasingly integrated into the value chain of the automobile manufacturers and frequently provide parts and components that are made specifically for one company.

The suppliers would be in a position of power if they were more highly concentrated than the entire industry. But in the automotive industry, the automobile manufacturers are more concentrated. In the past years the consolidation in the supplier industry has increased continuously, which means that the remaining suppliers were able to strengthen their position somewhat. Negotiating power as a result of forward integration appears less likely, since the financial resources are not available and strategic opportunities are frequently lacking.

In summary, it can be concluded that the negotiating power of the suppliers is least important as a competitive force in the automotive industry.

4.3.3 Challenges

The automobile manufacturers face the challenge of changing mobility demands in the different sales markets. The growing emerging markets will gain in importance for the automobile manufacturers, while the traditional markets are largely saturated. Motorization rates are currently still low and these countries can be expected to catch up with regard to mobility. Especially in the mature markets, automobile manufacturers must make an effort to fulfill the different customer demands or to address the various mobility types. Factors such as sustainability, individual mobility solutions and cost are gaining in importance for the customers. In the triad markets, the automobile is increasingly valued as a useful commodity and not so much as a status symbol.

Vehicle use and not ownership will be the dominant consideration in the future and the automobile manufacturers are under increasing pressure to offer individual mobility solutions. In order to assure the optimal integration of passenger cars with other forms of mobility, the product and service portfolio must be adjusted.[130]

In the BRIC countries the automobile will continue to be a status symbol, since ownership of a passenger car cannot be taken for granted. But in the mass market, the automobile manufacturers are facing the challenge of having to produce affordable small cars with constant quality. In the BRIC countries, customer needs such as functionality or affordability remain most important.

The observed tendency of allocating fewer resources to mobility or of readjusting budgetary priorities results in an increased demand for passenger cars in the more affordable segments (small car segment). The low cost segment is in strong demand in India and China already today. The observed "down trading" and "downsizing" poses challenges to the automobile manufacturers. Even within the premium segment, the development of smaller, lighter and more efficient passenger cars is a primary task.

---

[130] See Winterhoff, M., et al. (2009), p. 16.

All automobile manufacturers are increasingly trying to serve the segment of small cars in order to satisfy customer demands and establish a presence in the emerging BRIC markets. This also helps to compensate for existing excess capacities in the traditional markets. Especially for premium manufacturers it is of utmost importance to be present in the BRIC markets. They must develop new features of product differentiation in order to achieve differentiation from the volume manufacturers. The volume manufacturers in turn face the challenge of intensified competitive pressures especially from suppliers in China and India.

Presence in the highly contested volume markets of the low cost segment entails the risk of price wars and declining margins for the automobile manufacturers. The changed customer preferences will lead to enormous costs in research and development for them. Changes in societal values such as an increasing awareness of environmental issues and increasing fuel prices require the use of alternative engines that are more efficient and at the same time reduce emissions. Stricter environmental regulations imposed by politicians will cause additional costs for the automobile manufacturers. This in turn will lead to higher prices of the passenger cars produced. Many governments will provide comprehensive financial support to support the advancement of alternative drive technologies.

In the future, all automobile manufacturers will find themselves positioned in a field of tension characterized by steadily increasing development and production costs on the one hand and stagnating market volumes in the triad markets on the other hand.[131] These changes will affect the business models of the individual automobile manufacturers. Among other things, this includes the determination of the future positioning in the sales market and the precise definition of the target group segments by mobility types in the various sales markets. Especially the service offering must be modified, since the demand for comprehensive services and support will go up. These additional service offers must be aligned with the value chain and core competencies must be redefined.

The necessary competencies can either be established independently or via cooperations, strategic alliances and partnerships. Those types of global cooperation include the transfer of knowledge and resources. The utilization of synergies allows faster access to the sales market. In light of advances in globalization and the adaptation of innovation and development portfolios, these types of cooperations will increasingly happen, especially in the field of electromobility, both with partners within and outside the automotive industry.[132]

4.4 Electric Vehicles

4.4.1 Technological Developments

4.4.1.1 Alternative Drive Technologies

Following a presentation of the environmental drivers and the influence of competitive behavior on strategic developments in the automobile industry, the topic of electric vehicles will be analyzed in detail. As early as the year 1900, automobiles were powered by electricity, gasoline and steam power. Electric vehicles were not sufficiently powerful at the time

---

[131] See Winterhoff, M., et al. (2009), p. 14.
[132] See Winterhoff, M., et al. (2009), p. 14.

and just like steam powered cars were not successful.[133] Only gasoline powered vehicles were developed further and thanks to quick advances in technology became a global success.

The changed framework conditions of the 21st century such as limited crude oil reserves, tighter emissions standards as well as an increased environmental awareness of consumers forced the automobile manufacturers to reconsider their approach and hastened the development of new drive technologies, alternative fuels and the technology of electric engines. Figure 32 provides an overview of relevant current developments in drive technologies.

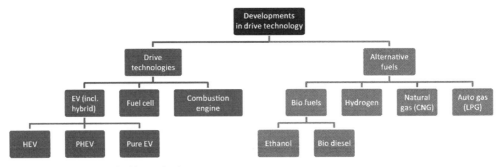

Figure 32: Developments in drive technology
Source: Authors' presentation

The hybrid technology is frequently described as an independent technology. But since it involves an electric engine, it is considered to be among the EVs in this chapter.

4.4.1.2 Technology of the Electric Vehicle

With regard to electric vehicles, a distinction is made between different types of "hybrid electric vehicles" (in the following: HEV), "plug-in hybrid electric vehicles" (in the following: PHEV) or pure EVs.

A HEV is a vehicle that employs both a combustion engine and an electronic motor. Several variations of the electronic motor exist, including "micro hybrid," "mild hybrid" and "full hybrid."[134] The micro hybrid provides sufficient energy to start the engine, while the mild hybrid already makes a contribution towards improving performance and efficiency. Driving without the use of a combustion engine is possible in general with a full hybrid.[135] The batteries of the EVs are charged via mechanical energy from the unused power of the combustion engines or via the electronic motor as generator.

A PHEV is a full hybrid with a combustion engine that is used to increase the range. The combustion engine takes over as soon as the battery is empty or it charges the battery which then continues to power the engine.[136] Sources of energy which are utilized by the PHEV are conventional fuel as well as electric power.[137]

---

[133] See Motavalli, J. (2010), p. 22.
[134] See Leschus, L., Stiller, S., Vöpel, H. (2009), p. 34.
[135] See Leschus, L., Stiller, S., Vöpel, H. (2009), p. 34.
[136] See Leschus, L., Stiller, S., Vöpel, H. (2009), p. 34.
[137] See Wirtschaftsministerium Baden-Württemberg, Fraunhofer IAO, WRS (2010), p. 7.

4.4 Electric Vehicles

The pure EV relies exclusively on an electric engine and therefore must be charged with electric power.

Some experts consider HEV and PHEV as interim solutions towards a pure EV. They assume that pure EVs will be successful over the medium to long term.

Of high relevance for the strategic development of the electronic vehicle are the following topics: battery technology, innovative materials needed to manufacture the vehicle, and necessary infrastructure. All of these areas are considered briefly in the following.

Battery

In addition to the electric engine, the battery is one of the main components of the EV. The major aim of an efficient battery is a high range. Up to date, the range is determined – because of the storage requirements – by the size of the battery and therefore has a major effect on the price of the passenger car.[138] Different types of batteries exist for the use in EVs. Figure 33 provides an overview of the different batteries – nickel, metal hybrid, lead acid and lithium – and shows advantages and disadvantages. At the moment, lithium-ion batteries are considered to be most suitable for EVs. This is due on the one hand to the high potential for optimization and development and on the other hand to a superior combination of safety, energy efficiency and power density.[139]

	Advantages	Disadvantages	Types of battery
Lead-acid Battery	• Established technology • Few safety cncerns • Recycling unroblematic	• Low energy density[140] • High weight • Acid stratification is possible	• Lead-gel battery • AGM battery • Flooded battery (standard)
Lithium batteries	• High energ density • Performnce • Flexible, any types • Great cyce stability (chargin/discharging)	• High self-discharge • Complex battery management • Complex safety features • Very high cost	• Lithium-polymer[141] • Lithium-ion (standard) • Lithium-iron phosphate • Lithium-cobalt oxide • Lithium-manganese oxide
Nickel-metal hybrid batteries	• Robust • Reliable • Great cycle stability	• Low energy density	

Figure 33: Advantages and disadvantages of various batteries
Source: Authors' presentation, based on ADAC Fahrzeugtechnik (2011), pp. 8ff.

---

[138] See Greeno, S. (2010), p. 36.
[139] See ADAC Fahrzeugtechnik (2011), p. 8.
[140] High energy density is important for a high range, while a high performance density (W/kg) is relevant for quick charging. Both cannot be optimized simultaneously. On that issue see Wirtschaftsministerium Baden-Württemberg, Fraunhofer IAO, WRS (2010), p. 11.
[141] Lithium-polymer batteries are advantageous especially when space is limited. However, they are about 10 percent more expensive than lithium-ion batteries.

Material

The battery also affects the materials used in manufacturing the automobile. In order to provide the required performance, currently available batteries are relatively heavy. A lithium-ion battery must weigh 540 kg in order to have a range of 500 km. In comparison, the diesel fuel needed to travel the same distance only weighs 33 kg.[142] The automobile manufacturers are looking for ways to counter the performance deterioration implied by the heavy weights. The use of lighter materials in the production of vehicles is a possible solution. These materials must still pass the safety requirements and therefore possess certain strength.[143] Carbon fibers for example are about 30% lighter than aluminum and even 50% lighter than steel.[144]

Infrastructure

To make EVs suitable for daily use, a corresponding infrastructure with charging stations and switching stations is required.[145] In China, one of the potentially largest sales markets for EVs, integration of the required charging infrastructure into existing gas stations is seen as the simplest and most efficient approach. However, this entails the need for fast charging or switching of batteries.[146] Whether such a switching station can operate successfully in daily business still remains to be seen. The company Better Place is the forerunner in this field and is in the process of installing a network of switching stations – starting initially in Israel and Denmark in 2011 and expanding to Australia by the end of 2011. The automobile manufacturer Renault-Nissan is delivering 100,000 EVs as test vehicles.[147] In addition to these public charging or switching stations it is also necessary that the batteries can be charged at home with the help of specific installations.[148]

In addition to the charging station, a corresponding power grid must also be available. An additional question in this context will relate to the way the charging of the battery can be billed. Adequate billing models are currently under development. It appears possible to either charge to the home utility bill, the electrical bill or separately.[149] The automotive industry, utility companies and independent integrators are asked to join forces and develop appropriate solutions.[150]

4.4.1.3 Competing Products and Developments

Drive technologies

Fuel cell

Use of a fuel cell makes it possible to efficiently power a passenger car without a combustion engine or a battery. The chemical energy of the fuels used is extracted and turned into electri-

---

[142] See ADAC Motorwelt (2011), p. 20.
[143] See The Engineer (2010), p. 2.
[144] See BMW Group (2011d), p. 20.
[145] See ADAC (o. J.d), Leschus, L., Stiller, S., Vöpel, H. (2009), p. 76.
[146] See Xinhua's China Economic Information Service (2010), p. 1.
[147] See Ross, A. (2010), p. 1.
[148] See Industrial Minerals (2010), p. 2.
[149] See Ernst & Young (2011), pp. 49–50.
[150] See Industrial Minerals (2010), p. 2.

cal power. Suitable fuels are either pure hydrogen or fuels that contain large amounts of hydrogen such as compressed natural gas. The degree of environmental pollution depends on the fuels used and their production. The range obtained with fuel cell passenger cars is comparable to that of conventional passenger cars.[151] A hindrance for the technology is the lack of an infrastructure and the elaborate manufacturing process for the fuels and the fuel cell.[152] Mercedes-Benz is the best known automobile manufacturer that supports this technology. Mercedes-Benz experimented with fuel cells in its fleet of busses already in the nineties. With the turn of the century, almost all major automobile manufacturers are experimenting with fuel cells in concept cars or are even testing several generations of vehicles. A specific campaign to illustrate the suitability for daily use of the fuel cell was conducted by Mercedes-Benz in January 2010 with the start of the Mercedes-Benz F-Cell World Drive. The goal was to complete about 30,000 kilometers in 125 days across the world in three automobiles of the B-Class. This project was completed very successfully.

Combustion engine

A shared goal of all automobile manufacturers is the continuous improvement of the existing technology of the combustion engine. BMW for example is developing engines with three instead of six cylinders. Thanks to the reduced weight and the increased efficiency of the three cylinder engine, gasoline use can be reduced further.[153] It is the dominant view in the automotive industry that the savings potential concerning fuel use and emissions of the combustion engine has not been fully exploited. The potential for further improvements over the next 10 years is estimated at approximately 25%.[154]

The advantages of this development are the existence of the required infrastructure as well as the familiarity of both customers and automobile manufacturers with the technology.[155] Therefore the customers are not shying away from the products. A disadvantage is the continued use of fuels such as diesel, gasoline or biofuel mixes. Thus no significant reduction of the dependence on crude oil can be achieved.

Alternative fuels

Biofuels

Depending on the raw materials used, a distinction is made between biofuels of the first and the second generation. Figure 34 provides an overview of these two types of fuels. In producing the first generation, fruits of plants are used, while the second generation utilizes remnants of plants, grass or wood. Examples of these fuels include biodiesel and ethanol.[156]

Burning these fuels does not release more pollutants than previously absorbed by the plants.[157] But the pollutants that are caused in production must also be considered. The com-

---

[151] See Guilford, D. (2010), p. 2.
[152] See Leschus, L., Stiller, S., Vöpel, H. (2009) p. 36 and p. 41.
[153] See Prem, M. (2011b).
[154] See Verband der Automobilindustrie (2011), p. 29.
[155] See Leschus, L., Stiller, S., Vöpel, H. (2009), p. 48.
[156] See Leschus, L., Stiller, S., Vöpel, H. (2009), p. 29.
[157] See Leschus, L., Stiller, S., Vöpel, H. (2009), p. 29.

plete CO_{2eq} balance[158] for ethanol produced from wheat with the help of lignite is worse than that of regular gasoline. If instead ethanol from sugar cane is used, CO_{2eq} emissions can be reduced significantly. Figure 35 provides a comparison of biofuels, hydrogen, natural gas and liquefied petroleum gas. It is apparent that especially second generation biofuels can provide a significant reduction of emissions.

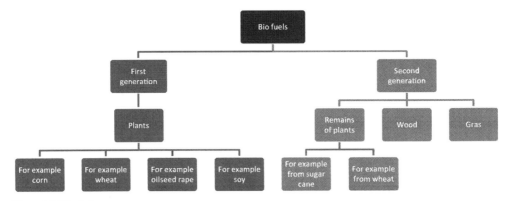

Figure 34: Bio fuels
Source: Authors' presentation, based on Leschus, L., Stiller, S., Vöpel, H. (2009), pp. 29–30

The biofuels of the first generation have the possible disadvantage of crowding out food production. At the moment the technical means are not yet available to produce biofuels of the second generation in sufficient quantities. Further innovation is needed.[159]

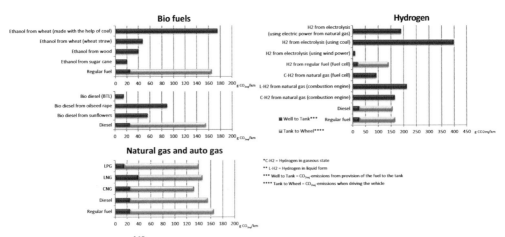

Figure 35: Overview of CO_{2eq}[160] balance of alternative fuels for 2010
Source: Authors' presentation, based on Concawe, EUCAR, European Commission JRC (2007), pp. 23, 28, 30, 35–36, 43, 50, 53

---

[158] CO_{2eq} comprises the polutants CO_2, CH_4 and N_2O.
[159] See Leschus, L., Stiller, S., Vöpel, H. (2009), pp. 30–31 and p. 40.
[160] CO_{2eq} includes the polutants CO_2, CH_4 and N_2O.

Hydrogen

Hydrogen must be produced from water utilizing technical processes such as electrolysis or gas reforming. The needed pure form does not occur naturally. This fuel can be used both in combustion engines and in fuel cells. The use of hydrogen in combination with a fuel cell appears more sensible, since a higher degree of efficiency is reached.[161]

Hydrogen does not cause any emissions when used as a fuel. But the production of hydrogen causes pollutants. These vary with the production process and the energy source utilized. Figure 38 also reveals that hydrogen produced with electrolysis utilizing wind power generates almost no CO_{2eq} emissions. Meanwhile, hydrogen produced with electrolysis in conjunction with coal power plants causes substantially higher emissions.

Current obstacles are the missing infrastructure for production and for refueling the passenger cars as well as the high costs of the fuel cell.[162] A different problem is the fear of the customers that hydrogen vehicles may not be safe in case of an accident. These fears are rooted in the high ignitability of hydrogen.

Natural gas (liquefied natural gas and compressed natural gas)

Natural gas can be used as fuel in two forms, liquid (liquefied natural gas) or compressed in the form of gas (compressed natural gas). The achievable reduction of emissions depends on the engine used and the drive technology. There are three types of natural gas vehicles. "Monovalent natural gas vehicles" are exclusively powered by natural gas, while the "bi-fuel" vehicle can use natural gas as well as gasoline. The gasoline is used as backup and cannot be used together with natural gas. Passenger cars with "dual fuel engines" use a mix of air and natural gas as the primary source of power and only utilize diesel fuel for the ignition of the engine.

Experts are of the opinion that even decades after crude oil has been used up, there will still be natural gas reserves. Scarcity is currently not a concern. The use of natural gas vehicles can mean cost reductions at the pump of up to two thirds for consumers.

Propane and Butane (liquefied petroleum gas)

The gases propane and butane, which are formed during the extraction and refining of crude oil and natural gas, are condensed and mixed under pressure. The result is auto gas, also called Liquefied Petroleum Gas (LPG). Technical modifications of the combustion engine make it possible to utilize LPG as fuel. LPG can also be used in bi-fuel vehicles.

The use of LPG can lead to a reduction of fuel costs of up to 50% compared to established passenger cars with gasoline or diesel engines. The advantage of auto gas compared to natural gas is the range which is up to three times larger for the same amount of fuel. However, harmful emissions are lower for natural gas.

---

[161] See Leschus, L., Stiller, S., Vöpel, H. (2009), pp. 35–36 and p. 38.
[162] See Leschus, L., Stiller, S., Vöpel, H. (2009), pp. 36ff.

> **Summary**
> Considering the different alternatives and their possible developments until the year 2020, it is likely that hybrid vehicles, as a component of electromobility, as well as combustion engines, will dominate the automobile market.
> - Combustion engines are based on a known technology and their saving potential has not been fully exploited.
> - Hybrid vehicles can serve as an interim solution until pure EVs are available in the mass market. The combination of old and new technology offers safety, reliability and a reduction of CO_{2eq} emissions.
> - Pure electric vehicles must make further progress with regard to the development of an adequate infrastructure, the battery; the materials used and related costs, before they are ready for the mass market.
> - Biofuels of the second generation require additional research and development until they can be produced for the mass market in sufficient quantities.
> - Hydrogen in connection with a fuel cell is unlikely to achieve the necessary cost reductions by 2020 to be affordable in the mass market.
> - Natural gas and auto gas generally offer the most limited savings potential concerning CO_{2eq} emissions and for that reason do not address the customers' heightened environmental awareness.

4.4.1.4 Strengths and Weaknesses of Electric Vehicles

To assess the strategic development opportunities in the field of electronic vehicles it is necessary to analyze strengths and weaknesses. Figure 36 provides a current overview of the strengths and weaknesses of electric vehicles in the year 2011 along a number of criteria. The criteria are again presented in more detail on the following pages.

Criteria	Strengths	Weaknesses

Range[163]	- Average journey per day (on 290 days per year) < 40 km
	- New business models:
	  - mobile charging station Angel Car®
	  - flexible exchange of passenger cars
		- an average of 150 km (only half of that in winter)
		- Customer expectations:
		  - 100 km: 10%
		  - 200 km: 20%
		  - 500 km: 31.5%
		- Customers fearful of insufficient range

Infrastructure (Charging or Switching Stations)	- EVs can be used as storage for optimizing the electric power grid	- Will only be demanded if infrastructure is sufficient - Investment in infrastructure only if there is sufficient demand - Lack of standards concerning connections or batteries

---

[163] Range relates to the maximum distance traveled before the battery needs to be recharged.

4.4 Electric Vehicles

Criteria	Strengths	Weaknesses
Time required to charge	- Improvements in the battery management system → possibility to charge faster - Several possibilities to charge: work, shopping, public places, at home	- Charging takes up to eight hours - Changes in the charging behavior of customers
Cost	- Battery prices are likely to decline - Battery leasing → purchase price of passenger car is similar to that of conventional vehicles - Lower maintenance costs, since the engines are less complex - Lower charging costs	- Up to two times higher purchase price - Large share of the costs relates to the battery - Amortization of higher purchase price takes about eight years - Little willingness of the customers to pay higher prices (just to protect the environment)
Battery life	- Reuse of the batteries and recycling of the materials are possible	- Service life of the battery is lower than that of the passenger cars - Loss of about 20% of original capacity during the service life - Negatively affects the value of the EV, since changing the battery involves high costs
Weight	- Weight reduction of EV possible using lightweight construction and new materials (carbon fibers, aluminum and magnesium technologies)	- Very heavy weight of batteries - New materials for weight reduction are very expensive and partially not available for mass production
Customer acceptance	- Possible increase in safety via certification - Study by Better Place shows relatively high customer interest in EVs – in five countries studied between 30% and 57%	- Uncertainties due to the above mentioned problems - Need for information about electromobility and EVs
Noise reduction	- Significant noise reduction for speeds up to 30 km/h	- Danger to be overlooked by other traffic participants
Opportunities for design	- Design of the EVs according to safety aspects and no longer mechanics	- Customers transfer their expectations if EVs do not differ from conventional passenger cars in design
Emission-free driving	- Share of renewable energies in energy mix is increasing - Higher efficiency	- To what degree the vehicle is emission-free depends on the way the electric power is produced - Considerably lower energy density of the batteries compared to other fuels

Figure 36: Strengths and weaknesses of the EVs
Source: Authors' research[164]

---

[164] Source: Authors' presentation based on Verband der Automobilindustrie (2011), pp. 7, 14, 16, 25ff.; Bhagaloo, M. (2010); Pehnt, M., Höpfner, U., Merten, F. (2007), p. 4; ADAC Fahrzeugtechnik (2011), p. 2; Leschus, L., Stiller, S., Vöpel, H. (2009), pp. 33, 64, 76, 78ff.; Pitour, M. (2010); LaMonica, M. (2010), p. 2; Greeno, S. (2010), pp. 46, 68ff., 75ff., 83ff.; Better Place (2009); The Engineer (2010), p. 2; Industrial Minerals (2010), p. 3.

Strengths and weaknesses

Range

The range of electronic vehicles depends primarily on the size of the batteries, weather conditions and driving style.[165] In order to neutralize customer fears about range, research is needed about battery performance, charging infrastructure and charging times. These worries are confirmed by experiments with small fleets of Smart EVs and Mitsubishi i MiEVs. In these field experiments 93% of the drivers of Smart EV were not willing to drive an electronic vehicle if the battery was charged less than 50%.[166] One possibility to reduce this fear of insufficient range is the introduction of Angel Car®, which was developed by the Swiss company Nation-E AG. It is a mobile charging station which can be integrated, for example in tow trucks. With this system, the battery can be charged in less than 15 minutes for a range of up to 30 kilometers. Thus the next charging station can be reached.[167]

Infrastructure

At the moment there is a lack of a developed and comprehensive network of charging or changing stations. More and more energy companies are joining forces with automobile manufacturers, since they have realized the potential of the EVs. The batteries of the EVs can continue to be used as temporary storage when energy production exceeds usage. This is especially the case when renewable energies such as wind and solar are used. When power demand exceeds production, the stored energy from the batteries can be fed back. According to estimates, 2.5 million EVs are sufficient to offset the electrical power fluctuations in Germany.[168]

The project "*Green eMotion*" which is supported by the European Commission has the aim to move forward the compatibility of charging systems in Europe and thus to assure electromobility across borders. The aim of the four-year project is the preparation of the European mass market for electronic vehicles. Developed are concepts to standardize connections and billing across borders. The cooperation is financed and conducted by 42 partners that come from energy providers, cities and municipalities, the automotive sector, research institutes and universities as well as other institutions.[169]

Charging times

Charging the batteries with a 230 volt connection can take up to eight hours, depending on the size of the battery and the level of discharge.[170] To reduce charging times, the battery management system can be optimized further so that more electric power can be processed. For this purpose, Leo Motors Inc., a Korean company has developed a powerful battery management system. When the fast charging mode is activated, a 30 kW Battery can be recharged in 15 minutes rather than in two hours. This development is currently tested for its suitability by manufacturers of batteries and EVs.[171]

---

[165] See Verband der Automobilindustrie (2011), p. 25.
[166] See Murphy, M. (2010), p. 1.
[167] See Business Wire (2010a).
[168] See Leschus, L., Stiller, S., Vöpel, H. (2009), pp. 53, 75, 78, Motavalli, J. (2010), p. 2.
[169] See Green eMotion (2011a), Green eMotion (2011b).
[170] See Greeno, S. (2010), p. 38.
[171] See Business Wire (2010b).

Cost

A cost comparison by the German automobile club ADAC between the Peugeot 107 (with combustion engine) and the Peugeot iON (EV) revealed that the purchase costs account for 96.3% of total cost in the case of the EV. In contrast, the share of purchase costs in total costs is only 73.7% for the gasoline vehicle.[172]

The purchase price of EVs can still be twice that of a conventional passenger car.[173] In Germany for example the Chevrolet Volt costs € 41,950[174] while the model Chevrolet Cruze (basic equipment) has a price of € 14,990.[175]

At the moment about 30 to 50%[176] of the costs of an EV are caused by the battery. One kilowatt-hour of power cost about € 800 in the year 2011.[177] Assuming a midsized passenger car that requires 20 kWh power, a battery price of about € 16,000 can be calculated. Current forecasts indicate that the prices could decline to about € 250 to € 300 by the year 2020. This would still imply a high share of the battery in the total price of an EV.[178]

The currently substantially higher purchase price of electronic vehicles thus continues to be the biggest obstacle for their suitability in a mass market.

Battery life

The durability of a battery depends on a number of factors such as the climate, the frequency of charging and the amount of energy involved in the charging process.[179] The Fraunhofer Institute for Systems and Innovation Research considers the expansion of the battery service life from seven to ten calendar years as essential for a successful market penetration.[180] Research on improving materials and combinations of materials and on battery systems or charging management systems has the aim of expanding the service life and of slowing down the reduction of available capacity.[181] Since up to 98%[182] of the lithium in the batteries can be reused, for example, the attractiveness is significantly increased.

Weight

In conventional passenger cars the vehicle body accounts for 40% and the chassis for 25% of the total weight.[183] Thus innovations in these areas provide the biggest potential for savings. These potentials are also available for EVs and should be utilized via lightweight construction technologies. New technologies are used in this process that are lighter, but at the same time maintain the same resisting power, so that the safety of the passengers is still assured. Examples for such materials are carbon fibers, aluminum and magnesium technologies.[184]

---

[172] See ADAC Fahrzeugtechnik (2011), p. 7.
[173] See Murphy, M. (2010), p. 2.
[174] See Chevrolet (2011).
[175] See Chevrolet (no year given).
[176] See Greeno, S. (2010), p. 82.
[177] See Verband der Automobilindustrie (2011), p. 11 and p. 25.
[178] See Verband der Automobilindustrie (2011), p. 11 and p. 25.
[179] See Verband der Automobilindustrie (2011), p. 25.
[180] Fraunhofer ISI, pp. 3ff.
[181] See Verband der Automobilindustrie (2011), p. 11.
[182] See Leschus, L., Stiller, S., Vöpel, H. (2009), p. 64.
[183] See Verband der Automobilindustrie (2011), p. 16.
[184] See Verband der Automobilindustrie (2011), p. 16.

Emission-free driving

Against the backdrop of an increased environmental awareness of the customers, "emission-free driving" is particularly important. An EV does not produce any CO_2 emissions during its journey. However, the entire amount of CO_2 generated by the EV is tied to the production of the electric power used. Figure 37 demonstrates differences in CO_2 emissions. Electric power from renewable energies, for example, causes about 5g CO_2/km, while the entire electric power mix in Germany in 2008 had a value of about 105g CO_2/km.[185] In contrast, the highest value of about 190g CO_2/km is obtained for electric power made from coal.[186] The degree of emission reductions of EVs thus primarily depends on the sources of the electric power used.

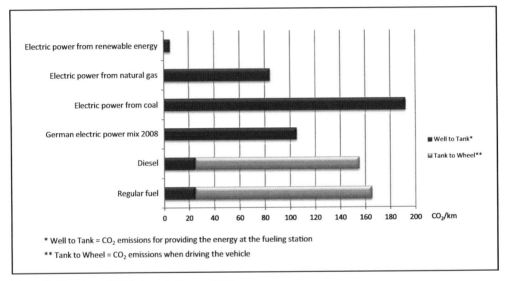

Figure 37: Overview of CO_2 balance in the year 2008
Source: Authors' presentation, based on Leschus, L., Stiller, S., Vöpel, H. (2009), p. 33

Estimates for the year 2020 assume a share of 30% of renewable energies in the entire energy mix[187] in Germany. This can lead to a significant reduction of CO_2 emissions for the German electric power mix.

EVs are able to use between 80% and 100%[188] of the energy. By comparison, combustion engines are effectively using up to 50%[189] of the fuel. The remaining energy is lost due to the mechanical process in the combustion engine. Combustion engines thus have significantly lower effectiveness and need more fuel for the same performance.[190] The lower range of the

---

[185] See Leschus, L., Stiller, S., Vöpel, H. (2009), p. 33.
[186] See Leschus, L., Stiller, S., Vöpel, H. (2009), p. 33.
[187] See Leschus, L., Stiller, S., Vöpel, H. (2009), p. 78.
[188] See Verband der Automobilindustrie (2011), p. 7.
[189] See Verband der Automobilindustrie (2011), p. 7.
[190] See Verband der Automobilindustrie (2011), p. 7.

4.4 Electric Vehicles

EVs is due to the lower energy density. It amounts to about 11,800 Wh/kg for diesel fuels, while lithium-ion batteries only achieve values of about 120–140 Wh/kg.[191]

Figure 38 provides an overview of selected electronic vehicles and their specifics from different manufacturers. With a range of 330 km, the e6 of BYD certainly stands out strongly. The other pure EVs only obtain a range between 100 km and 185 km. The hybrid vehicles of BMW stand out because of comparably high CO_2 emissions. This is explained by the high performance of the engine. The BMW Active Hybrid X6 for example has 485 PS, while the Toyota Auris only has 136 PS.

Manufacturer	Model	Type	Range	CO_2 emission	Maximum speed	Charging (normal)	# Seats	Purchase price	Market introduction
Toyota	Auris	Hybrid	–	89 g/km	180 km/h	–	5	€ 22,950	–
Toyota	Prius	Hybrid	–	92 g/km	180 km/h	–	5	€ 25,750	–
GM	Chevrolet Volt	Hybrid	600 km	–	161 km/h	3 h	4	€ 41,950	2011
Honda	Jazz Hybrid	Hybrid	–	104 g/km	175 km/h	–	5	€ 18,900	–
Honda	CR-Z	Hybrid	–	117 g/km	200 km/h	–	4	€ 21,990	–
Honda	Insight	Hybrid	–	101 g/km	182 km/h	–	5	€ 19,990	–
Peugeot	iOn	Pure EV	150 km	0 g/km	130 km/h	6 h	4	Leasing € 499	2010
Citroen	C-Zero	Pure EV	150 km	0 g/km	130 km/h	6 h	4	€ 35,165	–
Renault	Fluence Z. E.	Pure EV	185 km	0 g/km	135 km/h	6–8 h	5	€ 26,180[192]	2012
Renault	ZOE	Pure EV	160 km	0 g/km	140 km/h	6–8 h	5	–	2012
Renault	Twizy Urban	Pure EV	100 km	0 g/km	80 km/h	3.5 h	2	€ 7,690[193]	2012
BYD	e6	Pure EV	330 km	0 g/km	140 km/h	–	5	–	2009
BYD	F3DM	Hybrid	–	–	160 km/h	–	–	–	2008
BMW	Active E	Pure EV	160 km	0 g/km	145 km/h	4–5 h	–	–	–
BMW	Active Hybrid X6	Hybrid	–	231 g/km	236 km/h	–	–	€ 103,000	–
BMW	Active Hybrid 7	Hybrid	–	219 g/km	250 km/h	–	–	€ 105,900	–

Figure 38: Examples of current or future EV models
Source: Authors' presentation. Based on publicly available information from Toyota, Chevrolet, Honda, Peugeot, Citroen, Renault, BYD and BMW Germany

---

[191] See Leschus, L., Stiller, S., Vöpel, H. (2009), p. 64.
[192] Battery leasing is extra at € 79 per month.
[193] Battery leasing is extra at € 49 per month.

4.4.2 Sales Markets and their Future Development

4.4.2.1 Criteria for Selection and Analysis

When presenting the strategic developments in the area of electric vehicles, an assessment of the future sales markets is of particular relevance next to the analysis of strengths and weaknesses. Included in the analysis in addition to the major markets Europe, USA and Japan are also China and India. Since the countries Russia and Brazil are characterized by a relative abundance of raw materials, it can be expected that electric drives will only play a minor role.

Criteria	USA	Europe	Japan	China	India
Industry growth					
Sales figures[194] in 2010, million units	5.64	West: 12.98 Central & East: 0.82	4.21	13.76	1.95[195]
Forecast of sales figures in 2020, million units	7.57	West: 14.97 Central & East: 1.13	3.69	41.49	6.70[196]
Annual growth forecast until 2020	3.00%	West: 1.44% Central & East: 3.30%	−1.32%	11.67%	11.47%
Market share of the market leader in 2010[197]	18.8% GM	21.3% VW	33.6% Toyota	10.2% VW[198]	45.0% Maruti Suzuki[199]
Potential (Passenger car density 2008)	444	470[200]	454	12	8
Size of the passenger cars[201] in 2010 (largest share)	27.8% Midsized	43.4% Small vehicles[202]	35.8% Small vehicles	41.0% Compact cars	43.0% Subcompact
Share of EVs in 2025	42%	48%	46%	33%	n/a
Government support					
Research & development	Yes	Yes	Yes	Yes	n/a
Incentives for purchase	Yes	Partially[203]	Yes	Yes	No
Tax reduction[204]	Yes	Partially[205]	Yes	n/a	Yes
Overall assessment of development potential until 2020	Medium	Large	Large	Large	Medium

Figure 39: Overview of the criteria analyzed by region
  Source: Authors' presentation (Based on publicly available information)

---

[194] Relates to passenger cars sold – regardless whether these are conventional cars or EVs.
[195] Measured by sales between April 2010 and March 2011.
[196] Measured by sales between April 2010 and March 2011.
[197] Relates to passenger cars sold – regardless whether these are conventional cars or EVs.
[198] Measured by sales between January and September 2010.
[199] Measured by sales between April 2010 and March 2011.
[200] Based on the 27 member states of the EU.
[201] Regardless whether these are conventional cars or EVs.
[202] Measured by sales between January to November 2010.
[203] Differs from state to state. Available for example in France and Great Britain.
[204] For example waiver of motor vehicle tax or registration fees.
[205] Differs from state to state. Available for example in France, Great Britain and Gemany.

4.4 Electric Vehicles

An overview of the criteria considered is provided in Figure 39. For the criteria sales volume and annual growth forecast, a distinction was made between Western Europe and Central and Eastern Europe. This is due to the differences in development in these markets. The very high growth rates of China and India over the past years stand out. They can be explained by the currently low passenger car density and increases in per capita income.

4.4.2.2 USA

Growth of the automotive industry

Sales figures

In 2010, the American market witnessed a slight recovery from the severe declines in the years 2008 and 2009. Figure 40 shows a trend reversal for the year 2010 with 5.6 million passenger cars sold.[206] This marks an increase of 4.3%[207] compared to the previous year. The demand increase is due to a slight economic recovery and new technology in the models, also of the American automobile manufacturers.[208] The upward trend continued in the first quarter of 2011. Sales of 1.5 million passenger cars implied an increase of 18% compared to the previous year.[209]

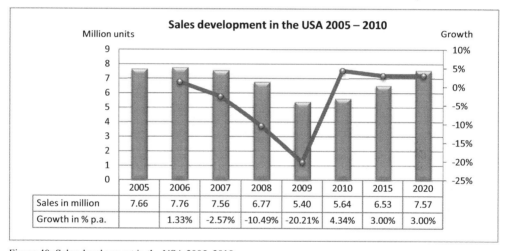

Figure 40: Sales development in the USA 2005–2010
Source: Authors' presentation, based on WardsAuto (2011)

Despite the slight market recovery in 2010 and the positive development in 2011, it will take quite some time before the pre-crisis levels will be reached again.

For the future sales development of passenger cars and "light trucks"[210] marginal growth is expected in the US. Purchases of new vehicles are largely limited to the replacement of existing

---

[206] See WardsAuto (2011).
[207] See WardsAuto (2011).
[208] See German Trade & Invest (2011e), p. 1.
[209] See German Trade & Invest (2011b).
[210] Light vehicles = Passenger cars and light trucks, weight category 1 to 3 (up to 6.4 t). See German Trade & Invest (2011b), p. 1.

ones. This is due to the high motorization rate. According to estimates, average annual sales growth of about 3%[211] can be expected until the year 2025. According to this calculation, approximately 7.6 million passenger cars[212] would be sold in the American market in the year 2020.

The market for passenger cars with alternative drive technologies is massively supported in the United States. Average sales growth of 3% also seems realistic.

Market share

In the year 2010 the three automobile manufacturers General Motors, Ford and Toyota had a joint market share of about 50%.[213] As can be seen from Figure 41, General Motors (GM) was the market leader in the year 2010 with a market share of about 19%.[214]

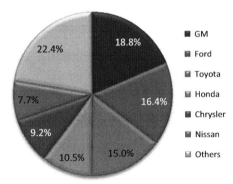

Figure 41: Market shares in the USA in 2010
Source: Authors' presentation, based on WardsAuto (2011)

The Big Three from Detroit – General Motors, Ford and Chrysler – used government support measures following the financial and economic crisis for a restructuring and repositioning. GM for example reduced its product range and focused on hybrid vehicles such as the "Volt."[215] European manufacturers were also able to increase their market share in the US compared to the previous year. Volkswagen (VW) for example witnessed an increase of about 9%.[216] On the American automobile market it seems possible that the domestic manufacturers will lose market share, especially to competitors from Asia.

Potential

The passenger car density in the year 2008 reached 444 passenger cars per 1,000 inhabitants. Within the triad markets and in the OECD countries, experts assume an annual growth rate of 1.3% until 2030 for the motorization rate.[217] Given the already high passenger car density, no significant growth potential of sales or motorization rates is likely in these saturated markets.

---

[211] See Roland Berger Strategy Consultants, Amrop (2011), p. 17.
[212] See WardsAuto (2011).
[213] See WardsAuto (2011).
[214] See WardsAuto (2011).
[215] See German Trade & Invest (2011b), p. 1.
[216] See WardsAuto (2011).
[217] See Leschus, L.; Stiller, S.; Vöpel, H.; et al. (2009), p. 13.

4.4 Electric Vehicles

Size of the passenger cars purchased

Figure 42 shows sales of passenger cars in the United States in the years 2010 by segment. Compact and mid-sized vehicles hold a combined market share of approximately 50%.[218] Despite the crude oil price development, the share of small cars was only 3%, while the segment SUV/Pickup was significantly larger at 20%.[219]

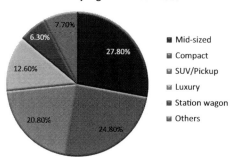

Figure 42: Sales by segments – USA 2010
Source: Authors' presentation, based on J.D. Power (2011), p. 2

Drive technology of the passenger cars purchased in 2025

Optimistic scenarios assume that the share of hybrid and pure electric vehicles in the United States could be as high as 42% of all newly registered vehicles by the year 2025.[220] Figure 43 shows that combustion engines will continue to dominate the market for new registrations at 58%, but that alternative technologies will significantly gain market share.[221]

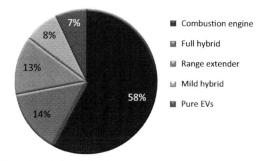

Figure 43: Market shares by drive technology 2025 in Northern America
Source: Authors' presentation, based on Roland Berger Strategy Consultants, VDMA (2011), p. 12

---

[218] See J.D. Power (2011), p. 2.
[219] See J.D. Power (2011), p. 2.
[220] See Roland Berger Strategy Consultants, VDMA (2011), p. 12.
[221] See Roland Berger Strategy Consultants, VDMA (2011), p. 12.

Government support

In an international comparison, the American government has implemented the largest and most comprehensive support programs for electromobility. The US government aims at one million EVs on American streets by 2015.[222] An additional goal is market leadership in this technology.

The immense investments in this industry are supposed to create future employment opportunities and strengthen the economy. The funds which were made available amount to approximately € 22 billion.[223] In the context of the American economic stimulus program in 2009, financial support for pilot projects concerning research and development in the field of electric and hybrid vehicles as well as their components was made available in an amount of US$ 2.4 billion.[224] Manufacturers of electric and hybrid vehicles were given the prospect of additional support and tax breaks totaling US$ 1.5 billion.[225] Individual federal states provided additional financial support in the form of subsidies and tax relief for electromobility. Depending on the state, either vouchers or rebates, for example for charging stations, electrical power, or conversion costs were provided. Furthermore, tax breaks, for example the exemption from the motor vehicles tax were granted.[226] As an example, buyers of a Chevrolet Volt can obtain a tax credit of up to US$ 7,500[227] in this way.

Especially the State of California was a strong supporter of electromobility in the year 2011.The "California Air Resources Board" (CARB) initially supported buyers of an electric vehicles with an award of US$ 5,000.[228] In the context of the "Clean Vehicle Rebate Project" (CVRP) funding in the amount of US$ 5.000[229] was approved for vehicles that are low in emissions. If this support program is added to the tax rebate of US$ 7,500, the total government support amounted to US$ 12,500 for the year 2011.[230] The Californian support program was very well received from the beginning and thus a reduction of the bonus payment to US$ 2,500[231] is likely.

4.4.2.3 Europe

Growth of the automotive industry

Sales figures

The traditional Western European market witnessed a sharp decline in the crisis year 2008.[232] Government support schemes such as the German scrappage bonus prevented further de-

---

[222] See US Department of Energy (2011).
[223] See German Trade & Invest (2010d).
[224] See German Trade & Invest (2010d).
[225] See German Trade & Invest (2010d).
[226] See German Trade & Invest (2010d).
[227] See Münchner Merkur (2011).
[228] See DailyGreen (2011).
[229] See DailyGreen (2011).
[230] See Münchner Merkur (2011).
[231] See DailyGreen (2011).
[232] The Western European market includes the EU-15 countries (Austria, Belgium, Denmark, Finland, France, Gemany, Greece, Ireland, Italy, Luxembourg, Netherlands, Portugal, Spain, Sweden, United Kingdom) and the EFTA countries (Iceland, Norway and Switzerland).

4.4 Electric Vehicles

clines in 2009. The sales decline in the year 2010 which is apparent in Figure 44 is primarily due to the expiration of government funded support programs. In the first five months of the year 2011, approximately 5.8 million passenger cars were sold in Western Europe.[233] A significant improvement compared to the previous year cannot be expected, given the immense public indebtedness in the Eurozone and the associated uncertainty on the capital markets. In selected Western European countries – especially in Germany with a growth rate compared to the previous year of 13%[234] – an upward trend is observable, but it remains unclear whether it can be maintained in the medium term.

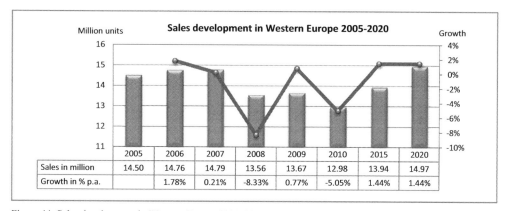

Figure 44: Sales development in Western Europe 2005–2020
Source: Authors' presentation, based on Association Auxiliaire de l'Automobile (AAA) (2011a)

Experts estimate the average annual growth rates for sales of passenger cars at only 0.4%[235] to 1.4%[236] in the years up to 2020. Given the comprehensive government support measures of electromobility in the individual member countries, annual growth rates of 1.4%[237] are a plausible scenario.

Figure 45 provides a detailed breakdown of sales in the countries France, Germany, Italy, Spain and Great Britain for the years 2005–2010. The tight economic linkages between these Western European countries find their expression in an almost identical development during the years under review. Especially against the backdrop of the sovereign debt crisis in Europe, these insights should be taken into consideration.

In the sales figures for the Central and Eastern European countries (the ten new member countries, called EU-10)[238] the effects of the financial and economic crisis in the year 2009 are clearly visible. Figure 46 very clearly shows the sales decline of close to 27%.[239]

---

[233] See Association des Constructeurs Européens d'Automobiles (ACEA) (2011).
[234] See Association des Constructeurs Européens d'Automobiles (ACEA) (2011).
[235] See Roland Berger Strategy Consultant, Amrop (2011), p. 10.
[236] See KB Investment & Securities (2010), p. 9.
[237] See KB Investment & Securities (2010), p. 9.
[238] EU 10: Bulgaria, Czech Republic, Estonia, Hungary, Lithuania, Latvia, Poland, Rumania, Slovakia, Slowenia.
[239] See Association Auxiliaire de l'Automobile (AAA) (2011a).

72 4 Strategic Development Potential of the Automotive Industry

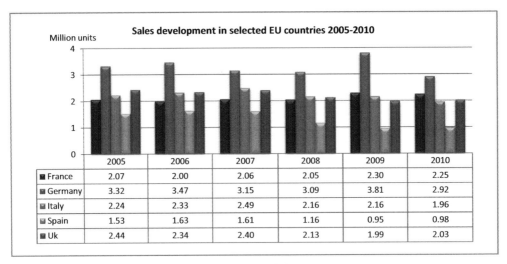

Figure 45: Sales development in selected EU countries 2005–2010
Source: Authors' presentation, based on Association Auxiliaire de l'Automobile (AAA) (2011a)

For the future development of the markets in Central and Eastern Europe, average growth of about 3.3% can be expected. One reason is certainly the still relatively low motorization rate in these countries, which continues to allow a significant number of new purchases.

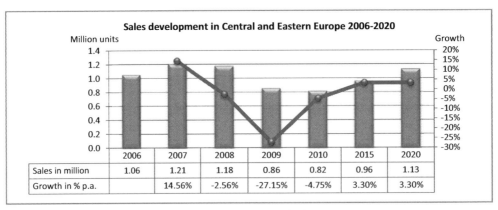

Figure 46: Sales development in Central and Eastern Europe 2006–2020
Source: Authors' presentation, based on Association Auxiliaire de l'Automobile (AAA) (2011a)

Market share

A breakdown of the market shares of the automobile manufacturers in the EU-27 member states and in Iceland, Switzerland and Norway for the year 2010 is presented in Figure 47. As can be seen easily, the Volkswagen Group is the undisputed market leader with 21.3%.[240] The European market is basically dominated by the domestic automobile manufacturers. The

---

[240] See Association Auxiliaire de l'Automobile (AAA) (2011b).

4.4 Electric Vehicles

three strongest European automobile manufacturers (Volkswagen, PSA, and Renault) share about 45%[241] of the entire market among themselves.

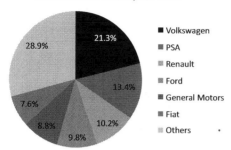

Figure 47: Market shares in Europe in 2010
Source: Authors' presentation, based on Association Auxiliaire de l'Automobile (AAA) (2011b)

No serious competition from Asian or American manufacturers must be considered over the medium term. Even Toyota/Lexus, still the world's largest automobile manufacturer only held a small market share of 4.4% in the year 2010.[242]

Potential

The high passenger car density of the European market is apparent when looking at motorization rates. In the 27 European member states there are about 470 passenger cars per 1,000 inhabitants.[243] But the passenger car density per 1,000 inhabitants in the Western European countries is significantly higher. In Germany, for example, there are 508 passenger cars per 1,000 inhabitants.[244] Significant growth cannot be expected. However, significant future growth potential appears possible in the case of the Central and Eastern European countries against the backdrop of a low passenger car density (approximately 400 passenger cars per 1,000 inhabitants).[245]

Size of the passenger cars purchased

An analysis of automobile sales in the year 2010 by segment as displayed in Figure 48 shows that the majority share of 72% is accounted for by small and lower midsized vehicles. The small vehicle segment advanced clearly compared to the previous years. This is attributable mainly to the government incentive programs in the crisis years 2008 and 2009. The share in the upper medium and premium segments increased only marginally.

---

[241] See Association Auxiliaire de l'Automobile (AAA) (2011b).
[242] See Association Auxiliaire de l'Automobile (AAA) (2011b).
[243] See Eurostat (2011).
[244] See Eurostat (2011).
[245] See Eurostat (2011).

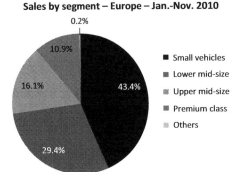

Figure 48: Sales by segment – Europe – Jan.–Nov. 2010
Source: Authors' presentation, based on Association des Constructeurs Européens d'Automobiles (ACEA)

Drive technology of the passenger cars purchased in 2025

On the combined European market the share of newly registered passenger cars with a combustion engine still dominates. Up to the third quarter of 2010, diesel engines alone had a share of about 50% in the Western European markets. The share of EVs in the entire fleet of passenger cars was less than 0.01%. As of 01 January 2011 only 2,307 of a total of 42 million passenger cars were powered by electricity.[246]

The share of vehicles with an electric drive is expected to increase significantly by 2025 and account for about 48% of newly registered vehicles.[247] As can be seen in Figure 49, the share of vehicles with a purely electric drive is expected at around 12%[248] of all passenger cars in the year 2025.

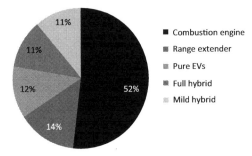

Figure 49: Market shares by drive technology 2025 in Europe
Source: Authors' presentation, based on Roland Berger Strategy Consultants, VDMA (2011), p. 12

---

[246] See Münchner Merkur (2011).
[247] See Roland Berger Strategy Consultants, VDMA (2011), p. 12.
[248] See Roland Berger Strategy Consultants, VDMA (2011), p. 12.

4.4 Electric Vehicles

Government support

The European Commission is especially trying to advance research and development in EVs by providing financial resources. With the "Green Car Initiative" in the context of the economic stimulus package of 2009, the European Commission provides one billion Euros[249] for research into alternative technologies and an efficient energy infrastructure. The European Investment Bank (EIB) provides loans in an amount of € 4 billion[250] to support the development of innovations and research. In March 2011 an additional amount of € 24.2 million[251] was provided in the context of the European initiative "*Green eMotion*" aimed at supporting electromobility. This initiative supports the vision of an interconnected Europe and calls for a reduction of CO_2 emissions by 60% until 2050.[252]

France

In 2009, the French government approved a four year support program with a total amount of € 400 million as part of the "Pacte Automobile."[253] In the same year, an amount of € 50 million[254] was paid into a fund that supports research and development of EVs. France has set itself the ambitious goal of having two million EVs in the streets by 2020.[255] Additional loans in an amount of € 250 million were made available for the development of environmentally friendly "low-emission products."

A subsidy of € 5,000 is provided for the purchase of an EV with CO_2 emissions below 60 g/km. Vehicles with CO_2 emissions of less than 135 g/km are supported with a subsidy of € 2,000.[256] In both cases that subsidy may not exceed 20% of the total purchase price.[257]

Germany

In Germany about one million EVs are supposed to be on the road by 2020.[258] In the context of the second economic stimulus program, the Federal Government has made available € 500 million[259] for development and research in the area of electromobility until 2011. The Federal Ministry of Education and Research provides an additional amount of € 160 million[260] especially for battery research and vehicle energy management.[261] Until the end of the legislative term in the year 2012, spending for additional research and development measures will total one billion Euros.[262]

---

[249] See Wirtschaftsministerium Baden-Württemberg, Fraunhofer IAO, WRS (2010).
[250] See Wirtschaftsministerium Baden-Württemberg, Fraunhofer IAO, WRS (2010).
[251] See EUROPA (2011).
[252] See EUROPA (2011).
[253] See ABC Carbon (2010).
[254] See ABC Carbon (2010).
[255] See ABC Carbon (2010).
[256] See ABC Carbon (2010).
[257] See ABC Carbon (2010).
[258] See Bundesministerium für Wirtschaft und Technologie (Bmwi) (2011), p. 11.
[259] See Bundesministerium für Wirtschaft und Technologie (Bmwi) (2011), p. 7.
[260] See Bundesministerium für Wirtschaft und Technologie (Bmwi) (2011), p. 14.
[261] See Bundesministerium für Wirtschaft und Technologie (Bmwi) (2011), p. 13.
[262] See Bundesministerium für Wirtschaft und Technologie (Bmwi) (2011), p. 20.

The government program on electromobility that was passed on 18 May 2011 does not entail direct subsidies for the purchase of electric vehicles. In contrast to the programs in many other countries, it is limited to non-monetary incentives. In particular road law requirements are altered to support EVs. This includes restricted parking spaces, waiver of access restrictions for EVs or the use of bus lanes and special lanes for EVs.[263] Tax incentives, for example for company cars are also supposed to strengthen electromobility. A tax exemption for ten years is planned for vehicles that are registered for the first time before 31 December 2015 and have CO_2 emissions below 50g/km.[264]

Great Britain

A number of support measures for EVs were passed in Great Britain during the last few years. Vehicle owners are exempt from the motor vehicle tax as long as CO_2 emissions are below 100g/km. The British government passed a support program totaling £ 230 million[265], which provides for a subsidy of 25%[266] of the purchase price for buyers of EVs and hybrids. The maximum amount of the subsidy is £ 5,000.[267]

4.4.2.4 Japan

Growth of the automotive industry

Sales figures

The Japanese automobile market was characterized by a slight stagnation already a few years before the economic crisis which continued until 2009. However, the sales decline was much milder than in Western Europe or the US. The stagnation in the years prior to the financial and economic crisis demonstrates the massive saturation of the Japanese automobile market. As is shown in Figure 50, sales recovered by about 7%[268] compared to the previous year in 2010, but this was due primarily to government support programs such as the scrappage bonus. The domestic automotive industry was also hurt by the fact that production was cut in half following the natural disasters in the spring of 2011.[269] The earthquake, the tsunami and the nuclear catastrophe in Fukushima in the year 2011 destroyed important production sites of the automobile manufacturers and the suppliers as well as parts of the country's infrastructure.[270] The outlook for the development of the Japanese automobile market is rather uncertain. Production continues to be slowed down by supply shortages for automobile parts and components. In part this even affects foreign automobile manufacturers, which depend on important supplies from Japan.[271]

---

[263] See Bundesministerium für Wirtschaft und Technologie (Bmwi) (2011), pp. 48ff.
[264] See Bundesministerium für Wirtschaft und Technologie (Bmwi) (2011), p. 50.
[265] See German Trade & Invest (2010a).
[266] See German Trade & Invest (2010a).
[267] See German Trade & Invest (2010a).
[268] See Japan Automobile Manufacturer Association (JAMA) (2011).
[269] See Japan Automobile Manufacturer Association (JAMA) (2011).
[270] See German Trade & Invest (2011d), p. 2.
[271] See German Trade & Invest (2011d), p. 2.

4.4 Electric Vehicles

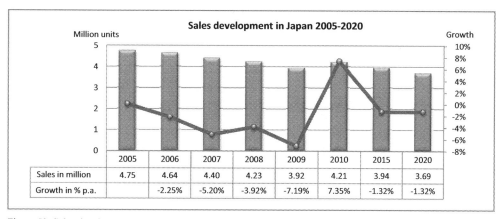

Figure 50: Sales development in Japan 2005–2020
Source: Authors' presentation, based on Japan Automobile Manufacturer Association (JAMA) (2011)

Prior to the natural disaster an average growth rate of minus 1.3% was expected until 2015.[272] Due to the deteriorating economic outlook for the years 2011 and 2012 this value is also used for the forecast of the sales development in Japan until the year 2020, which is displayed in Figure 50.

Market share

The Japanese market is characterized by a historic dominance of domestic automobile manufacturers. Their market share in 2010 was about 95%.[273] No significant entry of foreign competitors can be expected in the near future. Figure 51 shows that in 2010 Toyota was the undisputed market leader with a share of about 33%. Honda with 14.3% and Nissan with 13.4% market share follow at a clear distance.[274]

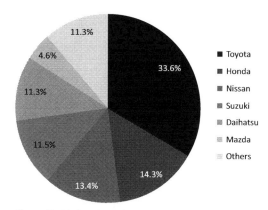

Figure 51: Market shares in Japan in 2010
Source: Authors' presentation, based on Japan Automobile Manufacturer Association (JAMA) (2011)

---

[272] See KB Investment & Securities (2010), p. 9.
[273] See Japan Automobile Manufacturer Association (JAMA) (2011).
[274] See Japan Automobile Manufacturer Association (JAMA) (2011).

Potential

The stagnation of the automobile market in the past years has its causes not only in the economic weakness of Japan, but also in the already advanced motorization rates. In Japan 1,000 inhabitants possessed on average about 454 passenger cars in the year 2008. Given this market saturation, no major growth potential can be expected in the future. Purchases of new vehicles will mostly serve to replace older ones.

Size of the passenger cars purchased

Purchases of new cars in the Japanese market are distinguished by size and categorized into small, standard and mini vehicles. As can be seen from Figure 52, the Japanese market is almost evenly split among the three segments.[275]

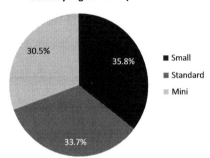

Figure 52: Sales by segment – Japan 2010
    Source: Authors' presentation, based on Japan Automobile Manufacturer Association (JAMA) (2011)

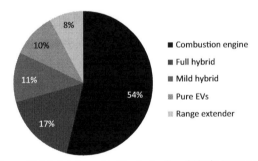

Figure 53: Market shares by drive technology 2025 in Japan and Korea
    Source: Authors' presentation, based on Roland Berger Strategy Consultants, VDMA (2011), p. 12

Drive technology of the passenger cars purchased in 2025

In the business year 2008/2009 already one million hybrid vehicles[276] were driving on Japans streets. This corresponds to approximately 1.7% of the entire automotive fleet. In the year 2010 the Toyota Prius with 316,000 vehicles[277] was the most frequently purchased hybrid.

---

[275] See Japan Automobile Manufacturer Association (JAMA) (2011).
[276] See German Trade & Invest (2011d), p. 3.
[277] See German Trade & Invest (2011d), p. 2.

4.4 Electric Vehicles

Pure EVs are available on the Japanese market since 2009, but only a few thousand have been sold since then.[278]

Japan is currently the leader in electromobility thanks to its many years of experience with hybrid cars and the strong research record in the field of high-performance batteries.[279]

In the future, the use of alternative drive technologies is likely to be accelerated even further. According to estimates, the share of electric or hybrid vehicles could be about 46%[280] by the year 2025. Figure 53 provides an overview of the expected market shares for the different technologies in the year 2025 in Japan and Korea.

Government support

The Japanese government has passed two comprehensive support programs for the spread of electric vehicles. In the year 2010, the Economic Ministry in Japan provided incentives for busses, taxis and company cars in the amount of ¥ 10.4 billion (about € 9 million).[281] In the context of the "Clean Energy Vehicle Promotion Program" additional incentives in the amount of ¥ 13.7 billion (about € 12 million)[282] were provided to private households. In addition, purchase bonuses were awarded for electric and hybrid vehicles as well as other environmentally friendly vehicles. The amount received depends on the type of vehicle.[283]

When purchasing the Nissan Leaf for example, a subsidy in the amount of ¥ 770,000 (approximately € 6,700) is paid. For the I-MIEV by Mitsubishi a subsidy of ¥ 1.14 million (about € 10,000) is due.[284]

In addition to financial incentives, tax exemptions were also implemented. The purchase tax for example is completely waived and the weight tax is due only after three years. In several regions, electronic vehicles are completely exempt from the motor vehicles tax for several years.[285]

4.4.3 China

Growth of the automotive industry

Sales figures

The Chinese market is witnessing a pronounced boom which began in 2005. In 2009, China became the biggest automobile market worldwide with 13.6 million passenger cars sold. This value was again significantly increased in 2010, when the market grew by more than 33% to more than 18 million vehicles sold.[286] Now China has replaced the US as the globally leading automobile market.[287] According to forecasts by experts, automobile sales in China will continue to witness average growth rates in excess of 11% in the coming years (see Figure 54).[288]

---

[278] See German Trade & Invest (2011d), p. 3.
[279] See German Trade & Invest (2010e).
[280] See Roland Berger Strategy Consultants, VDMA (2011), p. 12.
[281] See German Trade & Invest (2010c).
[282] See German Trade & Invest (2010c).
[283] See German Trade & Invest (2010c).
[284] See German Trade & Invest (2011d), p. 3; exchange rate used € 1 = ¥ 114.1.
[285] See German Trade & Invest (2010e).
[286] See German Trade & Invest (2011e).
[287] See Auto motor und sport (2011).
[288] See KB Investment & Securities (2010), p. 9.

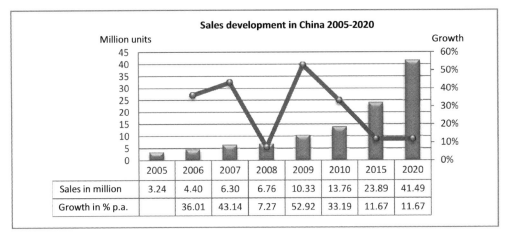

Figure 54: Sales development in China 2005–2020
Source: Authors' presentation, based on China Association of Automobile Manufacturers (CAAM) (2011)

Market share

American and European automobile manufacturers dominate on the hotly contested Chinese market. Many of the foreign manufacturers were able to establish a presence in the Chinese market with the help of joint ventures. It is the goal of the Chinese government to speed up the consolidation of the numerous domestic manufacturers in order to limit the dominance of the foreign producers and to enhance competition. Figure 55 provides an overview of the market shares in the year 2010 in which Volkswagen was the market leader with a share of 10.2%.[289]

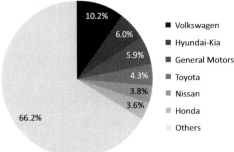

Figure 55: Market shares in China Jan.–Sept. 2010
Source: Authors' presentation, based on German Trade & Invest (2011e)

Potential

Due to the low motorization rates, the Chinese market continues to hold an enormous growth potential. In 2008 the statistics showed only 12 passenger cars per 1,000 inhabitants. This very low passenger car density implies a huge demand for initial purchases, which can be considered the driver of automobile sales.

---

[289] See German Trade & Invest (2011e).

4.4 Electric Vehicles

Size of the passenger cars purchased

The distribution of the vehicle segments for the year 2010, which is displayed in Figure 56, shows the dominance of compact and small vehicles in the Chinese market with a market share of about 60%.[290] In the overall market, all vehicle segments witnessed growth. With a share of 14%,[291] Sport Utility Vehicles (SUV) witnessed a sizeable increase and can now be found in third position.

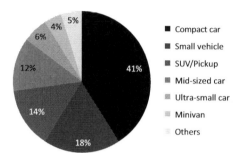

Figure 56: Sales by segment – China 2010
Source: Authors' presentation, based on J.D. Power (2011), p. 2

Drive technology of the passenger cars purchased in 2025

For the time period until 2025 it is expected that passenger cars with combustion engines will continue to dominate the Chinese automobile market. The share of full hybrids is estimated at 10%[292] in the future. The smallest sales potential is predicted for mild hybrids. Figure 57 shows the expected market shares of the different drive technologies in China for the year 2025.

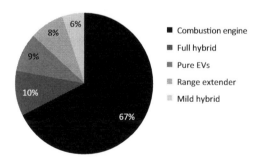

Figure 57: Market shares by drive technology 2025 in China
Source: Authors' presentation, based on Roland Berger Strategy Consultants, VDMA (2011), p. 12

---

[290] See J.D. Power (2011), p. 2.
[291] See J.D. Power (2011), p. 2.
[292] See Roland Berger Strategy Consultants, VDMA (2011), p. 12.

Government support

The Chinese government has set ambitious goals for the future development of electromobility. China aims at nothing less than global market leadership for alternative drive systems. By 2015 an annual capacity of one million electric and hybrid vehicles is expected to be in place. By the year 2020, a total of five million EVs are supposed to be driven on Chinese roads.[293] In order to reach this ambitious goal, the Chinese government plans to invest about € 11 billion in development projects. A conglomerate of 16 state-owned automobile manufacturers and utility companies was founded. The aim is to better connect the research and development activities of the individual producers of electric, hybrid, and fuel cell vehicles. This is supposed to accelerate the development of unified technology standards such as uniform plugs or a homogeneous charging infrastructure.[294]

At current, the Chinese government subsidizes electronic vehicles with RMB[295] 60,000 (about € 6,500) and hybrids with RMB 50,000 (about € 5,400).[296] Efficient drive technologies are supported with investments totaling about € 1billion,[297] while other pilot projects in more than 13 Chinese regions receive an additional € 2 billion in funding.[298]

4.4.3.1 India

Growth of the automotive industry

Sales figures

The Indian automobile market was characterized by above average growth in the past years. Sales did not even decline in the Indian market during the crisis years 2008/2009. Instead, the upward trend continued in the year 2009, as is shown in Figure 58. Close to 2 million passenger cars were sold in the year 2010.[299] This marks an increase of about 25%[300] compared to the previous year. The first quarter of 2011 showed another improvement by approximately 29% compared to the previous year.[301] This dynamic development can be explained by the economic situation, increases in income and planned support measures in India.[302] Since the motorization rate continues to be low, most passenger cars sold can be considered to be initial purchases.

For the coming years a continuation of the growth trend with annual average rates of 11.5% can be expected.[303]

---

[293] See German Trade & Invest (2011a).
[294] See German Trade & Invest (2011a).
[295] Renminbi Yuan.
[296] See German Trade & Invest (2011a); exchange rate used € 1 = RMB 9.2.
[297] Wirtschaftsministerium Baden-Württemberg, Fraunhofer IAO, WRS (2010), p. 37.
[298] Wirtschaftsministerium Baden-Württemberg, Fraunhofer IAO, WRS (2010), p. 37.
[299] See Society of Indian Automobile Manufacturers (SIAM) (2011).
[300] See Society of Indian Automobile Manufacturers (SIAM) (2011).
[301] See Society of Indian Automobile Manufacturers (SIAM) (2011).
[302] See German Trade & Invest (2011c), p. 2.
[303] See KB Investment & Securities (2010), p. 9.

4.4 Electric Vehicles

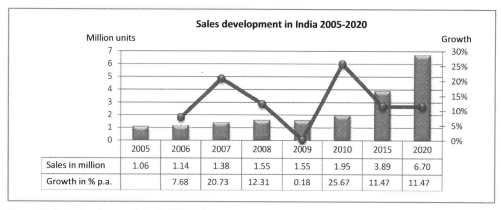

Figure 58: Sales development in India 2005–2020
Source: Authors' presentation, based on Society of Indian Automobile Manufacturers (SIAM) (2011);
Business year is from April to March

Market share

Domestic automobile manufacturers continued to dominate the Indian market in 2010. However, in most cases these manufacturers are involved in joint ventures with traditional companies. As can be seen from Figure 59, Maruti Suzuki with a market share of close to 45% was the undisputed market leader in India.[304] European automobile manufacturers continue to play only a minor role in India. As an example, the market share of Volkswagen in the year 2010 was merely 2%.[305] This is supposed to change in the future. European and American manufacturers plan to increase their sales in India and establish a stronger presence in this contested market.

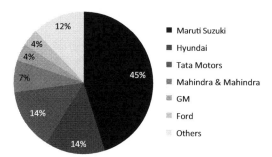

Figure 59: Market shares in India – April 2010–March 2011
Source: Authors' presentation, based on J.D. Power (2011), p. 2

Potential

An enormous growth potential can be expected for the future development of the Indian market. This is due to the low motorization rates: in the year 2008 only eight passenger cars per 1,000 inhabitants were recorded in India. As Figure 60 makes clear, India has the lowest

---

[304] See German Trade & Invest (2011c), pp. 2–3.
[305] See German Trade & Invest (2011c), pp. 2–3.

passenger car density of all the international markets analyzed. But the demand for mobility will grow above average in the years to come. To a large part this can be explained by the steady growth of the middle classes and their income as well as the generally favorable economic outlook for India as an emerging economy.

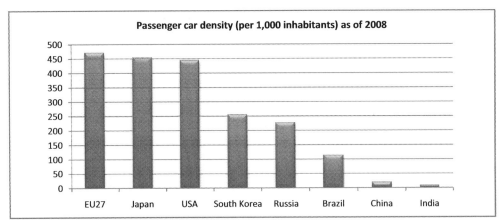

Figure 60: Passenger car density (per 1,000 inhabitants) as of 2008
Source: Authors' presentation, based on Eurostat

Size of the passenger cars purchased

Inexpensive very small and small cars are most frequently purchased. These entry level models had a market share of about 80% in 2010.[306] As can be seen in Figure 61, the sales figures in the premium and luxury segment are relatively small at 2%.[307] However, growth rates of up to 42% are expected in this segment for 2011.[308]

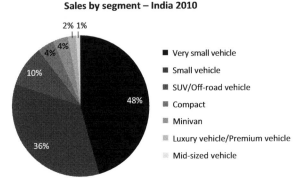

Figure 61: Sales by segment – India 2010
Source: Authors' presentation, based on J.D. Power (2011), p. 2

---

[306] See German Trade & Invest (2011c), p. 2.
[307] See German Trade & Invest (2011c), p. 2.
[308] See German Trade & Invest (2011c), p. 2.

Government support

Most automobiles in India are powered by natural gas or diesel. Electric vehicles only play a minor role in India. To date, the support of electromobility was more or less neglected. Electric drives mostly play a role for two-wheelers. In 2009/2010 an estimated 80,000[309] electric vehicles were manufactured, almost exclusively two-wheelers. But the Indian government is planning to support electromobility in the future. At the moment only limited subsidies are provided to the automotive industry. For example import duties in the amount of 14%[310] were waived until the year 2013 for components of electric vehicles such as batteries or charging equipment. Nonetheless, the electric vehicle will continue to be of minor importance in India. Reasons are high purchase prices and customer preferences for inexpensive small vehicles.[311]

Summary

The biggest development potential in the area of electromobility is in the Chinese automobile market. Above average growth rates for sales of passenger cars in general and a relatively high share of EVs will be achieved by 2025. This development is supported by comprehensive government measures.

The share of electric vehicles will go up in all markets of the triad. Since these markets are by and large saturated, an exchange of conventional vehicles for electric vehicles will take place. In addition, electromobility receives particularly strong support in these countries.

Least important for the breakthrough of electric vehicles is India. The lack of government support and comparably low income levels hinder the spread of electric vehicles.

---

[309] See German Trade & Invest (2010b).
[310] See German Trade & Invest (2010b).
[311] See German Trade & Invest (2010b).

5 Product Policies in the BRIC Countries

5.1 Executive Summary

While the traditional automobile markets in Western Europe, North America and Japan are stagnant or even in decline, the BRIC countries (Brazil, Russia, India and China) exhibit high annual growth rates.[312] As a consequence, the BRIC countries are increasingly important for the German automobile manufacturers. It is the aim of this Chapter to derive an optimal distribution and product strategy for the individual BRIC countries and to provide recommendations for action.[313]

5.2 Scope of the Analysis

5.2.1 Status Quo of Automobile Distribution in the BRIC Countries

The economic advance of the BRIC countries which was observable in the past years is now also beginning to have a positive impact on the automotive industry. An analysis of the global sales figures of the last years reveals that the strong growth rates for the BRIC countries that were frequently predicted did in fact materialize. Figure 62 gives an overview of newly registered vehicles in the largest automobile markets.

It is apparent that the markets in Brazil, India and especially in China witnessed considerable increases compared to 2008, the year before the crisis. None of the traditional automobile markets such as Germany, USA or Japan are growing at a similar speed. This forces the globally active automobile manufacturers to readjust their target markets and to put greater emphasis on the BRIC countries.[314]

However, the BRIC countries also require a careful analysis. Even today, experts think it very likely that excess capacities in the automotive industry will also develop in these markets over the next five years.[315]

Due to the attractiveness of the BRIC countries for premium as well as volume manufacturers, both categories of automobile manufacturers will be considered in the following sections. Possible differences in market cultivation strategies will be developed. Since Volkswagen and BMW will be used as examples for the two categories, the current strategy of these manufacturers in the BRIC countries is analyzed initially.

---

[312] See Avantalion (2012).
[313] We thank Karolina Engenhorst, Michaela Kraus and Michaela Mittelstädt for their support in the topic area of "Product policies in the BRIC coutries." Their work has made the success of this book possible.
[314] See Thiele, M. (2010), p. 8.
[315] See KPMG (2010a), p. 11.

International Car Sales Outlook						
	1990-99	2000-08	2009	2010	2011	2012f
			(millions of units)			
TOTAL SALES	39.20	49.55	50.42	56.82	58.89	61.39
North America*	16.36	19.01	12.61	13.96	15.22	16.10
Canada	1.27	1.60	1.46	1.56	1.59	1.61
United States	14.55	16.39	10.40	11.55	12.73	13.50
Mexico	0.54	1.02	0.75	0.85	0.90	0.99
Western Europe	13.11	14.48	13.62	12.98	12.80	12.16
Germany	3.57	3.28	3.81	2.92	3.17	3.24
Eastern Europe	1.18	2.73	2.58	3.14	3.90	4.25
Russia	0.78	1.54	1.47	1.91	2.65	2.95
Asia	6.91	10.97	17.68	22.47	22.50	24.23
China	0.43	3.14	7.32	9.41	10.04	10.94
India	0.31	0.83	1.43	1.87	1.95	2.09
South America	1.64	2.36	3.93	4.27	4.47	4.65
Brazil	0.94	1.46	2.53	2.69	2.64	2.74

*Includes light trucks

Figure 62: International car sales outlook
Source: Scotiabank (2012)

BMW

BMW currently serves the automobile market in the BRIC countries with a "conventional" network of dealers, which is also used, for example in Germany. A decision is made case by case whether the dealership is run by BMW in the form of a BMW branch or whether an independent dealer sells BMW automobiles at his own risk. The same structures are in place as in Germany and the decision criteria are also not materially different. The focus is on urban areas, since rural areas in the BRIC countries are considered to offer no or only very little potential for automobile sales.[316]

County	Type	Location	Product
India	Assembly	Channai	
China	Development	Beijing	
	Plant	Shenyang	5 Series, 3 Series Limousine
	Distribution		
Russia	Assembly	Kaliningrad	
	Distribution		
Brazil	Distribution		

Figure 63: International activities of the BMW Group
Source: Authors' presentation based on data provided by BMW (2010b): Company profile – Locations

BMW has both a production site and development facilities in China. In India, BMW works with an external partner and operates its own assembly line. Independent companies with responsibility for distribution are operating in Russia and Brazil. In order to meet the re-

---

[316] See BMW (2010a).

quirements of the emerging markets, the automotive company expanded its distribution network in the BRIC countries. About 100 new facilities were opened in these countries in 2010. Figure 63 again summarizes the status quo for BMW at the end of the year 2010.

Volkswagen

The Volkswagen Group, which possesses volume as well as premium brands, is not fundamentally different from BMW with regard to distribution. It also relies on a network of dealers that is set up by the local company.[317]

Figure 64 shows which brands or products were manufactured in the individual BRIC countries at the end of 2010. Volkswagen maintains its own distribution sites in all BRIC countries. The focus is also on urban areas.

Country	Type	Location	Product
India	Plant	Pune	Skoda Fabia, VW Polo
	Plant (Skoda)	Aurangabad	Fabia, Octavia, Superb, Jetta, Passat, A4, A6
China	Plant	Shanghai	Fabia, Octavia, Superb, Polo, Lavida, Santana, Passat, Touran, Engines
	Partner	Changchun	
	Partner	Chengdu	
	Partner	Dalian	
	Plant	Jiading	Transmissions
	Plant	Loutang	Engines
	Plant	Nanjing	
Brazil	Plant	Anchieta	Gol, Saveiro, New Saveiro, Polo (Classic), Parati, T2, Engines, Transmissions, Foundry
	Plant	Curitiba	Fox, Golf
	Plant	Sao Carlos	Engines
	Partner	Sao Paulo	Engines, Axles, Cabs, Trucks, Bus companies
	Plant	Taubaté	Gol, Voyage
Russia	Plant	Kaluga	Tiguan, Octavia, SKD Models, VW Commercial Vehicles, Audi

Figure 64: International activity of the VW Group
Source: Authors' presentation based on data provided by Volkswagen (2010a)

Concerning the distribution structure of the two manufacturers BMW and VW in the markets under consideration, it must be pointed out that customer retention plays a huge role both in sales and after sales. When purchasing a "high interest product" such as an automobile, which is characterized both by high investment costs and a long service life, personal advice is particularly important all over the world. This factor can be seen as the decisive reason for the adherence to a distribution strategy developed specifically for the local market.

---

[317] See Volkswagen (2010a).

5.2.2 The Four P's – Product as the Crucial Success Factor

The four P's which are displayed in Figure 65 are also called marketing mix. They are the tactical tools that can be influenced in order to evoke specific customer reactions.

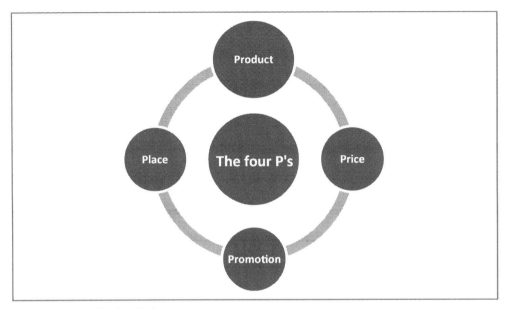

Figure 65: The four P's of marketing
Source: Authors' presentation

"Price" refers to the pricing strategy. Examples are high price strategies or penetration strategies. **"Place"** means the type and location of the distribution network, which in the automotive industry tends to be organized in the form of a dealer network. **"Promotion"** relates to the marketing instruments that can be used, such as television advertising.

In the following analysis, the focus in on the "P" that stands for **"Product."** In our definition, the product refers not only to the automobile, but also includes all additional company services. In the case of the automobile manufacturers this also includes loans provided by a financial services company tied to the manufacturer or spare parts. Thus "Product" spans the entirety of all goods and services that are in the portfolio of a company.[318]

For the product "automobile," a number of possibilities for adaptation and combination stand out. On the one hand, it becomes possible to precisely cater to specific customer needs. On the other hand, the possibility of very high production costs is a disadvantage. Every new option for a new combination reduces the degree of standardization. The following section deals specifically with standardization and adaptation.

---

[318] See Kotler, P., Armstrong, G. (2010), p. 18.

5.2.3 Standardization or Integration and Adaptation or Differentiation

Depending on the degree of standardization or differentiation, there are four possibilities to approach foreign markets in marketing. Figure 66 displays these possibilities.

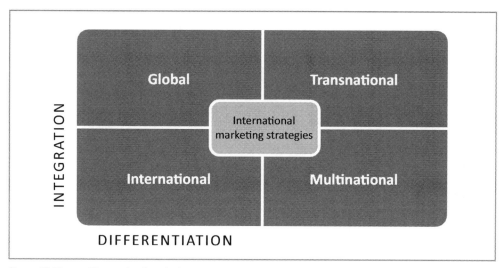

Figure 66: Types of international marketing
Source: Authors' presentation based on Sheth, J. N, Parvatiyar, A., (2001)

The term standardization refers to the organizational integration of a foreign company into the internationally active parent company. Differentiation in contrast refers to the degree of adjustment of the marketing mix to local or national customer demands.

When the degree of standardization and differentiation is low, the marketing approach is considered to be international. This strategy is most frequently used by small and medium sized companies which frequently do not possess the necessary financial means required for the further development of their activities. Significant standardization leads to global marketing. Coca Cola represents that approach. The soft drink is based on the same recipe all over the globe and the local companies predominantly follow the lead of the American parent. The term multinational is used when marketing activities are largely tailored to meet local requirements and at the same time, the local company remains largely independent. Transnational marketing for the most part only makes sense for very large groups, since it requires the strong integration of the national company as well as differentiated marketing. The classical example is McDonalds.

With regard to differentiation, the 4P model is usually applied to an assessment of the entire marketing mix. However, the product is usually at the center of the analysis. This Chapter will primarily deal with the opportunities available to an automobile manufacturer in the context of product differentiation. This will involve a particular focus on multinational marketing, while the organizational perspective will not be considered. The approaches which are called multinational in this context could also be called transnational. This would require taking the organizational level into consideration. Higher market shares and returns are often strategic aims of product adaptations. If an internationally active company does not adapt its product plan to the local market reality, domestic competitors will frequently imitate it and at the same time achieve superior alignment to the specific local customer needs. For that reason, higher market shares and returns are strategic aims of product adaptation.[319]

However, a comprehensive product adaptation to local specifics is associated with high costs and possibly a dilution of the brand. Comprehensive development activities can have grave effects on company earnings, since the required development costs can frequently be substantial.

The decisive success factor is the ability to strike the appropriate balance between adaptation and standardization. It must be assured that customer needs are addressed without excessively straining costs.

5.2.4 Importance of Product Adaptation for Automobile Manufacturers

As a consequence of the high development and manufacturing costs in the automotive industry, the implementation of optimized processes is of major importance. Furthermore, the adequate degree of adaptation and standardization that is required to assure profitability must be carefully considered.[320] This is in conflict with the fact that especially a car, as a major household expense, should closely meet specific customer needs.[321] In the opinion of decision makers, this necessity of product adaptation to the specific customer demands in the local markets is a major challenge for their companies.[322]

A few examples for possible product adaptations by automobile manufacturers are presented in the following. The successful market appearance in the increasingly important BRIC countries is given specific consideration.

5.3 Relevance of the BRIC Countries for the Automotive Industry

5.3.1 Brazil

Brazil became the largest production site for German automobile manufacturers in 2006 and in 2009 it was already among the five largest automobile production sites globally.[323]

Macroeconomic stability has increased since 2004. This has provided Brazil with high growth rates and large investments. The efforts of the past years and the related investment spending are starting to pay off. Margins are up, also in comparison to other regions.[324]

It is known that Brazilians adore their automobiles almost as much as Germans. It is said that the delayed modernization from the 1930s until the 1960s together with the effects of neoliberalism in the 1990s are slowly but surely putting Brazil into a leading role in the development of the automotive industry of the future.[325]

---

[319] See Kotler, P. (2009), pp. 286ff.
[320] See Janovsky et al. (2011).
[321] See Haslbeck, A. (2006), pp.18–19.
[322] See KPMG (2010a), p. 24.
[323] See Keese, S. (2010), p. 11.
[324] See Keese, S. (2010), p. 4.
[325] See Gegner, M. (2008), pp. 216–217.

5.3 Relevance of the BRIC Countries for the Automotive Industry

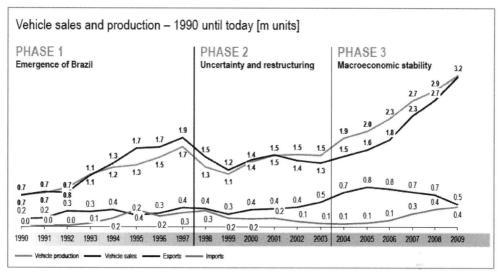

Figure 67: Vehicle sales and production – 1990 until 2009
Source: Vgl. Keese, S. (2010), p. 5

Figure 67 displays the different development stages of automobile sales in Brazil since 1990 and its positive development.

5.3.2 Russia

The Russian automobile market was opened for foreign companies only in the late nineties. This makes it the youngest market for foreign manufacturers among the BRIC countries. While this implies a large sales potential, it is also true that the development of the market is hard to predict.[326] Predicting the future market development in Russia is made even harder by the strong dependence on external factors such as commodity prices.[327]

The unpredictability of the Russian market also became apparent in the aftermath of the financial and economic crisis. In the first half of 2008, more automobiles were sold in Russia than in Germany, previously the largest automobile market in Europe. This development led many experts to predict that in 2009 at the latest, Russia would replace Germany as the largest automobile market in Europe.[328] But sales in the Russian market collapsed sharply in the second half of the year, a development that even accelerated in 2009. Sales in the automotive sector again declined by 50% compared to the previous year.[329] A main reason for the sales decline was the worsening of financing conditions for purchases of new vehicles as a consequence of the financial crisis. 50% of automobile purchases in Russia are credit financed. In addition, the purchasing power in Russia declined as a consequence of higher unemployment and lower real wages.[330]

---

[326] See Lange, N.S., Maurer, S. (2010), p. 16.
[327] See Lange, N.S., Maurer, S. (2010), p. 5.
[328] See Hones, B. (2010), p. 1.
[329] See Lange, N.S., Maurer, S. (2010), p. 16.
[330] See Schulze, G. (2009), p. 1.

Most affected were the Japanese brands. As an example, Toyota sales were down by 63%. In comparison to other volume producers, VW did well and only suffered a sales decline of 28%. Volkswagen maintained its position as second most successful foreign automobile dealer with sales of 94,018 vehicles. Much less affected by the economic crisis were premium manufacturers. As an example, BMW only recorded a sales decline of 11%.[331]

To reinvigorate the Russian automobile market, the scrappage premium was introduced in March 2010. Buyers received a certificate valued at RUR 50,000 for scrapping a car that was at least ten years old. However, these certificates could only be applied towards the purchase of cars manufactured in Russia.[332]

Looking forward, a recovery of the Russian automobile market is expected. However, it will take until 2014 before the sales figures of 2008 will be reached again.[333] It remains open at the moment whether Russia will indeed be able to replace Germany as the largest and most important automobile market in Europe.

Numerous factors support the long-term growth of the Russian market. For one thing, the Russian fleet is relatively old; more than 50% of automobiles are older than 10 years.[334] In addition, the passenger car density in Russia compared to other Western European countries such as Germany or France, is relatively low.[335]

The Russian market is also attractive for foreign manufacturers, because profit margins are higher than in Western Europe. One reason is the fact that there is no need for dealerships to grant rebates, since the demand for foreign models is high.[336] Additionally Russian customers prefer foreign brands with numerous extras. This also supports favorable margins.[337] An additional argument in favor of the Russian automobile market is the comparably low degree of competition relative to other BRIC countries.[338]

The Russian Minister for Industry and Trade Christenko estimates growth of the market volume of new vehicles to 3.6 million by 2020. Martin Winterkorn, CEO of Volkswagen AG even forecasts a market volume of up to 5.6 million automobiles in Russia by 2018.[339] Compared to these forecasts, sales in the record year 2008 of 2.8 million vehicles and in the year 2009 of about 1.4 million vehicles appear rather modest.[340]

The share of foreign manufacturers in the Russian automobile market has increased steadily in the past years.[341] Since 2009, the Russian government has been actively involved in counteracting this development by providing subsidies to the two Russian manufacturers Avtovaz and GAZ. As an example, Avtovaz, the manufacturer of the Lada, had received € 1.67 billion

---

[331] See Root, S. (2010), p. 6.
[332] See Broese, M. (2010), p. 42.
[333] See Lange, N.S., Maucrer, S. (2010), p. 16.
[334] See Tselikov, S. (2007), p. 8.
[335] See Ernst & Young, (2010), p. 9.
[336] See Tselikov, S. (2007), p. 9.
[337] See Revill, C. (2008), p. 1.
[338] See Capgemini (2009), p. 10.
[339] See Hones, B. (2010), p. 1.
[340] See Schulze, G. (2009), p. 12.
[341] See Begley, J. (2008), p. 7.

in financial support from the Russian government by November 2009.[342] It remains to be seen how these subsidies will affect the competitive position of foreign manufacturers. Since Russian producers have invested only moderate amounts in new technologies and models to date, it can be doubted whether they will be able to successfully compete with Western manufacturers over the long term.[343]

5.3.3 India

In the past years, China has been the largest growth market among the BRIC countries. But a number of forecasts assume that India will become the number one by 2020. By the year 2035, India will have a population of 1.45 billion people and thus surpass China. These two developments not only offer many opportunities, but also several risks for foreign automobile manufacturers.[344]

Especially the market for so-called Ultra-Low-Cost Cars (ULCC) – cars that are priced between US$ 2,500 and US$ 5,000 – will grow drastically in India by the year 2020.[345] The number of Indian citizens with a purchasing power of US$ 2,500 to US$ 5,000 was already 208 million in 2008. It is expected that this number will increase to 439 million by 2020. Figure 68 shows the expected global development of the ULCC segment in the largest markets in which it is relevant.[346]

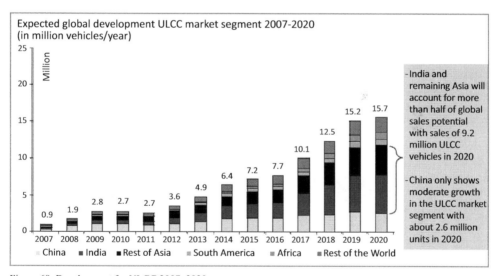

Figure 68: Development for ULCC 2007–2020
Source: Mayer, S., Rattey, F., Pleins, R. (2007) Mega-Markt für Ultra-Low-cost, pp.1ff.

---

[342] See Willershausen, F. (2010), p. 2.
[343] See Broese, M. (2010), p. 44.
[344] See Reiche, L. (2010).
[345] See Lange, N.S., Maurer, S. (2010).
[346] See Lange, N.S., Maurer, S. (2010).

An increasing number of young Indians use their education to advance economically. Especially this segment of the population forms the growing Indian middle-class. While the middle-class will remain sensitive to price and prefer inexpensive basic models, the dependability of an automobile will increasingly be valued.[347] This customer group represents the ideal market for low-cost cars or inexpensive midsized vehicles.

Next to the fast growing middle-class, there are also numerous earners of high incomes in India, who are the target group for luxury vehicles.[348] Thus the Indian automobile market also offers major sales potential both for volume and premium manufacturers.

5.3.4 China

A successful market entry in China is of major importance for every automobile manufacturer. In the year 2008, China accounted for 53% of the total sale volume in the BRIC countries. By the year 2016, this share is even expected to increase to 61%.[349] The timely establishment of a presence or even an active role in the Chinese market is particularly important, since more and more domestic manufacturers will enter the market by 2020. As is shown in Figure 69, experts anticipate a significant increase in the share of Chinese automobile manufacturers over the coming years.

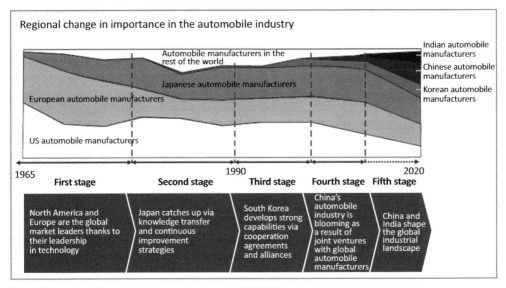

Figure 69: Regional change in importance in the automobile industry
Source: Mayer, S., Rattey, F., Pleins, R. (2007), pp.1ff.

---

[347] See Soellner, F.N., Rattey, F., Stolle, W. (2006), pp. 1ff.
[348] See Roeder, A. (2009), pp. 46ff.
[349] See Lange, N. S., Mauerer, S. (2010), pp. 20ff.

5.4 Customer Demands and Requirements in the BRIC Countries

5.4.1 Brazil

Infrastructure and climatic conditions

Due to the economic developments from the 1930s to the 1960s, the neoliberal approach in the 1990s and the associated city planning, which was fundamentally new and very supportive of automobile traffic, the automobile has steadily gained in relevance in Brazil.[350]

The architecture of today's megacities in Brazil strongly favors one form of transportation, namely the automobile. Cities do not support a network of public transportation that can be compared to European standards. Even the capitol Brasilia only has one metro line. Pedestrians and cyclists are highly at risk in the streets, which tend to be mostly expressways. Only those who cannot afford a car will walk or use a bicycle, since both are considered to be unsafe, even during the day. Vehicles are even used for distances as short as one kilometer.[351] Outside the currently 14 major metropolitan areas such as Sao Paulo, Rio de Janeiro or Brasilia, the streets tend to be poorly developed. The country with a size of more than 8.5 million km^2 is dominated by tropical and subtropical regions. In some parts of the country, especially in the Amazon Basin, enormous amounts of precipitation are recorded. These specific climatic conditions pose significant challenges to the automobile manufacturers concerning their product offering.

A broad market appearance and thus the development of sub-brands will be necessary in order to cover the entire range of Brazil with its specific economic and climatic conditions.

Target group segments

With an overall economic performance (GDP) of US$ 2.1 billion, average per-capita income amounted to US$ 11,127 in the year 2010.[352] Despite the remarkable economic development of the country in the past years, the percentage of those living in poverty still amounts to significantly more than 20% of the total population of 195 million inhabitants.[353] The share of the urban population amounts to approximately 51%.

In Brazil, the automobile is a lot more than just a means of transportation; it also confers status to its owner. Automobiles are used to demonstrate distance to the lower classes and to document social advancement. Those who are without a car in Brazil are considered to be among the informal segment of society. Chances for social advancement require participation in the motor vehicle boom. Especially the upper middle class and the upper class attempt to achieve noticeable differentiation from the lower middle class with their possession of exclusive automobiles.[354] What is more, success in Brazil is frequently not only a matter of personal definition, but rather manifests itself via visible status symbols.[355]

---

[350] See Gegner, M. (2008), pp. 213ff.
[351] See Gegner, M. (2008), pp. 213ff.
[352] See World Bank (2011).
[353] See World Bank (2012).
[354] See Gegner, M. (2008), pp. 213ff.
[355] See Fuchs, C.-M. (2009), p. 284.

Especially volume manufacturers can play a major role on the Brazilian automobile market. They are in a position to market inexpensive automobiles to the vast population segment with low and medium income.[356] With regard to the rural population, the poor infrastructure implies major opportunities especially for SUVs.

Country-specific demands

Customer demands concerning environmental standards that are globally relevant and observed by all manufacturers are efficiency and eco-friendliness.[357] In the case of Brazil, these customer demands are not nearly as important as in the European countries. Much more relevant are initial investment needs and ongoing maintenance costs.

Especially for the German automobile manufacturers this cost awareness implies that mere cost optimization of existing models will not be sufficient to address the price sensitivity of the buyers. Instead it would be necessary to offer automobiles in a significantly lower price segment. Certain automobile manufacturers, for example from India and China could serve as role models in this regard.[358] In fact, a third group of the German automotive industry, namely the group of super low cost providers, is missing at the moment.[359] Continuing this train of thought, the ongoing maintenance costs must also be addressed, since they cannot remain at the European level. In this regard, the further development of drive technologies and the necessity to innovate existing technologies play a major role. Especially in Brazil, drive technologies involving ethanol must be considered. Brazil grows 45.5% of the global supply of sugar cane, which serves as the basis for the production of ethanol.[360] If only ten percent are added to the fuel mix, CO_2 emissions can be reduced by up to 20% and emissions of carbon monoxide by up to 13%. The company Bosch has already developed a FlexFuel System which no longer requires one type of fuel to drive a vehicle, but instead allows the user to vary.[361] The broad use of this system can be recommended to both premium and volume manufacturers. VW invested approximately one billion Euros in Brazil between 2006 and 2011. The funds were largely used for product adaptation.

In summary it can be stated that it will be absolutely necessary for the automotive industry to be more innovative with regard to new developments. An approach to product development that is merely evolutionary will not be sufficient for two reasons. First, it is necessary to maintain margins and protect profitability despite the steadily accelerating price war. And second, customers must be won over in order to maintain the competitive position in the struggle among the automobile manufacturers. This is true for Brazil in particular, since the level of income remains relatively low and therefore it is not possible to charge high prices. In addition, competitive pressures are likely to intensify. More and more manufacturers will establish a presence in Brazil. This will lead to excess capacities before long.

---

[356] See Meyer, D. (2006), p. 4.
[357] See KPMG (2010b).
[358] See Meyer, D. (2006), p. 1.
[359] See Deck, S. (2009).
[360] See Gegner, M. (2008), pp. 226ff.
[361] See Meyer, D. (2006), p. 2.

5.4.2 Russia

Infrastructure and climatic conditions

The climatic conditions in Russia put very specific demands on an automobile. The automobile must be able to start even at temperatures as low as minus 40 or 50 degrees Celsius. Temperatures like these also require a strong heating system; it should be possible to heat windshields and exterior mirrors to prevent freezing. An all-wheel drive is also preferred in rural areas of Russia. The Mercedes S600 for example is not available as an all-wheel drive. For that reason it is almost impossible to sell, even in Moscow.[362] Especially small cars offer a lot of potential for development in these areas.

The infrastructure is an additional problem in Russia. A lot of roads are in poor condition and some important road links are completely missing.[363] Due to the poor street conditions and the weather situation, there is strong demand in Russia for big and top-quality off-road vehicles. An estimated 18% of all automobiles sold in Russia are off-road vehicles, while the share in Western Europe is merely 8%.[364] Of course, the "normal" automobile models also need to be adapted to the street conditions in Russia, for example by using specific tires or wheel suspensions. This point will be dealt with in more detail under 5.4.3 India.

Target group segments

Russia has a very rich upper class which likes to display wealth openly. No other city has more Maybachs and luxury limousines than Moscow.[365]

Consumption in general is of major social importance in Russia.[366] Russians enjoy the open exhibit of wealth.[367] The automobile is a very important status symbol for all population levels. For that reason, some Russian consumers are willing to spend more than 50% of their annual income for an automobile. In the US by comparison, the majority of buyers spends less than 25% of their annual income on an automobile.[368] There is a strong preference for Western brands on the Russian automobile market.[369] The majority of Russian consumers even support the view that a used Western car is better than a new vehicle from a Russian manufacturer.[370] One reason for this is the frequently inferior quality of Russian products, since research and development were ignored for a long time in the Soviet Union due to a lack of competition.[371]

The price of an automobile is used in Russia as an indicator for its quality. This means that expensive products are equated with high quality. Similarly well-known Western brands are associated with quality.[372] Particularly popular are big models. During a visit to Russia in

---

[362] See Geiger, T. (2008).
[363] See Guyette, J. (2008), pp. 69–70.
[364] See Revill, C. (2008), p. 1.
[365] See Geiger, T. (2008).
[366] See Busse, N. (2006).
[367] See Amann, S. (2006).
[368] See Capgemini (2009), p. 7.
[369] See Clarke, I. (2002), p. 27.
[370] See Busse, N. (2006).
[371] See Schmid, S. (2004), pp. 167ff.
[372] See Schmid, S. (2004), pp. 215ff.

2008, Martin Winterkorn remarked: "… at the moment, the Russians love big cars such as the Audi A8, the Phaeton, Touareg and Passat."[373]

Due to the high prestige of Western brands and the fact that Russians had to live without them for decades, they prefer to purchase the same models that are also available on the market in Europe, Japan and the United States.[374] Any automobile specifically made for the Russian market will therefore face tough times, particularly in the premium segment.

Since 2007, VW has repeatedly announced its intentions to manufacturer an inexpensive vehicle specifically for the Russian market. These plans were shelved repeatedly until VW announced at the beginning of June 2010 the intention to develop a VW Polo limousine with the name Polo Sedan exclusively for the Russian market. The vehicle has features which are tailored to the demands of the Russian market. Prices will start at € 10,000.[375]

Russian customers rarely buy cars with just the basic equipment. They particularly value extras and top-quality equipment.[376] There is a huge demand for special colors, audiovisual electronics, lights and so forth.[377] For that reason, numerous extras should also be offered for small cars.

Country-specific demands

Russia is among the countries with the highest rate of accidents globally. According to a study by the OECD, 939 of 1 million motorists suffer a deadly accident in Russia. This gives Russia the worst record among the OECD countries. In Germany, for example there are only 90 road casualties per one million vehicles.

Despite these frightening figures, safety is a purchasing criterion for only 8% of all Russian buyers.[378] For that reason, the topic of safety is not addressed by the manufacturers. Advertising for example does not stress the issue of safety technologies such as ESP or airbags.[379] But precisely the high accident rates offer a massive potential for differentiation from the cheaper, but qualitatively inferior Russian competition. For that reason, it would be a task of the marketing departments to clarify to consumers the value added that the use of modern technology brings with regard to safety. One possibility would be a joint campaign of several automobile manufacturers, which demonstrates how airbags can save lifes.

Gasoline use of a vehicle is currently a purchasing criterion for only 5% of all buyers. Environmental protection plays almost no role in Russia and is not discussed much in public.[380] The climatic conditions discussed above, the preference for big automobiles and the size of the country also put alternative drive technologies in a difficult position. It is doubtful whether Russian buyers are willing to spend more money for automobiles with alternative drive technologies.

---

[373] Kurylko, D. (2008), p. 20.
[374] See Lange, N. S., Maurer, S. (2010), p. 17 as well as Schmid, S. (2004), pp. 160ff.
[375] See Razumovskaya, O. (2010).
[376] See Revill, C. (2008), p. 1.
[377] See Guyette, J. (2008), p. 70.
[378] See Ernst &Young (2007), p. 19.
[379] See Santer, B. (2008).
[380] See Ernst &Young, (2007), p. 19.

5.4.3 India

Infrastructure and climatic conditions

A major problem in in India is the traffic infrastructure, which is in very bad shape in some areas and massively falls behind the development of the Indian high-tech industries such as the information and communications industry. Only about half of the network of streets with a total length of 3.3 million kilometers is paved. Thus vehicle construction must take these infrastructural factors into consideration.[381]

The uneven road surfaces in particular make it necessary to specifically protect certain components such as underside, shock absorbers and tires. This problem could be solved with an additional off-road mode or supplemental fixtures. Alternatively, specific tires or suspensions as already discussed in Section 5.4.1 Brazil and 5.4.2 Russia could be a solution. This point will be taken up again in Section 5.4.4 China.

Since 2003, tire pressure control systems for new vehicles are a legal requirement in the United States. With such a control system, the current tire pressure is monitored, taking the tire temperature into consideration.[382] If the tire pressure is too low, the "Intelligent Tire System" of Continental for example will directly report to the cockpit and thus to the driver. The optimal adjustment of the tire pressure to the vehicle and the framework conditions such as the weather helps the driver to safe energy and reduces tire wear. Insufficient tire pressure is also a frequent cause of accidents and tire punctures. This is a problem especially in rural areas of India, where the next repair shop can be far away.

A combination of run-flat tires and tire pressure control could always assure that the driver can continue the journey until the next repair shop is reached. Run-flat tires are tires with an integrated emergency system. An additional rubber element inside the tire prevents its collapse even when the pressure is lost.[383]

An increasing number of automobile manufacturers are offering run-flat tires for their new vehicles, since upgrading is more expensive and in some cases even impossible. A different approach was chosen by the company Michelin. Since 1998 it is offering an airless tire. A supporting ring which is fitted on the rim allows a continuation of the journey in the event of a puncture over a distance of up to 200 km at a speed of 80 km/h despite a complete loss of pressure. With such a tire system a tire pressure control system would not be required.[384]

Both tire technologies are particularly interesting for markets such as India and China with a partly insufficient road network and poor road surfaces. A consideration would be to include these tire systems as a standard for every new vehicle. This is more cost efficient and easier to handle.

---

[381] See Logwin (2009), pp. 5ff.
[382] See Wiesinger, J. (2009).
[383] See Wiesinger, J. (2009).
[384] See Sandor, J. (2010).

Target group segments

Many Indians wish to achieve a basic standard of mobility.[385] In India the lower income levels are still dominant, for that reason the price of a vehicle as well as the maintenance costs must be low.[386]

In the low cost segments the margins are small and the pressure to keep costs under control is rather high. In order to keep manufacturing costs at a minimum, it is not sufficient to simply downsize existing models that were not initially developed as Ultra Low Cost Car or Low Cost Car. To obtain sustainable cost savings it may be advisable to directly move production to India or at least to relocate parts of the process. First, low wages can contribute to a lowering of the manufacturing costs and second, transport routes are shortened and thus cheaper. Also India charges high import duties for "completed" vehicles. For that reason it would even be beneficial if an automobile manufacturer only moved the final manufacturing stages to India.

Standard models of high quality, which are tailor-made for the Indian market will not only lead to savings, but in addition may imply faster development cycles.[387]

Despite low profit margins and massive cost pressures, automobile manufacturers will increasingly make investments in the segment of Ultra Low Cost Cars or Low Cost Cars in order to obtain an entry point into the quickly growing markets of the BRIC countries. At the same time, the cost pressure forces the automobile manufacturers to increasingly consider more cost-efficient alternatives and ideas. This leads to the development of revolutionary materials, modules and processes.[388]

Next to the population segments that only have low income, there is also a segment of Indians with significant income that can even afford a personal driver.[389] Automobile manufacturers should react to this fact and offer extra-large rear compartments that offer additional space or long versions of existing models.

Country-specific demands

The Indian upper, middle and lower class is very similar to the Chinese population with regard to the demands concerning a vehicle. But unlike China with its one child policy, India is still the country of large families. For that reason a vehicle for the Indian mass market should be rather compact, because of the traffic situation in most cities, but at the same time offer sufficient space for up to five persons and their luggage.[390]

An additional peculiarity of the Indian market is the choice of the automobile color. There is a preference in India for simple and elegant automobile colors that are not too intense. These preferences were also taken into consideration by Volkswagen, when the range of colors was determined for the Polo which was developed specifically for the Indian market. The main choices are white, silver and black plus a traditional rich red as trend color.[391]

---

[385] See Soellner, F.N., Rattey, F., Stolle, W. (2006), p. 1.
[386] See Scheider, W.-H. (2007).
[387] See Scheider, W.-H. (2007).
[388] See Wyman, O. (2007), pp. 20–21.
[389] See Roeder, A. (2009), pp. 46ff.
[390] See Kakar, S., Kakar, K. (2006), p. 196.
[391] See Roeder, A. (2009), pp. 46ff.

In summary it can be concluded that in many regards the Indian market demands the same automotive features as the other BRIC countries. But the Indian culture also leads to a few specific wishes, such as the need for space and the choice of color. These points can be addressed rather easily by an adaptation of the European models and the standardization for the Indian market.

5.4.4 China

Infrastructure and climatic conditions

Even though China invested heavily in its infrastructure over the past decades, the roads, especially in rural areas, continue to be a major challenge for vehicle traffic. They are frequently poorly maintained and some of them are still not paved. Especially underside, shock absorbers, tires, steering system and brakes are affected by the poor road quality. Since the streets are not asphalted, broken wind shields as a result of flying gravel are common. In order to achieve specific protection for the components mentioned, the vehicles should be equipped with a specific underbody coating. Shock absorbers and tires should be of high quality, tires should have a coarse tread. Another possibility would be the inclusion of an additional off-road mode, which would be an alternative to full off-road models. For such an off-road mode, the manufacturers could adapt functionalities of already existing off-road or all-road models such as the Toyota Land Cruiser or the Porsche Cayenne.

Toyota improved the off-road qualities of the Land Cruiser with the help of three assistance systems: at the push of a button a "Multi-Terrain Select System" adjusts handling and braking response to the current surface. The so-called "Crawl Control" allows the setting of five different speed levels without the need for the driver to apply gas pedal or brakes in difficult territory. Furthermore the "KDSS" (Kinetic Dynamic Suspension System) of the Land Cruisers adjusts the effectiveness of the stabilizers at the front and back axles, which reduces the tendency of the vehicle body to roll while negotiating curves.

For its model Cayenne, Porsche favors two technologies in particular: first, the "Porsche Traction Management" (PTM), which consists of an active all-wheel-drive system with an electronically variable map-controlled multi-plate clutch automatic brake differential (ABD) and anti-slip regulation (ASR). The off-road handling of the vehicle is enhanced, since the PTM, jointly with the Porsche Stability Management (PSM) assures the optimal distribution of the drive power between rear axle and front axle in response to different surfaces and driving situations.[392]

Second, for the Cayenne, the Porsche Active Suspension Management (PASM) has a similar function as the Toyota KDSS. Depending on the condition and type of the road as well as the driving style, it actively and continuously regulates the damping force via an electronic adjustment of damper stiffness in order to reduce unsteadiness of the vehicle body.[393]

While these assistance systems were developed specifically for off-road vehicles, they can also be used in countries such as China as the standard in serial production.

---

[392] See Porsche (2010a).
[393] See Porsche (2010b).

Target group segments

The demands placed on their automobiles by Chinese users are similar to those of Indian buyers in many respects.

As in the remaining BRIC countries, a separation exists between the wealthy upper class and a broad lower class. But in recent years a middle income segment is developing and wages are increasing rapidly.[394] These three income segments differ vastly in the demands that they have with regard to products in the high interest area such as automobiles. Especially the Chinese upper class that lives in congested major cities likes to indulge in the luxury of a personal driver. For these customers, status and the open display of luxury goods are most important, while the costs of an automobile are in the background. In order to meet their high demands for comfort, it is suggested to offer automobiles with an oversized rear compartment or long versions of existing models. This leaves sufficient space in the interior of the vehicles for the desired and even demanded special equipment and installations such as an entertainment system or a refrigerator.

In contrast to the upper segment, different product features are most relevant for the purchasing decision of the Chinese middle class. This segment of buyers has only recently come into existence in China. The income situation in China will continue to improve rapidly so that this consumer group will also become an important target group especially for small and medium sized vehicles.[395] Since the income in this segment will be significantly below that of the upper class, the price sensitivity is high in that customer segment. This target group is looking for a functional and inexpensive automobile, which satisfies their desire for mobility. Cost effectiveness continues to be the main consideration.[396]

In this case the challenge is to satisfy the desire of the customer to get an inexpensive vehicle that is nonetheless equipped with current technology. The solution for automobile manufacturers is to provide standardized products without any special equipment.

Country-specific demands

The inhabitants of the Chinese megacities are continually exposed to extreme traffic density and smog. In order to reduce the air pollution in the cities, the Chinese government has passed a new emissions law, which will become effective in 2013. Additionally China also strongly supports the use of electric vehicles. The aim is not only a lowering of pollution levels, but also the reduction of crude oil and fuel imports.[397] When purchasing a hybrid or electric vehicle, buyers obtain a subsidy of up to US$ 8,000 from the government.[398] At the Shanghai Motor Show 2009 almost all Chinese automobile manufacturers presented at least one hybrid or electric vehicle either as concept car or in some cases even as production vehicle.[399] And German manufacturers as well are planning electric drives for the Chinese market. As an example, BMW was planning to introduce a fleet based on the electro development "BMW Concept Active E" in China in 2011. And according to Norbert Reithofer

---

[394] See Müller, V. (2010).
[395] See Mayer, S., Rattey, F., Pleins, R. (2007), pp. 1ff.
[396] See Soellner, F.N., Rattey, F., Stolle, W. (2006), pp. 1ff.
[397] See Höhn, J. (2009), p. 10.
[398] See Höhn, J. (2009), p. 10.
[399] See Gottwald, A. von (2009), pp. 16ff.

(CEO of BWM AG) the Megacity Vehicle is to be developed by 2013. This city vehicle with a pure electric drive is to target especially the demands of singles in a megacity. Especially in the more than 40 cities in China where the population exceeds one million, a vehicle, especially if made by a premium manufacturer such as BMW, does not need to cover a huge range, but instead needs to be chic, small, light, versatile, practical and safe. Due to the still high manufacturing costs, these vehicles are suitable only for the target market of the upper class.[400] But in general both premium and volume manufacturers should invest in the further development of different drive technologies in order to secure additional market share in China and to be in a position to lower production costs in the future and thus to offer more affordable electric vehicles.

Thus it is not necessary to develop a completely new model for the Chinese market. Already existing models can be modified slightly and especially in the luxury segment they can be offered with additional equipment in order to meet the demands of Chinese customers.

5.5 Recommendations for Action

Figure 70 once again summarizes the options presented in the context of a multinational (possibly transnational) approach:

Needs / Demands	Implications
Brazil	
Infrastructure and climatic conditions • Very good road conditions in the major cities and very poor conditions in rural areas	• Broad product range and possibilities for combinations with corresponding influence on the price • Increased protection for underside and shock absorbers • Assistance systems such as off-road mode • Tire pressure control systems • Run flat tires
Target group segments • Large middle class and lower class with low income but very high need for mobility • Strong need for differentiation from lower classes by the upper middle class and the upper class	• Large demand for low cost vehicles • Maintenance costs of the vehicles should be low (Optimize drive technologies) • Optical alteration of the vehicles (luxury segment)
Country-specific demands • High levels of pollution especially in the megacities	• Increase efficiency and environmental compatibility of the vehicles

---

[400] See Höhn, J. (2009), p. 10.

Needs / Demands	Implications
Russia	
Infrastructure and climatic conditions	
• Climate: extremely low temperatures in certain regions	• Extras such as windshields and mirrors that can be heated may have to be included in the basic equipment of the Russian models • All-wheel drive for all models
• Very poor infrastructure: streets are in poor conditions or not existent	• Expand offering of off-road vehicles, offer opportunities to combine standard models and off-road vehicles • Increased protection of underside and shock absorbers • Assistance systems such as off-road mode • Tire pressure control systems • Run flat tires
Target group segments	
• Upper class with high income	• Further expand the offering of luxury limousines, existing models may have to be adapted to the climatic conditions in Russia, for example by including an all-wheel drive
• Automobile is a very important status symbol for all classes, therefore high willingness to pay	• No ultra-low cost car specifically for the Russian market, instead provide a high-quality small car for the lower and middle classes • Continue the strengthening and further positioning of the brands
• Automobiles are rarely purchased in the basic equipment, but rather with numerous extras. This is true for all population segments	• Automobiles in Russia should generally be offered with basic equipment of higher quality • Offering of numerous extras and accessories; also for small and medium sized cars
Country-specific demands	
• To date low demand for safety technologies despite high rate of accidents	• Value added of safety technologies must be made clear to customers, for example with the help of advertising campaigns
• Gasoline consumption not a purchasing criterion to date • No or little interest in alternative drive technologies	• Currently alternative drives should not be offered in Russia; focus should continue to be on combustion engines

5.5 Recommendations for Action

Needs / Demands	Implications
India	
Infrastructure and climatic conditions	
• Underdeveloped infrastructure	• Increased protection of underside and shock absorbers • Assistance systems such as off-road mode • Tire pressure control systems • Run flat tires
Target group segments	
• Upper class with high income	• Oversized rear compartment, long versions • Ability to install extras
• Growing middle class	• Small and medium sized vehicles
• Low average income	• Low cost and ultra-low cost cars • Low operating costs
Country-specific demands	
• Indian preferences for colors	• Specific range of colors with muted tones and a dominant red
• Extended families	• Need for space despite small size of vehicles
China	
Infrastructure and climatic conditions	
• Poor infrastructure	• Increased protection of underside and shock absorbers • Assistance systems such as off-road mode • Tire pressure control systems • Run flat tires
Target group segments	
• Upper class with high income	• Oversized rear compartment, long versions • Ability to install extras
• Growing middle class	• Small and medium sized vehicles
• Low average income	• Low cost and ultra-low cost cars • Low operating costs
Country-specific demands	
• Strong environmental pollution especially in the megacities: new emission law in 2013	• Increase efficiency and environmental compatibility of the vehicles • Development of alternative drive technologies

Figure 70: Customer demands in the BRIC countries and implications for the automotive industry
Source: Authors' presentation

From the overview of customer needs in the various countries and the implications for possible product adaptations, the following recommendations for action for the automotive industry in the BRIC countries can be derived:

1. Infrastructure:
   Robustness of vehicles is an important consideration in all BRIC countries due to the poorly developed infrastructure. This would help to increase the degree of standardization and thus lower costs of production.
2. Target group segments:
   With the exception of Russia, a strong differentiation into several segments should generally be considered.
   Especially in Brazil, India and China, development efforts should be increased in order to obtain new and cost-efficient processes and materials to lower production costs. These lower costs should be passed along to customers in the form of an ultra-low cost car. There is a large potential for volume manufacturers such as the Volkswagen Group, which could open up a completely new segment with the development of a low cost car.
   The growing upper class in all four BRIC countries attempts to achieve differentiation from the middle and lower classes by openly displaying their status and wealth via luxurious automobiles. This need can be satisfied by providing comprehensive special equipment such as entertainment systems or other luxury features. This offers major potential especially for manufacturers in the premium segment such as BMW.

The product adaptations mentioned above are similar for all BRIC countries and therefore offer a large potential for standardization among the four countries.

However, all of the four countries are also characterized by specific needs. The implementation of all product adaptations must be checked for economic validity. This is necessary to secure a market share in the growing BRIC countries.

6 The Changing Business Field of the Automotive Financial Service Providers

6.1 Executive Summary

Over the past years, the market for automotive financial services has become one of the major sources of revenue for the automobile manufacturers. The divisions which service this market, the so-called Captive Finance Companies (CFCs), financial service providers that are tied to the manufacturer, have gradually expanded their product portfolios from classical leasing and financing products to banking products such as deposits and mobility services. In the major automobile markets such as the US, Europe and Japan, the primary tasks of the CFCs are the promotion of sales and customer retention. Against the backdrop of the economic and financial crisis, the CFCs gained in importance as a strategic refinancing instrument of the manufacturers. Furthermore they are indispensable as manufacturers expand into new growth markets such as India and China with a financial infrastructure that is still underdeveloped.

The ongoing changes within the automotive industry in the area of electromobility as well as the changed mobility requirements of the customers make it absolutely necessary for the automobile manufacturers and their associated financial service providers to align their existing business models to the new mobility trends and to expand their offering of products and services in line with these changes. Since drivers increasingly value the use of a vehicle and not so much its ownership, these changed mobility demands must be met via new concepts such as car sharing, location based services or corporate car sharing. The development of new drive technologies will increase the relevance of electric vehicles in the future. New, tailor-made financing and leasing products must be developed quickly by the CFCs in order to allow the strategic positioning in these new business segments.[401]

6.2 Basic Terms and Scope

Captive Finance Company (CFC):
A CFC in the automotive industry is a business unit which is owned by the manufacturer and which provides primary and derivative financial services in the market.[402] These services are related directly or indirectly to the motor vehicle and are generally offered by specialized companies in the market. In contrast to universal banks, which offer the entire range of bank-

---

[401] We thank Helena Ehrstein, Oliver Elsoud, Klaus Wassermann and Andrea Zedlitz for their support in the topic area of financing and leasing of CFCs. Their work has made the success of this book possible.
[402] See Lorenz, J. (2001), p. 29.

ing and financial service offerings, the CFCs focus particularly on products in the field of financing and leasing.[403]

Depending on the product portfolio offered, country-specific demands, strategic requirements or strategic positioning, the CFCs are present in the respective markets either as leasing or financing companies, fleet companies or automobile banks. In the following analysis, the term CFC subsumes all the specializations mentioned.

If CFCs also want to offer banking products (the majority of CFCs present in the German market does this or is planning to do this), they are subject to the German banking law and require a banking license. In addition they are required to use the term "bank" in the company name. The term "automobile bank" is derived from this requirement and is used as a label for this segment of the financial services industry.

With regard to company law, these CFCs are predominantly legally independent subsidiaries or divisions within the group.[404] The most common legal forms are "AG" and "GmbH." The global names of the German CFCs are BMW Financial Services, Daimler Financial Services and Volkswagen Financial Services. In the German market they are present with their operative units BMW Bank GmbH, Mercedes-Benz Bank AG and Volkswagen Bank GmbH.

Due to the fact that Germany has one of the most developed markets worldwide for automobile financial services, the following analysis is based on that representative market. Advantageous for the analysis is the fact that the German automobile financial service providers have their headquarters with global responsibilities in the domestic market and that the operative units that are responsible for the market all have a banking license. Furthermore, new products in the area of alternative mobility concepts and electromobility are frequently tested in the German market. The relevance of these characteristics of the German market for automobile financial services is made clear in the following sections.

6.3 Classification of the Market for Automobile Financial Services

6.3.1 Captive and Independent Financial Service Providers

Due to its profitable business opportunities, the market for automobile financial service offerings has witnessed an enormous increase in the number of market participants. In addition to the captive financial service providers, which will be considered in more detail in the following, a large number of independent financial service providers has also become active in this market in recent years.

The Association of German Leasing Companies represents the majority of all providers of leasing services in Germany. Among them are 112 companies that specialize in the leasing business with passenger cars and occasionally also with commercial vehicles.[405] Well known examples of these independent financial service providers are ALD Lease Finance GmbH,

---

[403] See Kratzer, J., Kreuzmair, B. (2002), p. 21.
[404] See Stenner, F. (2010), pp. 1ff.
[405] See Bundesverband deutscher Leasinggesellschaften e.V. (2011).

6.3 Classification of the Market for Automobile Financial Services

Deutsche Leasing AG or KBC Lease GmbH & Co. KG.[406] Subsidiaries of well-known commercial banks in Germany are also offering leasing and financing solutions for private and commercial customers in the automotive sector. Examples include Deutsche Bank, ING-DiBa or the Savings Banks.[407]

The working group of the banks and leasing companies in the automotive industry unites the twelve largest captive financial service providers, which represent a majority of the established automobile manufacturers in Germany.[408] These twelve companies and the associated automotive brands which they represent are displayed in Figure 71.

Figure 71: Overview of the twelve captive financial service providers and their brands
Source: Arbeitskreis der Banken und Leasinggesellschaften der Automobilwirtschaft (2011)

Compared to the non-captives, the proximity to the manufacturers provides the CFCs with a competitive advantage, especially in the segment of new vehicles. In addition to the transfer of the positive brand image of the manufacturer at the point of sale during the financing talks, there are also advantages when setting the contract terms. These include the possibility for cross-financing with the automobile manufacturers in order to generate attractive conditions for new vehicles, the informational advantage when setting the residual value or model-specific special conditions that may be offered to enhance sales. From the perspective of the CFCs, the network of authorized dealers is of particular strategic relevance. Despite the abundance of information sources, the authorized dealer is still the partner of choice for the purchase of an automobile. This opens up an opportunity for the CFC to successfully place its leasing and financing products at this important interface between customer and automobile manufacturer and to use and expand its competitive advantage over non-captives.

6.3.2 Financing of the Own Brand Versus Financing of Other Brands by the CFCs

It is the primary goal of the CFCs to support group sales with its financing and service offering. In close cooperation with the group brands, the CFCs also strengthen customer loyalty towards the automobile brands and support private and commercial clients as well as dealers. Differences in the brand appearance of the CFCs can be captured quite well when looking at German CFCs in their home market.

---

[406] See Bundesverband deutscher Leasinggesellschaften e.V. (2011).
[407] See Jünigk, T. (2009), p. 26.
[408] See Arbeitskreis der Banken und Leasinggesellschaften der Automobilwirtschaft (2011).

Volkswagen Financial Services AG for example is active in the German market with its operative subsidiaries Volkswagen Bank GmbH, Volkswagen Leasing GmbH and Volkswagen Versicherungsdienst GmbH. VW Financial Services is offering its customers financing and leasing products as well as insurance solutions and direct banking for the brands Volkswagen, Audi, Seat and Skoda to its customers. The financing activities for new and used automobiles are conducted by Volkswagen Bank GmbH with its independent brands Volkswagen Bank, Audi Bank, Seat Bank, Skoda Bank and AutoEuropa Bank.

BMW Financial Services in contrast is offering its financing, leasing and banking products in the German market for all three group brands BMW, Mini and Rolls-Royce exclusively via the BMW Bank GmbH. A differentiated brand appearance is not part of the company strategy in this case.

With the rewriting of the group exemption regulation in the year 2002, the captives are facing new challenges with regard to the financing of outside brands. The regulation assures the liberalization of the European automobile market by offering the opportunity to dealerships of opening up sales and service branches that are independent of automobile manufacturers.[409] It has led to a continuous increase in the number of automobile mega-dealers. In the year 2007 every seventh automobile in Germany was already sold by a so-called "multi-brand dealership."[410]

For the CFCs the issue of financing external brands necessarily increased in relevance. On the one hand, the financing via multi-brand dealerships offered the opportunity of reaching a significant number of customers of external brands. On the other hand, multi-brand dealerships are obviously also the target group of other CFCs and non-captives. This involves the risk of losing some of the customers to the competition. It is the clear strategy of the German CFCs with regard to the financing of external brands not to support any cannibalization of the group brands. For that reason they have chosen a purely internet-based market appearance with neutral brand names (BMW Bank with Premium Financial Services, Volkswagen Bank with AutoEuropa Bank and Mercedes-Benz Bank with Creditracer). Mercedes-Benz Bank has meanwhile terminated its Creditracer webpages and integrated the offering into its own webpages.

6.3.3 Corporate Affiliation and Legal Separation of the CFCs

Figure 72 displays the major differences with regard to position and legal standing of the CFCs of the three German automobile companies Daimler AG, BMW AG and Volkswagen AG. This look at the status quo of the positioning and legal treatment of the CFCs is relevant among other things for the possibility of implementing bank branches and the internationalization of the CFCs, which is dealt with in later sections.

At Volkswagen and Daimler the business area of global financial services is organized in legally independent subsidiaries. Daimler Financial Services AG and VW Financial Services AG are independent legal entities and normally conduct their operative business in the respective countries via subsidiaries. In contrast the designation BMW Financial Services is a business designation of the BMW Bank GmbH and a segment within BMW AG. The operative BMW Financial Services units are tied to the automotive manufacturer in different ways in the various countries (department, subsidiary or others).

---

[409] See Brachat, H., Dietz, W., Reindl, S. (2011), pp. 131ff.
[410] See Institut für Automobilwirtschaft (2008).

6.3 Classification of the Market for Automobile Financial Services

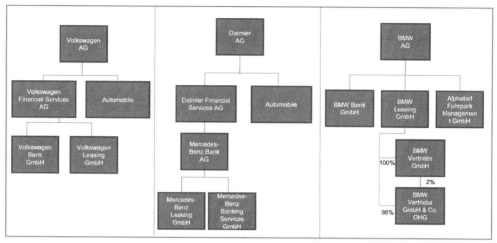

Figure 72: Group structure of Volkswagen AG, Daimler AG and BMW AG (as of 2010)
Source: Authors' presentation

Depending on the classification and strategic understanding of the overall group, the external appearance also differs. As an example, VW Financial Services AG is an independent part of the group with its own annual report and a very detailed and descriptive internet appearance. Daimler Financial Services AG and BMW Bank GmbH appear only as a sub-segment in the annual report of the automobile manufacturers and only provide rudimentary information in their internet appearance.

6.3.4 The Classical Product Areas of the CFCs

6.3.4.1 Retail Leasing

The two most relevant types of leasing in the automobile business are operating and finance leasing. The two types differ mostly in the assumption of the investment risk, i.e. the residual value risk.[411] Utilization of these types depends on the motivation of the user and the use of the leasing object. The differing legal, balance sheet and tax treatments play a role in choosing the type of leasing product, especially for corporations.

Operating leasing is a short-term rental contract that can be cancelled at any time. The investment and payment risk is with the lessor, i.e. the CFC. Since the lessor is interested in a continuation of the rental, maintenance and service costs are the responsibility of the CFC.[412]

In contrast to the above model, the investment object is first rented and later purchased in the case of finance leasing. Thus it is a hire purchase. The investment risk is with the lessee, who is also responsible for maintenance and service.[413]

---

[411] See Göller, K. (2008), pp. 119ff.
[412] See Städtler, A. (2009), pp. 18–19.
[413] See Bundesanstalt für Finanzdienstleistungsaufsicht (2009).

6.3.4.2 Retail Finance

In addition to leasing activities, standard financing and financing of the final installment continue to be of central relevance. Characteristic for financing are the higher monthly charges that the borrower incurs. He is not only interested in the use of the vehicle, but also has the intention to purchase it.

Standard financing takes the form of a classical loan contract. Via monthly installments which are set in advance, the entire sum needed for the purchase of the vehicle is paid over a predefined period of time.[414] As long as the loan contract is in effect, the relationship between borrower and bank is characterized by the right of use. Ownership rights to the financed vehicle are transferred once the loan has been completely repaid.

In the case of three-way financing contracts, customers decide at the end of the financing period whether they want to return the vehicle, refinance the remainder of the loan, or pay it off in cash.

6.3.4.3 Wholesale Finance

Central distribution channel for the automobile manufacturers is the proprietary sales organization. To finance the automobiles which are taken over by the dealers, specific arrangements are needed. Wholesale financing enables the dealership to finance the vehicles on hand, required operations and needed investments. This is done via Captive Finance Companies.[415] Since automobile manufacturers and dealerships are in a position of mutual dependence, it is the role of the CFCs to support the automobile dealerships at the point of sale by providing the needed financing. The CFCs with their financing offers for the dealerships play a decisive role in maintaining the current operations with new and used vehicles and showroom models.

With the liberalization of the market as a result of the new group exemption regulation of 2002 and the focus of other competitors on the business area of automobile financing, competition in the field of wholesale finance has intensified considerably. Non-captives are attacking the market with attractive terms and commission schemes. In order to maintain the lucrative wholesale finance business (average share of 15% to 25% in the volume of claims outstanding[416]), the CFCs are increasingly challenged to offer attractive terms not only to end users, but to dealerships as well.

6.3.4.4 Fleet Business

Fleet business or fleet management refers to the systematic planning, structuring and management of a fleet of vehicles for corporate customers.[417] It comprises all strategic and operative responsibilities that are needed to maintain the fleet. This includes the analysis, organization and administration of the fleet.[418] A corporate customer that makes use of this service

---

[414] See Olfert, Reichel (2005), p. 143.
[415] See Stenner, F. (2010), pp. 214–215.
[416] See Stenner, F. (2010), pp. 214–215.
[417] See Stenner, F. (2010), p. 115.
[418] See Stenner, F. (2010), pp. 115–116.

can outsource the entire administration of the fleet of company vehicles. Figure 73 summarizes the tasks involved in fleet management in detail.

Fleet analysis	Fleet organization	Fleet management
Situation analysis:	Vehicle selection/ Vehicle procurement	**Invoice controlling:**
▪ Repair costs ▪ Vehicle costs	Vehicle registration/ Vehicle logistics	▪ Controlling, payment and archiving of invoices
Choice of vehicle:	Financing alternatives/ Structuring of contracts	**Reporting:**
▪ Regular/Diesel/Alternative drives (hybrid/gas…)	Services	▪ Cost developments, Vehicle comparisons
Car Policy:	Vehicle disposal	
▪ Rules for company cars ▪ Leasing contract for company cars		
Insurance:		
▪ Management of existing and development of new insurance concepts		
Choice of repair shop:		
▪ freie Independent repair shops/ Managed workshops		
Replacement planning:		
▪ Replacement of existing vehicles		

Figure 73: Overview – Different tasks of fleet management
Source: Stenner, F. (2010), p. 115

6.3.5 Strategic Relevance of the CFCs

The concept of the automobile industry to offer financial services as part of the downstream strategy has turned out to be a lucrative business over the past years. Downstream strategy is the strategy of the CFCs to establish long-term customer relations that extend beyond the vehicle purchase. Between 1997 and 2008 the volume of claims from leasing and financing in Germany has more than doubled and amounted to more than € 88 billion in the year 2008. The penetration rate, which measures the share of vehicle purchases financed via loans or leasing in total vehicles registered, increased from 39% in the year 2004 to an average of 46.2% in the year 2008.[419] Thus in 2008 for the first time more than four out of ten new vehicles in Germany were financed or leased via captive automobile financial service providers.

---

[419] See Arbeitskreis der Banken und Leasinggesellschaften der Automobilwirtschaft (2009).

This development shows the major strategic relevance of the CFCs as part of the automobile companies.

Some of the reasons for the growing relevance of the CFCs include the stagnating automobile market, global excess capacities of the automobile manufacturers, the declining profitability of the manufacturers and dealerships as well as the increasing intensity of competition.[420]

The strategic aim of the automobile manufacturers with regard to the CFCs is the pursuit of profitable activities in the financial service sector and a diversification of their portfolios. Their subsidiaries in the financial sector generate additional earnings for the automobile manufacturers that serve as stabilizers even in times of crisis. As an example, the finance subsidiary of the Daimler group made a profit of € 457 million in the very difficult year 2008 and thus contributed more than 32% to the total earnings of the automobile manufacturer.[421]

A fundamental reason for the current popularity of the CFCs could also be the "one-stop-shopping" mentality of the customers. Apparently modern customers prefer to receive individually tailored products from financing to disposal of the vehicle from one source. The CFCs thus not only support automotive mobility, but also provide financial mobility to their customers.

Supplementary financial services and an effective customer relations management particularly serve to strengthen brand loyalty and customer retention. This in turn has a positive effect on repeat purchases of the customers (see Figure 74).

Figure 74: Summary of the strategic relevance of the CFCs
Source: Authors' presentation

---

[420] See Roland Berger Strategy Consultants (2005), p.9.
[421] See Daimler Group AG (2008).

6.4 Leasing and Financing Today – An Overview of the Market for Leasing and Financing

The German leasing and financing market is dominated by captive financial service providers. In 2010 they had a market share of 68% of all newly leased and financed vehicles (2009: 63%).[422]

The contract volume from leasing and financing activities amounted to approximately € 84 billion (–6% compared to the previous year). € 24 billion were attributable to new contracts (–7%). In Figure 75 the volume of new leasing and financing activities for private and commercial vehicles is presented.

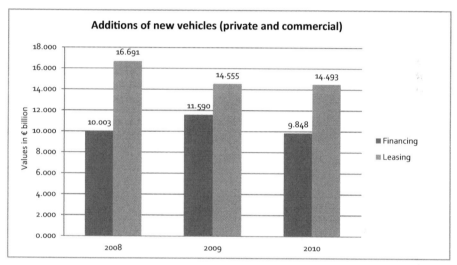

Figure 75: Additions of new vehicles 2008–2010 (in Euro billion)
Source: Arbeitskreis der Banken und Leasinggesellschaften der Automobilwirtschaft (2010a)

In that same year, 2.9 million vehicles were newly registered in Germany. The number of new contracts for financing and leasing amounted to 1.1 million. This translates into a penetration rate for new leasing and financing contracts as a share of total new registrations of 38% for the year 2010. The development of new leasing and financing contracts in the years 2008–2010 is displayed in Figure 76.

In the year 2010 a strong decline was registered in the private sector. The number of new vehicles declined strongly with regard to both financing contracts (–38%, 405,443) and leasing contracts (–37%, 82,457). The commercial business in contrast was very successful. The number of newly financed vehicles amounted to 121,962 (32%) and new leasing contracts also increased to 511,643 (11%).

---

[422] See Arbeitskreis der Banken und Leasinggesellschaften der Automobilwirtschaft (2010b).

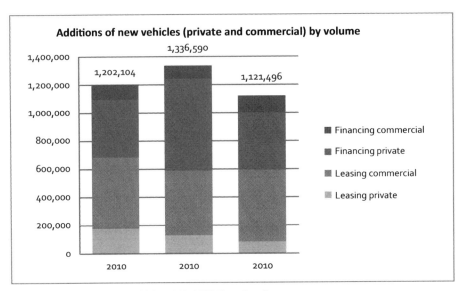

Figure 76: Additions of new vehicles 2008–2010 (by volume)
Source: Based on Arbeitskreis der Banken und Leasinggesellschaften der Automobilwirtschaft (2010a)

The entire European leasing market has grown by 4% in 2010 and reached a volume of € 224 billion (2009: € 210 billion); 4,886,284 contracts were added.[423] The growth rate in the segment of vehicle leasing was 8% compared to the previous year. There was only moderate growth of 3% in commercial leasing, which is due to the fact that few companies upgraded their vehicle fleets.

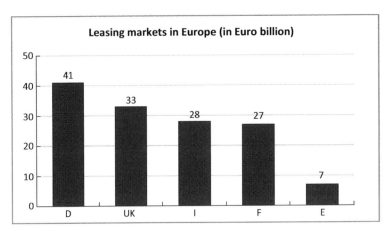

Figure 77: Top 5 leasing markets in Europe (in Euro billion)
Source: Bundesverband deutscher Leasinggesellschaften e.V. (2010)

Figure 77 demonstrates that Germany holds the leading position among the five largest leasing markets. Especially commercial vehicle leasing is popular in Germany, since companies can obtain tax advantages and balance sheet improvements by leasing their vehicle fleet.

---

[423] See Leaseurope (2010a).

Additionally, Germany has the largest number of suppliers of leasing products, which leads to the provision of a diversified market offering of leasing opportunities.

6.5 What are the Current Business Approaches of the CFCs?

In order to derive strategic management options for the CFCs, an analysis of current business practices is mandatory. Automobile financial services can be broken down into the two fundamental approaches of "classical captive finance" and "advanced automotive banking." Figure 78 compares the main products of the classical captive finance approach with those of the advanced automotive banking approach.

Captive Finance Approach	Advanced Automotive Banking Approach	Advanced Automotive Banking Approach
• **Leasing** – Operating leasing – Finance leasing • **Financing** – Standard financing – Financing of the final installment – Dealership financing	• **Financial services related to mobility** – Full-service leasing – Fleet management – Automobile insurance – Maintenance contracts	• **Financial services unrelated to mobility** – Direct banking – General insurance – Credit cards – Securities products

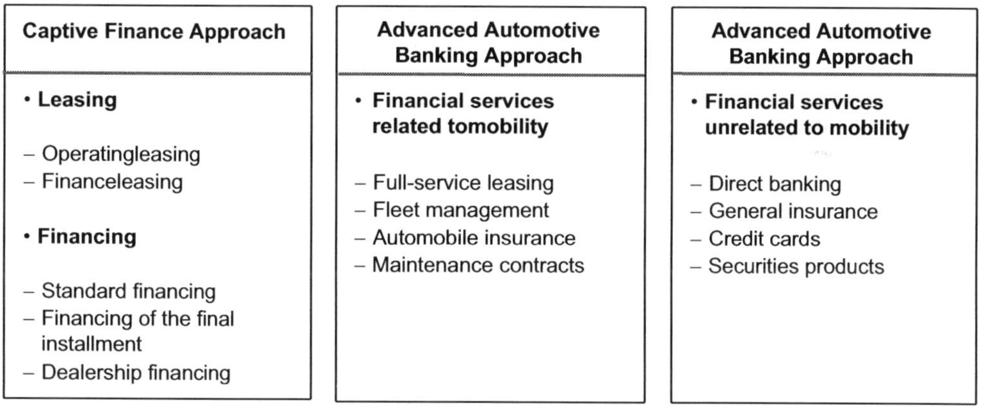

Figure 78: Product range of the CFCs
    Source: Authors' presentation

6.5.1 The Classical Captive Finance Approach

The focus in the classical captive finance approach is on sales support via leasing and financing products for private and corporate customers. In this business approach the captives concentrate on the provision of financing solutions for final customers via the primary distribution channel of company-owned trading organizations at the point of sale. Normally the financing of company brands in the business with new vehicles dominates the market activities. Next to traditional credit financing, the leasing business has massively gained in importance over the last decades. The classical captive finance approach is frequently chosen when finance or leasing companies enter a new market.

6.5.2 Advanced Automotive Banking Approach

Since the mid-nineties the captive financial service providers have successively expanded their product portfolio along the value chain by offering more banking services. With the expansion of their product range and intensified activities to strengthen customer loyalty, the captives moved in the direction of the so-called advanced automotive banking approach. In this case the product portfolio additionally comprises services that are related to mobility as well as services unrelated to mobility such as direct banking, but also insurance and brokerage products.

Of central relevance for the development opportunities and management options of the captives are their strategic market positioning and business policies. The market positioning as well as the product portfolio of a captive can differ significantly from country to country.

In line with market requirements, the three German automobile banks have continuously expanded their range of products and services and added new building blocks. The aim was and continues to be the discovery of new target segments for the group, which can be familiarized with the company brands. In addition to gaining new customer segments and revenue sources, an additional aim was the opening up of new sources of financing via the banking products offered (for example money market accounts and time deposits).

With the continuous expansion of their financial services offering, the automobile banks were able to achieve a certain independence from the developments in the automobile industry and to generate not only interest income but also fees.

Of particular interest, also with regard to the repositioning of the automobile banks on the European market by establishing bank branches, which will be discussed later, is their positioning in the home market. It makes a difference whether the CFC is positioned as the first or second bank of the customer. The approach of Volkswagen Bank AG is an example of the strategic positioning as the first bank for the customer which is also offering checking accounts and even ATMs. Mercedes-Benz Bank AG and BMW Bank GmbH are examples of banks that position themselves as the second banking relation in Germany with a clear focus on selected products.

6.5.2.1 Services Related to Mobility

The portfolio of services linked to mobility includes offerings that stand in direct relationship to the core business of the automobile manufacturer such as additional services for vehicles. The increasing demand for "one stop shopping" of private and commercial customers increasingly challenges the CFCs to personalize and expand their offerings at the point of sale. Among the services which are linked to mobility are mainly car insurance, fleet management and full service leasing.

Car insurance

Taking the entire German insurance market as the basis, car insurance accounts for 11.3% of all premium payments received. In the year 2010 this amounted to a sum of € 20.16 billion.[424] Numerous CFCs are already offering car insurance products as intermediaries. In addition to the premium income, these products give CFCs the option to use the customer contact for the placement of additional services and repairs from the same company in case of a claims settlement. This is an opportunity to counter the observed trend of taking repairs away from the authorized service center. Revenues from these services and the spare parts business have meanwhile become an essential component of the earnings of automobile manufacturers. The business with insurance policies will continue to offer major growth potential to the CFCs, since the penetration rates in this area continue to be relatively low.[425]

---

[424] See Gesamtverband der deutschen Versicherungswirtschaft e.V. (2011).
[425] See Arbeitskreis der Banken und Leasinggesellschaften der Automobilwirtschaft (2006).

Full service leasing and fleet management

Full service leasing is an extension of operating leasing. Full service leasing offers include additional services of the CFCs such as tire service, management of fuel cards, insurance and claims management in addition to the basic leasing services. Especially corporate customers use full service leasing and auxiliary fleet management. With the fleet management offering, the CFCs provide comprehensive services for the entire fleet of vehicles to corporate customers. The customers are freed from administratively complex tasks such as fleet analysis, procurement and maintenance of vehicles, accounting and reporting.[426] Figure 79 displays the schematic setup of operating leasing and additional building blocks to extend that service offering, including fleet management.

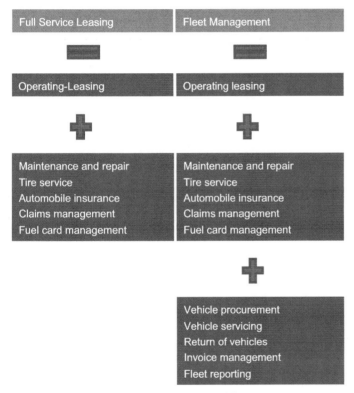

Figure 79: Stylized setup of full service leasing and fleet management
Source: Authors' presentation

6.5.2.2 Services Unrelated to Mobility

Services unrelated to mobility are all services that are not directly related to the core business of the automobile manufacturer, namely the automobile. Among the German CFCs, VW Financial Services AG, BMW Financial Services and Daimler Financial Services AG for example are offering comprehensive services that are not related to mobility. Meanwhile

---

[426] See Stenner, F. (2010), pp. 115ff.

almost all captives in the German market have a banking license for their operative units. The German Banking Act allows them to offer the entire product range of banking and financial services.

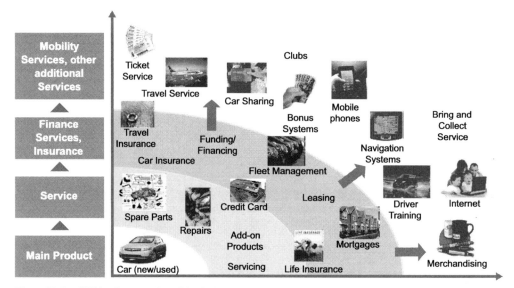

Figure 80: Possibilities for expansion of the CFCs
Source: Authors' presentation based on Daimler Chrysler (2004)

Especially the business with direct banking products (including overnight deposit accounts, time deposits and saving plans) has significantly gained in importance for the CFCs over the past years. As already discussed, establishing the deposit business provides the CFCs with very attractive refinancing opportunities. Figure 80 provides an overview of the product offering which ranges from classical leasing and financing products to services without a direct link to mobility.

6.5.3 Cross-selling and Crossover in the Automobile Financial Services Sector

In today's hotly contested automobile market, professional and sustainable Customer Relationship Management (CRM) is indispensable to increase the earnings potential of the customer base. With the introduction of additional banking products, the CFCs opened up new possibilities for cross-selling and the method of crossover (see Figure 81). The aim of cross-selling is to interest existing customers who hold leasing or financing contracts for new banking products and vice versa. The primary goal of the crossover method is to win over owners of other brands for the own vehicles in the context of CRM activities. Given the fact that the majority of deposit customers at German automobile banks drive other brands, crossover and cross-selling hold significant earnings potential.[427]

---

[427] See IBM (2009).

6.5 What are the Current Business Approaches of the CFCs?

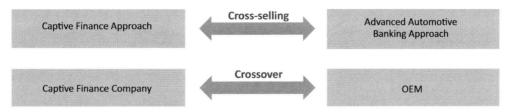

Figure 81: Stylized presentation of cross-selling and crossover
Source: DaimlerChrysler (2004)

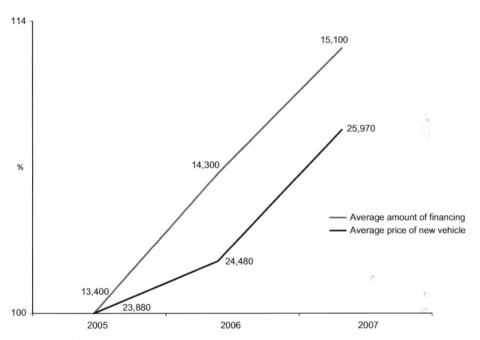

Figure 82: Trend towards more valuable vehicles
Source: Arbeitskreis der Banken und Leasinggesellschaften der Automobilwirtschaft (2009a)

With regard to the classical leasing and financing products, the focus of the CRM activities is on the realization of so-called upselling potential.

In the automobile industry the term upselling refers to the sale of vehicles or equipment versions of higher value as the result of targeted sales support which includes leasing and financing contracts.[428] The offer of an attractive monthly rate in place of the full payment of the total amount can help to trigger the upselling effect. In practice, the customer frequently chooses a stronger engine or additional equipment and deviates from his initial plans. Between 2005 and 2007 the average price paid by the customers for a new vehicle increased by 8.8% (see Figure 82). Clearly visible is also the increase of the average financing amount by 12.7% during the same time period.[429] This increase can be justified among other factors by the restraint of the dealers to give rebates for cash purchases during the boom phase until

---

[428] See Ueno, S. (2006), p. 5.
[429] See Arbeitskreis der Banken und Leasinggesellschaften der Automobilwirtschaft (2009).

2007. Compared to a cash purchase, automobile dealerships reduced the rebates granted for financing or leasing between 0.1% and 4%. At the same time the vehicle price was increased by between 0.5% and 5% because of upselling effects.[430]

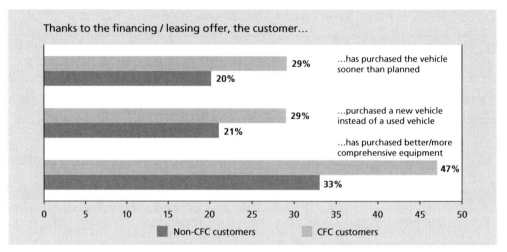

Figure 83: Purchasing behavior in the new vehicle business
Source: Arbeitskreis der Banken und Leasinggesellschaften der Automobilwirtschaft (2009)

The influence of the financing and leasing offering of the CFCs on customers is described in a study of the working group of the banks and leasing companies in the automobile sector which analyzes customer behavior when purchasing a new car (see Figure 83). A comparison of customers of CFCs and customers of other banks reveals that the CFCs have a much larger influence on the buying behavior and thus make a valuable contribution to the automobile manufacturers.

6.6 CFC – Quo Vadis?

6.6.1 The Strategic Options of the CFCs

The previous sections provided a market overview and specifically a presentation of the business models and product portfolios of the captive financial service providers. Several questions concerning the future development can be derived from this analysis:

- What are the immediate fields of action for the captives in the developed automobile markets USA, Europe and Japan to assure a sustainable and positive contribution to the earnings of the parent company?
- How can the automobile manufacturers include the CFCs as strategic instruments in their initiatives in the growth markets?

---

[430] See Lorenz, J. (2001b), pp. 88ff.

- Which business and operating models promise to be successful for the captives in the future?
- Which recommendations for action can be derived for the new growth markets?
- What are the most promising answers for the new mobility trends?
- Which business opportunities are offered by the topic of electromobility for automobile financial service providers?

6.6.2 The Fields of Action for the Developed Automobile Markets in the Triad

6.6.2.1 Accelerate Financing of Used Vehicles

Despite massive government intervention aimed at stabilizing sales of new vehicles in the established automobile markets in the triad (USA, Europe and Japan) the volumes have reached levels that are about 20% below the record year 2007. Growth forecasts for this segment are also not pointing toward a recovery in the next years. Considering these developments, the captives should clearly focus on the market for the financing of used cars. A look at the penetration rates for used cars of the three major captives in Germany of about 20% reveals that there is a great need to catch up.[431] Core components of a comprehensive concept should include among others:

- Positioning of the distribution processes for the financing of used cars as an integral component of the end-of-term and remarketing process
- Development of specific training programs for the dealerships
- Development of specific leasing and financing products including pricing concepts as well as service components for the used car segment
- Implementation of a suitable incentive program for the dealerships
- Development of appropriate IT-solutions at the point of sale (internet or dealer), which optimize the distribution processes for used car financing

6.6.2.2 Develop or Expand the Business with Fleet Customers

According to current figures, the fleet business with commercial customers is on the rise. In the relevant German market for fleets, growth of new registrations of 16.9% was achieved compared to the previous year.[432] The development of the fleet business with commercial customers depends like no other market on the overall economic environment. And at current it is hard to predict when the economies with major automobile markets will stabilize and growth will return. The challenge for the CFCs during the crisis lies in the positioning of new strategies, business models and vehicles. The following are major building blocks needed in the further development of the fleet business:

- Adjustment of the vehicles in the fleet to the new ecological framework conditions
- Expansion of existing service components in the fleet business with the aim of facilitating operations for commercial customers

---

[431] See IBM (2009).
[432] See Dataforce news (2011).

- Expansion of the offering of small and very small fleets (1–19 vehicles)
- Introduction of fleet management services across countries for both large and small customers, which support the increasing internationalization of the customers
- Positioning of offerings for multi-brand fleets

6.6.2.3 Introduce or Expand the Offering of Products with Risk Adjusted Pricing

The economic and financial crisis not only hit the financing of new vehicles, but also resulted in a significant increase in loan default rates. While average loan default rates stood at about 1–2% in the past years, a significant increase with a correspondingly detrimental effect on earnings can be expected going forward. In order to be prepared for this expected development, the captives are challenged to significantly enhance their offering of leasing and financing contracts with differentiated interest rate conditions, or in some cases to implement such an offering for the first time. The concept of risk adjusted prices takes specifically those risks into consideration which are unique to the customer. These are applied in addition to the standard parameters such as refinancing rates and administrative costs. The goal of this more differentiated approach is to put greater weight on the credit standing of individual customers when setting the terms of a loan. In addition to mathematical models for the calculation of potential credit default risks, which were promoted by the introduction of Basel II, but which are not considered further at this point, the following issues are important for a successful implementation of risk adjusted pricing models:

- Target process definition at the point of sale to integrate risk-adjusted pricing into the sales process
- Establishment of a specific communication concept for the dealerships
- Development of a strategic marketing concept for the new loan terms
- Introduction of a supporting concept for the provision of collateral, which includes the possibility of adjusting financing terms in case adequate collateral is provided

6.6.2.4 Establish Bank Branches

With the introduction of the European passport in the year 1996, financial institutions in the European Union are allowed to make use of a simplified approval procedure for setting up branches in a member country of the EU. The founding of branches can be supported without much administrative burden and costly effort from the home country. For the auto banks and their parent companies the establishment of bank branches offers a multitude of strategic options.

With the establishment of a network of bank branches for their auto banks, the automobile manufacturers can open up new strategic opportunities for integrated liquidity, refinancing and risk management.

Due to the comparatively high savings rate in Germany, this market is well suited for offers of direct banking products such as overnight money or time deposits. Especially in the beginning of the year 2009, the auto banks of the German automobile manufacturers were able to collect significant amounts of customer funds by offering attractive terms for deposits. If a network of banking branches is established, these customer funds can also be used abroad as attractive sources of refinancing for leasing and financing contracts with end customers and the financing of dealerships. Figure 84 shows both the positioning of an auto bank with branch offices in the overall structure of the company and the various refinancing possibilities discussed above.

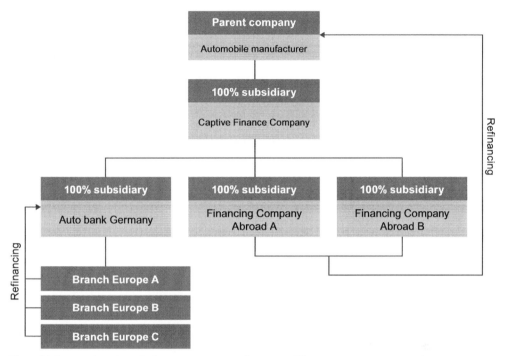

Figure 84: Presentation of a typical company structure of an automobile company
Source: Authors' presentation

Especially in times of tightened credit standards, the concept of refinancing via deposits at direct banks appears to pay off. The placing of a bond of the Daimler group on the capital markets in the year 2009 required interest charges of 4–9% as a result of the credit standing, while deposits at the direct bank in the form of money market accounts paid an interest rate of 1.9%.[433]

Additional advantages relate to the central allocation of funds across the entire company and an expanded Europe-wide loan portfolio, which can be utilized for ABS transactions. Both features serve to lower costs and to improve risk management and will be discussed again later.

Daimler Financial Services for the first time opened up a European branch location of Mercedes-Benz Bank AG in Spain in May 2008. And VW Financial Services as well is already represented in eight countries with subsidiaries of VW-Bank GmbH in Europe. Daimler Financial Services is present in 39 countries with financing companies, but only in Spain, Poland and Russia via the branches of the German auto bank (Mercedes-Benz Bank AG).

---

[433] See Daimler Group (2009).

The following key aspects in the target country must be assessed before making a decision about the establishment of bank branches:

- Legal framework conditions and taxation
- Structure of market supervision
- Portfolio development in the leasing and financing business
- Requirements for organizational structure and processes in the areas of liquidity, refinancing and risk management
- Implementation of information technology
- Strategy of market entry: establishment of a new bank branch or purchase/takeover of an existing financing or leasing company

6.6.2.5 Convert to a Bank Holding Company

Only with the severe crisis on the international financial markets did the American concept of converting CFCs into bank holding companies receive broad public attention. A bank holding company is a vehicle which has control over one or several banks and is regulated by the Federal Reserve Bank, the US central bank (see Figure 85). Bank holding companies make concessions with regard to capital requirements and control mechanisms, which are also in effect for other commercial banks. In exchange they receive facilitated access to government support.

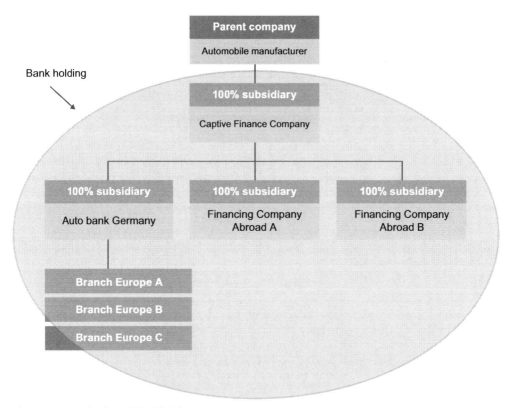

Figure 85: Example of a CFC bank holding
Source: Authors' presentation

Since the outbreak of the financial market distortions, numerous well known American companies have undertaken the restructuring process to become a bank holding company. Among them are for example Goldman Sachs, American Express and GMAC. The case of GMAC makes it clear that the conversion is not without consequences for the current owners. They have to relinquish control in the form of ownership shares for a specified period of time to an independent government-appointed fiduciary. Until the end of 2008 the private equity company Cerberus and the automotive group General Motors held 51% and 49% in the financial service provider GMAC. With the status as bank holding these shares were reduced to 33% and 10% and at the same time, GMAC was given access to funds from the American rescue funds for banks which has a total volume of US$ 700 billion.[434] In addition, GMAC was obliged to differentiate its product portfolio and make its financing offers available to everybody.

For the European CFCs the conversion to a bank holding company would also open up new perspectives with regard to the flexibility of internal and external refinancing. A conversion significantly facilitates the transfer of funds across borders, since the bank holding can be considered a central superordinate construct. But in Europe a conversion would only make sense against the background of adjusted legal framework conditions. A detailed analysis which also takes into account issues related to the topic of founding a bank is thus indispensable before a far-reaching decision such as the conversion to a bank holding company can be implemented.

6.6.2.6 Rework Governance Structures and Operating Concepts

The market coverage of the captives is currently characterized by a large number of local companies that act largely independent of each other. Depending on their strategic orientation, the captives have headquarters with global responsibility, which are normally domiciled in the home country of the parent company (Daimler Financial Services in Berlin, BMW Financial Services in Munich and VW Financial Services in Braunschweig). In some cases regional concepts, mainly for the coordination of the areas distribution and marketing, are implemented in the organization. The corresponding operating models usually comprise all units of the organization along the defined processes (among others distribution, processing of applications, contract management, finance, controlling, risk management, accounting, personnel, legal and information technology).

A weakness of almost all globally active captives is their relatively unfavorable cost structure with limited economies of scale as a result of their decentralized setup compared to competitors in the field of banking. Compared to other banks, the share of internal contributions along the entire value chain in the leasing and financing area is significantly higher.

For the captives, declining financing volumes for new vehicles, especially in the core markets of the triad, might imply cost problems going forward. Notably the growing regional convergence of the framework for supervision, taxation and legal issues suggests that the implementation of the following measures has the potential to achieve savings:

- Implementation of new governance concepts at a global and regional level
- Centralization of tasks in the areas of finance, controlling and accounting
- Establishment of shared service centers across borders for the areas of customer relations, contract management and accounting on the basis of harmonized business processes

---

[434] See Reuters Deutschland (2009).

- Harmonization and standardization of the information technology at a global and regional level for the areas of wholesale finance, retail finance as well as accounting and business analytics
- Review of the core processes that are completed in-house and possibly outsourcing of process components or complete processes and services

6.6.2.7 Optimize the Areas Refinancing, Liquidity Management and Risk Management Jointly with the Automobile Manufacturers

The economic crisis in 2009 has resulted in significantly increased refinancing costs on the capital markets despite historically low central bank rates. The entire automotive industry was hit particularly hard by the fact that debt financing had become expensive and hard to obtain during the sales crisis. Refinancing costs for the CFCs went up significantly as well for two reasons. First, the banks that provided financing assumed higher default rates in the loan portfolios of the CFCs. Second, it had to be assumed that the liquidity of the CFCs would decline as a consequence of the reduced demand for leasing and financing contracts. The direct dependency on the rating of the automobile manufacturers made the situation even more difficult for the CFCs. A worsening of the rating of the automobile manufacturers directly resulted in increased refinancing costs for the CFCs. In the hotly contested market for automobile financial services this implied an enormous competitive disadvantage compared to the independent providers of financing.

The iTraxx Europe Index is a suitable instrument to clarify the development of the return spreads. This index contains the 125 most frequently traded credit default swaps in Europe (see Figure 86). It shows the difficult situation CFCs and in particular automobile manufacturers were facing during that year.

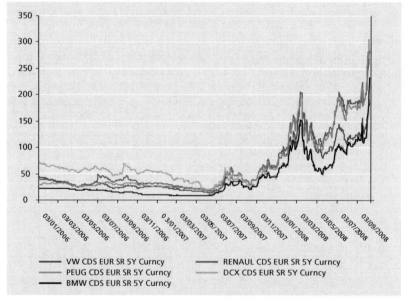

Figure 86: Development of Credit Default Swaps (CDS) in the automotive industry
Source: Deutsche Bank Equity Research (2008)

At this point the increasing strategic relevance of the CFCs for the automobile manufacturers becomes particularly apparent. With the implementation and combination of some of the strategic management options for the CFCs such as

- Founding of bank branches,
- Establishing alternative and independent ways to access capital markets and
- Developing a sophisticated and integrated liquidity, refinancing and risk management system,

the automobile manufacturers will be in a much better position to survive the crisis in the major sales markets, which is likely to continue for a number of years.

6.6.3 Recommendations for Action in the New Growth Markets

6.6.3.1 Establish Financing Companies in Brazil, Russia, India and China

Since the financial and economic crisis erupted in the year 2008, the BRIC countries have turned into the growth engine for the global automotive industry. The outstanding sales figures of the US-American, German and Japanese automobile manufacturers in the years 2010 and 2011 are due predominantly to market success in China. Forecasts for the years until 2015 continue to predict high growth rates for new vehicle sales in the BRIC countries.

Among the German automobile manufacturers, Daimler AG and BMW AG currently only have a weak presence of both their automobile operations and their financial services in the BRIC countries. In contrast, VW has a much stronger presence in China and Brazil because of its broader range of vehicles and brands.

Especially in the BRIC countries, which are characterized by low income and large financing needs, market support for the automobile manufacturers by the CFCs is appropriate and promising in our opinion. It must be the goal of the CFCs to gain market share and new customers in these growth markets by offering specific and attractive financing conditions, for example in the form of micro loans for small vehicles. Local requirements and legal framework conditions in the respective countries continue to limit the scope of the CFCs in some cases. In China for example, financing activities continue to require the cooperation with a local company.

While the CFCs are facing only limited growth potential in the traditional regions and should predominantly pursue the aim of increasing customer loyalty, they can specifically take on the task of acquiring new customers in the growth countries.

6.6.3.2 New Operating Strategies for the Growth Markets

If the market entry with a proprietary local financing and leasing company is an option for the fast growing and populous BRIC countries, several peculiarities must be taken into consideration with regard to strategy. These include:

- Very high expected annual growth rates for new financing
- Rather limited number of software companies that can provide solutions for the leasing and financing business
- In some areas major and continuous change in supervisory regulations due to the early development stage of the markets for financial services

- Lack of resources with needed technical competencies
- High share of manual processes due to a lack of technology

If all these issues are taken into consideration, the development of an independent operating strategy by the CFCs is indispensable. The following aspects could be components of such a strategy:

- Cooperation with other captives at the local level concerning selected business processes
- Establishment of joint IT service companies by the CFCs for operation, maintenance and further development of software
- Outsourcing of business processes to local banks
- Outsourcing of needed IT activities to IT service providers
- Cross-border cooperation with other group companies
- Cross-border establishment of resources with specialized knowledge

6.6.4 Promising Answers to New Mobility Trends

It is one of the biggest challenges of automobile financial service providers to develop financing solutions which address new mobility trends. If it is the task of the manufacturers to construct ecological and energy efficient vehicles, the captives are challenged to develop new financing solutions in support of these promising mobility concepts.

While the desire of the manufacturers to support individual mobility solutions for society by providing private passenger cars is understandable, it must be weighted critically against the goal of protecting the climate and resources. Motorization rates of the Chinese population that are similar to those in the US do not appear very desirable. In response to higher fuel prices and tighter environmental regulations, customers are also reassessing their purchasing decisions. Highly motorized vehicles and SUVs are increasingly viewed with skepticism by environmentally conscious consumers, due to their high CO_2 emissions and gasoline use.[435]

What are possible contributions of the automobile financial service providers in the context of these new mobility trends? While financial products were previously linked to the ownership of a vehicle, they must now be developed more in the direction of use-based billing. Additionally, offers must be developed that take into consideration new mobility trends and the related mobile use of the internet. In the following three promising offerings are presented which have the potential to significantly enhance the product portfolio of the automobile financial service providers. These are car sharing, location based services and corporate car sharing.

6.6.4.1 User-based Mobility via Car Sharing

Many drivers, especially in the developed industrial nations, have developed a new understanding of mobility for themselves. Due to the high degree of interconnectedness of public transportation and the lack of adequate parking in major cities, vehicle ownership is less and less attractive. Since individual mobility needs continue to be high, several providers have developed the concept of car sharing. Car sharing is "[…] the organized and joint use of motor vehicles."[436]

---

[435] See Bernhart, W., Zollenkop, M. (2011), p. 281.
[436] See Bundesverband Carsharing e.V. (2011b).

Car sharing is particularly suitable for people who live in agglomerations and who do not depend on the daily use of their vehicle. It can be used to supplement the public transport offerings of the cities or the railroad system. The advantages for users are mostly of a monetary nature.[437] Costs only accrue if the customer actually uses the vehicle. For persons who only infrequently need a vehicle, car sharing is significantly more cost-effective than ownership. Additional advantages are a certain independence from gasoline prices as well as the fact that service, cleaning and repairs are included. Flexibility with regard to the type of vehicle is also an advantage for the customer. In contrast to the purchase of a vehicle, many car sharing providers offer the right vehicle for every occasion.[438]

What are the opportunities provided to the automobile manufacturers and their captive financial service providers in the context of car sharing? A particularly relevant field for the captives is the processing of payment services for the manufacturer. In addition to the generation of fees, this service can also be used as a suitable platform for customer acquisition and retention. If the automobile manufacturers are able to convince the customers who use their own car sharing offering of the quality of the vehicles used, this can be a decisive argument for a purchase at a later point in time. Automobile manufacturers who run their own car sharing programs must put a specific focus on a high service quality in addition to superior product quality and brand loyalty. Especially in this regard, the captive financial service provider can offer additional value. A successful and long-term service relationship opens up the opportunity to collect valuable customer information which can be used to derive new mobility demands and corresponding offerings. The automobile manufacturers have realized that the use of customer data, especially of young people with a preference for car sharing, can open up future sales potential for their vehicle brands.

From a strategic perspective, the introduction of car sharing by automobile manufacturers opens up the profitable opportunity to take away market share from rental companies. Persons who do not own a vehicle, but still want to be mobile on certain occasions, are usually forced to rent a vehicle for an entire day. Car sharing offers the opportunity to adjust the rental period to their needs. If the manufacturers decided to extend rental periods with the help of specific long-term rates for car sharing, a scenario of serious competition against rental car companies appears possible.

Additional aspects that support the introduction of car sharing by automobile manufacturers and their financial service providers are the large potential and the growth opportunities provided by corporate customers. 13% of all kilometers travelled in Germany every year are related to business. Automobile travel accounts for a large share of this. Companies that do not maintain their own fleet can realize huge savings by utilizing car sharing offerings.[439]

Car sharing also gives the automobile manufacturers the opportunity to consider the market for used cars as well. In case of weak economic fundamentals of the used car market, used cars could be added to the proprietary car sharing fleet.

From a geographic perspective, especially the emerging economies in Asia offer an enormous potential for car sharing. Except for a rather small population segment that is rich, the majority of the population will not be able to afford their own vehicle. Nonetheless, there is a

---

[437] See Bundesverband Carsharing e.V. (2011a).
[438] See ADAC (2011a).
[439] See Bundesverband Carsharing e.V. (2010).

demand for a certain degree of individual mobility. Car sharing offers an opportunity to be mobile for these population segments. The automobile manufacturers can secure this major potential by providing the corresponding offering.

Risks that must be taken into consideration by the automobile manufacturers refer to possible competitive pressures. Since barriers to market entry are low for this line of business, while returns are high, more and more new providers that are not tied to manufacturers are entering the market. These might take away market share from the automobile manufacturers and therefore reduce the profitability of the business.

It can thus be concluded that the idea of car sharing provides several opportunities for both automobile manufacturers and captive financial service providers to open up an alternative source of revenue and to secure future sales potential.

6.6.4.2 Location Based Services – Participation in Mobility Services that are Not Linked to the Vehicle

"LBSs are services accessible with mobile devices through the mobile network and utilizing the ability to make use of the location of the terminals. LBS provide specific, relevant information based on the current location to the user."[440]

Location based services are an expansion of the product portfolio and can constitute an additional source of revenue for the automobile manufacturers and their financial service providers in the area of alternative mobility concepts.

BMW AG was the first automobile manufacturer that decided to make comprehensive investments in alternative and sustainable mobility solutions. For this reason, the new sub-brand BMWi was introduced in February 2011. It combines both activities with electric vehicles and mobility services.[441] The two aims are the design of holistic mobility solutions for the customers and the generation of new sources of revenue that do not depend on mobility for the company.[442] The BMWi Ventures Fund which was founded for this purpose in New York is to be endowed with up to US$ 100 million. The first investment of the BMWi Ventures Fund was the New York based provider of location based services "MyCityWay" with a volume of US$ 5 million.[443]

The investment in this technology enables BMW to deliver the services of a comprehensive mobility and information provider also to interested parties that do not own a vehicle. All users of MyCityWay can always find the closest attractions, leisure activities or similar sites on their smartphones. It is possible, for example, to get directions to the nearest movie theatre while on the road, to obtain programming information and at the same time reserve tickets. BMW acts as intermediary between providers and customers via MyCityWay. If contact is established via the application, the provider is required to pay a fee to MyCityWay and the automobile manufacturer receives a share of that fee. In the future, MyCityWay could be extended in a way that payment for services is made via the application. A captive financial service provider could be responsible for the entire payment transaction in such a case and generate new revenues.

---

[440] See Reichenbacher, T. (2004), p. 40.
[441] See BMW i (2011).
[442] See GreenTech (2011).
[443] See Techcrunch (2011).

These types of alternative mobility platforms for services also can be used by the automobile manufacturers as a lasting and durable advertising forum. A clever analysis of the interests of the users, for example, can be utilized to supply specific target groups with advertising for the company and its manifold products. When looking for attractions in Munich, for example, the BMW Museum and the BMW World are always listed near the top. This implies a direct positioning of the brand with the aim of getting the user interested in BMW. Other companies that want to have their products appear at the top of the list of searches are frequently willing to pay an additional fee. This can translate into additional revenues for the automobile manufacturers from the new platform.

A program to optimize travel is also an option that should be considered in the future. Location based services always point the user to the quickest, cheapest or possibly also the most CO_2-efficient route to his destination of choice. Automobile manufacturers could combine this function with their own online-based car sharing or rental car portal and thus guarantee comprehensive customer service from one source. Peugeot has taken a first step in this direction and offers via its platform "Mu by Peugeot" the possibility to rent automobiles, commercial vehicles, accessories, scooters as well as bicycles of the automobile manufacturer in selected cities.[444] In combination with a car sharing strategy, such a platform would provide the user with the optimal form of mobility at each point in time. For the automobile manufacturers and their financial service providers, enormous opportunities are present in such a holistic approach to mobility and information systems. What sounds like science fiction at present may well be considered a standard service by the year 2020.

6.6.4.3 The Expansion of Fleet Management – Corporate Car Sharing: The Model of Siemens

A third promising mobility concept which can be used by the automobile manufacturers and their financial service providers to expand the existing business, especially with regard to fleet management for major corporate customers, is corporate car sharing. The idea behind corporate car sharing will also be called "Siemens model" in the following. The name is derived from the origin of the idea. In 2010 Siemens AG started a field experiment on the topic of electromobility with its own staff. The company provided 100 electric vehicles, which could be used by its workforce for private occasions on favorable terms. In exchange, the company received relatively inexpensive feedback necessary which was used to make improvements in the area of electromobility. For Siemens AG the value was in testing electromobility under normal conditions. The users were required to report their experiences and suggestions for improvement to the developers in the company.[445] A win-win situation was created for Siemens and its employees.

In the area of alternative mobility concepts it is conceivable that additional companies make their proprietary fleet of vehicles available for overnight use or during the weekend. This would be a form of car sharing. The company can generate additional revenues from its fleet which is usually not utilized during these time periods. The advantage for the employees is the availability of a vehicle at favorable conditions and when needed. It can be rented, for example, for a major shopping tour in the evening and returned the next morning on the way

---

[444] See Mu by Peugeot (2011).
[445] See Siemens AG (2011).

to work. Billing of the costs can be done via the payroll of the employee. The vehicle can be opened and locked, for example, with the company chip card, which is handed out to employees in many companies.

Up to now, automobile manufacturers are normally only responsible for providing the fleet of vehicles for companies, while the captive financial service provider is responsible for the fleet management. The companies, meanwhile, must always make an effort to keep down costs or the size of the fleet of vehicles they own. If some of the costs can be covered with the approach described, cost pressures can be eased. For the automobile manufacturers this would have the advantage that the dangers of fleet reductions could possibly be avoided. Since billing of the private use of the vehicles in the fleet would normally mean enormous additional costs for the company in question, the captive financial service provider has the opportunity to take over this service for the customers in the context of an expanded fleet management.

Especially the provision of electromobility for companies offers large growth potential for the automobile manufacturers in the area of corporate car sharing. Electromobility is one component in the environmentally conscious and cost efficient mobility of the future. Specifically environmentally conscious companies will attempt to align their fleets to this trend and to also offer these vehicles to their employees for private use. The management and handling of this new value chain offers notable potential for the automobile manufacturers and their captive financial service providers. The BMW subsidiary Alphabet with its offering "AlphaCity" was the first captive financial service provider to fully embrace this business model.[446]

6.6.5 New Leasing Models in the Area of Electronic Vehicles

Modern companies are increasingly influenced by issues of sustainability. Considering global warming, the scarcity of fossil resources and the fear of nuclear disasters, consumers have started to rethink their priorities. The aim is to shape a future in which resource use is ecological, CO_2-neutral and economical. With electric vehicles among others, the automotive industry will follow this trend of sustainability and create new forms of mobility. As already discussed, electric vehicles currently have a few deficits with regard to price, range and availability of an adequate infrastructure. For automobile manufacturers this leads to the challenge of marketing electric vehicles under current conditions with new financing and leasing solutions. Of particular relevance are the financial details of the leasing contract and the related chances and risks.

6.6.5.1 Splitting Battery and Vehicle Leasing

At the moment, electric vehicles constitute the technology of the future. They are not only considered to be "clean" in comparison to standard combustion engines, but are also in line with current societal preferences for sustainability trends. Numerous electric vehicles are already available on the market, but purchase prices far exceed those of conventional automobiles. This is due to the high cost of the batteries. What is more, the service life of the batteries is limited to only a few years at present. Thus only a few consumers are considering the purchase of electric vehicles at the moment.

---

[446] See alphabet.de (2011).

6.6 CFC – Quo Vadis?

One possibility to increase the demand for electric vehicles can be the financial decoupling of battery and vehicle. Customers are purchasing the vehicle "empty" (without battery) at the conventional purchase price and additionally lease the battery, for example from the captive financial service provider. The automobile manufacturer or a third party is responsible for purchase and maintenance of the battery and the ultimate disposal.

The advantage of the separate leasing for the customer is quite clearly the cost reduction compared to the purchase and the permanent availability of the battery. Currently Renault is offering the Kangoo in the zero-emissions version for € 23,800 plus € 85.68 monthly leasing rates (term: 48 months, 10,000 km annually, including sales tax).[447] This makes the Kangoo about € 9,000 more expensive compared to the same model with a diesel engine. In addition the total leasing charges for the battery add up to € 4,113.[448]

From the perspective of the automobile manufacturers it is questionable whether it can be profitable for them to assume the investment costs for the battery and be responsible for maintenance and upkeep. When comparing the leasing income in the above example with the purchase costs, it appears to be an unprofitable transaction at first sight. In the following a simple calculation is used to assess the conditions for the profitability of battery leasing.

The following assumptions are used:[449]

The useful life of the battery is t years. During this time interval, earnings and costs are defined as follows:

- Cost of the battery per unit of energy: x_1 €/Wh,
- Maintenance costs of the battery per unit of energy per year: p €/Wh/year
- Annual leasing income: x €/Wh/year,
- Income from secondary battery use per unit of energy: q €/Wh (Following the use of the battery in the vehicle, it can still be used in smaller networks.),
- Annual interest on the receipts is paid at α.

Thus the total receipts from leasing C are:

$$C = x + \frac{x}{(1+\alpha)} + \frac{x}{(1+\alpha)^2} + \frac{x}{(1+\alpha)^3} + \ldots \frac{x}{(1+\alpha)^{(t-1)}}$$

The income from secondary battery use is:

$$Q = \frac{q}{(1+\alpha)^t}$$

The maintenance costs of the battery are:

$$P = p + \frac{p}{(1+\alpha)} + \frac{p}{(1+\alpha)^2} + \frac{p}{(1+\alpha)^3} + \ldots \frac{p}{(1+\alpha)^{(t-1)}}$$

When considering all these conditions, battery leasing is profitable only if $C + Q - P - x_1 > 0$.

---

[447] See Renault.de (2012).
[448] See Renault.de (2012).
[449] See Li, Z., Ouyang, M. (2011), pp. 3224ff.

6.6.5.2 Chances and Risks in the Area of Electromobility

Electric vehicles are supposed to guide the mobility of the future. At the same time the current state of electromobility is characterized by major deficits, which entails both chances and risks for the automobile manufacturers.

At current the comprehensive coverage with charging stations for batteries cannot be guaranteed. This may be one of many reasons why electric vehicles are not yet popular with automobile buyers. Here the automobile manufacturers have the opportunity to form strategic alliances with utilities aimed at providing the infrastructure to strengthen their business model.[450] In addition to charging stations, service stations for the maintenance and repair of electric vehicles are also needed. An integration of these components of the value chain could allow the automobile manufacturers to obtain enormous returns in the long term.

A further deficit is the low range of the electric vehicles. The average car battery only allows distances of about 100–150 km, even with an efficient driving style.[451] According to a survey of the ADAC only about 10% of the respondents would accept such a range.[452] Additional usage factors that affect the time it takes to discharge the battery are speed or additional use of air conditioning or heating as well as external factors such as the outside temperature. Thus a longer drive on the highway is not possible with the given state of technology. However, range should not be a criterion for exclusion in big cities.

The automobile manufacturers could install charging stations in cooperation with the public transport system or with parking deck operators, were owners of electronic vehicles can park and charge their vehicles while they go about their business.[453] In some bigger German metropolitan areas this model is already established. Since parking spaces are scarce in downtown areas, park and ride parking spaces that are established specifically for electronic vehicles can provide relief.

The Californian company Better Place can provide a solution concerning the inadequate number of charging stations and the problems with the current range of the vehicles.[454] The model of the company is to establish a network of automated battery switching stations. To do so, the vehicle must be driven on a specific platform, were the entire process is fully automated. Below the vehicle the empty battery is removed and replaced by a charged battery. The empty batteries are checked in a storage area below ground and charged for the next use. It takes about two minutes to exchange the battery. With a broad implementation of the switching stations, for example at gas stations, the low range of the current batteries would no longer be an issue. Drivers could simply turn into the next gas station and a few minutes later continue their journey with a charged battery.

Automobile manufacturers have the possibility to cooperate with Better Place. This is demonstrated for example by Renault.[455] Starting in 2012, Renault will market an electric vehicle in Australia that was developed in cooperation with Better Place and that has a battery which

---

[450] See Roeder, R. (2011), p. 27.
[451] See Elektroauto-Fahren (2011).
[452] See ADAC (2011b).
[453] See Roeder, R. (2011), p. 28.
[454] See Better Place (2011).
[455] See Mein Elektroauto (2011).

6.6 CFC – Quo Vadis?

is compatible with the battery switching stations. In this approach the electric vehicle is purchased without a battery from Renault, while the battery is leased from Better Place.

By outsourcing the battery leasing operations to companies such as Better Place, automobile manufacturers could obtain advantages, since purchasing costs for the battery are no longer an issue. A comprehensive coverage with switching stations could provide customers with another argument in support of purchasing an electric vehicle. However, especially German automobile manufacturers are critical of the concept of Better Place.[456] They are afraid that an early standardization of the automobile batteries will be detrimental to research. Additionally the automobile manufacturers want to assure their individuality by not succumbing to the demands for unification of the underside of the vehicle.

When weighing all the above issues it can be concluded that the electromobility of the future will provide numerous revenue opportunities also with regard to leasing and financing offers. The automobile manufacturers and their captive financial service providers have the opportunity to actively participate in the design of future mobility concepts and the related infrastructure. They should not fail to embrace the sustainability trend and to shape its economic contours. The captive financial service providers should recognize the changes in the classical leasing and financing business and tailor their products to the new developments in electronic markets.

---

[456] See Mein Elektroauto (2010).

7 Mobility Needs and Mobility Concepts

7.1 Executive Summary

One of the most important success factors for automobile manufacturers is the early identification of new mobility demands of their customers in order to develop and offer suitable mobility or mobile user concepts. The exploration of dynamic mobility demands has as its starting point the analysis of its determinants, the major societal fields of development. These are morality, economy, demography, urbanization, ecology and technology. Changes in moral values of a society include the desire to take the environment into consideration when making mobility choices. The idea of the automobile as status symbol is being eroded and the automobile is increasingly turned into an object with a clearly defined practical purpose. This supports trends in favor of alternative usage concepts such as leasing or car sharing, which gain in importance. Since individual ownership is no longer needed for the "consumption" of mobility, significant economic challenges lie ahead for automobile manufacturers. Against the backdrop of demographic change, including an increasing number of smaller households and an ageing population in the major industrial countries, the willingness to try alternative mobility concepts and approaches to mobile usage on the one hand and to simple and age adequate mobility on the other hand will go up.

The continued global urbanization with its resulting increase in traffic density will also lead to calls for cleaner mobility, a clean environment as well as small and efficient automobiles or alternative mobility solutions. Technological developments have already created completely new requirements such as the ever present connectivity via the internet, increased safety demands of the customers, higher demands on entertainment as well as increased efficiency with regard to new mobility solutions and mobile usage concepts. The analysis of already implemented or planned approaches (for example "Mu by Peugeot", "Better Place", "Car Sharing", "PRT 2getthere" as well as "BMWi") shows that they already are, or soon will be, in a position to provide answers to future mobility demands.

It is an exciting challenge to identify mobility solutions and mobile usage concepts that are not available at present but can also satisfy future customer demands. One example of a mobile usage approach of the future is the dual concept "Car Packaging and Pooling" which will be presented later in this Chapter. With a "Car Package" the mobility customer would be able to purchase access to a number of vehicles that is tailored to his individual mobility demands. He could alternate the use of several vehicles over different time windows. With the second building block "Car Pooling," the unused vehicles could in turn be rented by other consumers. Such a concept would provide simultaneous solutions for a number of societal fields of development. The second, even more visionary mobility concept is also aligned along future determinants by combining and enhancing the mobility concepts "Better Place" and "PRT." Since current and future changes in the field of mobility are likely to accelerate, similar considerations from the automobile manufacturers will be required in order to be successful in the competition for mobility customers. This competition will also come from companies positioned in other segments of the mobility value chain, which are the beneficiaries of changed mobility demands.[457]

7.2 Definition of Terms

Definition of mobility

Several definitions of the term mobility exist in the literature. Next to the Latin term *mobilitas*, which means "agility, quickness, fickleness," the following definition also exists: *"Mobility in general refers to the movement of people and things. The movement can be physical, intellectual or social."*[458] An additional definition for mobility is found in Bähr (1983): *"Mobility refers to the movement of an individual between defined units of a system."*[459] This means, for example, that an individual is moving from one location to another. As is also stated by Kristofferson & Ljungberg, mobility today is frequently seen in connection with an auxiliary aid such as an automobile, which supports the movement of the individual and increases his mobility beyond normal capacities. Following Kristofferson & Ljungberg, we define mobility as physical movement with the help of an auxiliary aid.

Definition of need

A need is generally defined as a "collective term for material and non-material things or states, which are absolutely required or targeted by individuals. Elementary needs are aimed at self-preservation and safety. Acquired (secondary) needs relate to social recognition, self-respect and self-realization. Since needs vary between different cultures and are always influenced by psychological and subjective feelings and assessments, they differ markedly with respect to the required quantity or intensity and the individual degree of satisfaction achieved."[460]

Definition of mobility need

In this Chapter a mobility need is defined as "the need of an individual to move and to travel over distances as well as the possibility to change the location of goods, services and information across space. Apart from the individual desire of humans to be mobile, to travel to a vacation destination or to enjoy leisure activities in different places, the demand for mobility is also motivated by the possibility to satisfy basic needs, such as the procurement of food and clothing or the ability to commute to the place of work."[461]

---

[457] We thank Daniel Bickert, Markus Lechner and Mathias Wesinger for their support in the topic area of "Mobility demands and mobility concepts." Their work has made the success of this book possible.
[458] Montes de Oca (2007), p. 4.
[459] Bähr, J. (1983). According to Kristofferson & Ljungberg (1999) it is hard to provide a correct definition of the term mobility. Either certain conditions are not in place or the definition is too vague. Nonetheless, it is relatively easy to define mobility with reference to a number of examples such as "automobile." Despite this claim, a number of definitions of mobility can be found in the literature.
[460] Schubert, K., Klein, M. (2006), p. 25.
[461] See Weinreich (2003), p. 43.

Definition of concept

The term concept as used in this Chapter means the draft of a new product or a new service. During the concept development stage, a concept is advanced from a rough sketch to a more concrete product definition. A concept contains both structured and unstructured information about the product design. During the associated concept development stage, a life cycle view on the available information is provided.[462]

Definition of mobility concept

A mobility concept is not only useful for society at large as a comprehensive approach, but can also be applied in a microeconomic setting, for example for a company. The Baden-Wuerttemberg Ministry for the Environment and Transport defines the term mobility concept as follows: *"Mobility concepts of companies include their aims and measures targeted at conducting company traffic in a way that is both economic and ecological."*[463] This could also include commuter traffic and customer service for example. The same is true at the macroeconomic level. In a region (for example a municipality, a city or a state) a concept, similar to that at the company level, is established for the implementation of (private) mobility, which includes environmental factors or other goals (for example with regard to corporate profits). This concept can be situated for example in the area of public transport, but can also address completely new niches in its desire to support the mobility of people. The idea of a mobility concept that is targeted at the environment and takes a comprehensive approach must be differentiated from a mobile use concept that focuses more on the individual as recipient of a service and user.

Definition of mobile use concept

In contrast to the already defined mobility concept, a mobile use concept does not address new ways of mobility provision, but rather deals with the use of already existing mobility alternatives. A mobile use concept thus does not enhance the number of existing mobility solutions, but increases the number of alternative uses. Concepts of this kind also include services that give center stage to the user and enable him to be mobile without ownership of the means of transportation.

7.3 Determinants of Future Mobility Needs

7.3.1 Societal Developments

The human need for mobility can be satisfied by utilizing different mobility concepts respectively mobile use concepts. The chosen concept will be the one that most fully satisfies the needs. In order to develop suitable concepts, the mobility needs of the future and their specific features must be analyzed. The first step is an identification of the determinants which shape these needs. These determinants, which are in turn driven by different developments in society, can be used to make predictions about future mobility needs. An overview of se-

---

[462] See SAP (2010a) for an alternative definition of the term concept: "Concept refers to the description or the design of the functioning of systems," following Enzyklo (2010).

[463] Ministerium für Umwelt, Naturschutz und Verkehr Baden-Württemberg (2010).

lected development fields in a society is provided in Figure 87. In the following the focus will be on the societal development fields of morality, economy, demography, urbanization, ecology and technology.

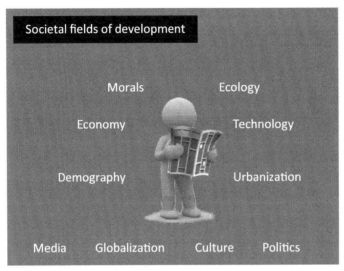

Figure 87: Selected societal fields of development
Source: Authors' presentation

7.3.2 Moral Developments

Moral developments today

A closer look at the historical development of a country or a society reveals that individual or group-specific factors such as values, morals, cultural life, emotions, expectations and similar attributes are subject to constant change. Any attempt to compare the moral values of two generations would surely reveal the lack of any stringent development. Certain moral standards have subjectively improved, some have deteriorated, but certainly moral values have changed overall. A number of moral values today take the awareness of political correctness or appropriate ecological behavior as their starting point. Frequently published are examples of individuals that act in violation of societal moral values and are more interested in their own well-being than the well-being of society at large. For that reason the current economic climate is frequently determined by thinking about one's own interests and advantage. Private live and family are more important than social activity, integration into society and group considerations. This development is strengthened by a rural exodus, since the anonymity of a major city increasingly affects moral change in a society.

Moral developments tomorrow

Especially the global challenges facing our society such as climate change, exploding population growth and the scarcity of natural resources necessitate a general discussion and the development of appropriate solutions. Individuals are not really in a position to change the ecological damage or overall emissions, which threaten the global climate. Only joint and coordinated action can lead to movement and change. The moral of the masses must be

7.3 Determinants of Future Mobility Needs

changed towards "responsibility" for the planet and for society. The seeds of this development are already visible on a global scale and could continue to grow in the future as well. Especially with regard to mobility there has been fundamental change, which must be advanced further if the above targets are to be pursued.

Effects of these moral developments on mobility

While it was still completely acceptable fifty years ago to smoke in public, in restaurants or during social events, an increasing moral aversion against smoking has developed over the years and by now smoking is prohibited in many public places in order to protect those who do not smoke. Similar developments can also be expected with regard to mobility. While in the US, for example, considerations concerning an automobile used to be dominated by size, performance and cylinder capacity, ecological and compact cars with a high mileage are now increasingly in demand, especially for city traffic. And the emotional radiance of the automobile as a status symbol seems to be on the decline as well, according to the management consultant Peter Kruse, who stresses this result of in-depth interviews with consumers. According to his findings, the automobile has lost its attractiveness concerning design and emotions. Especially the vehicles in the upper segment continue to be further away from the ideal than smaller vehicles.[464]

However, any moral and emotional change is not autonomous, but largely influenced by external forces. Increased education, scarcity of resources, heightened awareness of our responsibility towards future generations, cost consciousness, ecological factors, technical progress and other factors also affect our thinking about mobility, the way we want to travel and what is appropriate or inappropriate in this regard. Two dimensions of human morality can be distinguished. On the one hand, moral actions that are reflective of reality and on the other hand moral rules that are imposed by society, for example by politicians and the law and for that reason are considered to be "valid."[465] The combination of these two moral dimensions leads to moral thinking and actions in society. The automotive industry can only achieve the former dimension; it is obliged to meet legal guidelines such as emission standards, noise regulations or safety requirements. Still, it can directly reach customers and society with its moral actions. As an example, efforts have been strengthened over the past years to highlight the combination of emotions as a typical feature of the brand and an awareness of corporate "responsibility," the responsibility of the manufacturer towards society. This provides a whole range of arguments concerning design and driving pleasure, but at the same time for low emissions as a result of alternative technologies and modern engine design such as hybrids or electric drives.[466] The challenge for the automotive industry will thus be to give the customer the impression – via the product and its image, in other words with the help of advertising and communications – that all moral standards with regard to ecological behavior are met, while driving pleasure and comfort of the automobile are maintained.

In summary it can be maintained that the automobile and mobility demands are determined by changes in moral values. The automobile must be more than just a status symbol; compact, unpretentious and useful appear to be the new buzzwords. Coupled with the moral standard of ecological responsibility, these attributes gain in popularity. People want to be mo-

---

[464] See Schneider, M. (2010).
[465] See Thieme, S. (2007), p. 1.
[466] See Allgayer, F. (2009), p.34.

bile, but in an environmentally conscious fashion. Automobiles should have low emissions or no emissions at all. But especially this idea must be considered along the entire value chain. This means that the energy consumed by an automobile must also be climate neutral in order to fully comply with the moral aspects of ecological responsibility.

7.3.3 Economic Developments

Economic developments today

The economy has changed tremendously over time. In modern society it is considered a given that all types of consumption goods and services are available for purchase.[467] And this can be done even with insufficient funds, since credit finance and loans are typical in many countries. Ownership is a defining element of our society. Establishing wealth in order to prepare for retirement, to purchase a home or to buy status symbols such as automobiles is considered to be important in our society. Companies are able to offer consumption goods at very low prices because of high degrees of specialization. The use of machines lowers personnel costs and furthermore reduces the potential for error. At the same time energy costs and investments in information technologies are on the rise. And competition between companies is intensifying due to the removal of global economic barriers and the activities of international financial investors. A look into the future and related studies undeniably points to a change in our understanding of the economy.

Economic developments tomorrow

The economy of tomorrow brings with it changes in the way we think and act as a society that are similar to the ones already described when discussing moral developments and their effects on mobility. The well respected Yale economist Robert Shiller sees a weakening of the established economic structures; especially in times that are characterized by repeated shocks and economic crisis. He thinks that it is necessary, for example, to change the current market structures. In his opinion, the dominance of supply and demand as a market mechanism will be reduced. Consequently the state should do more than just provide a general framework in the form of competition and consumer law. A new economic structure must be developed, which also does justice to the new demands on an economy.[468] And the consumption behavior of society is also subject to permanent change. Especially the segment of investment goods witnesses a trend away from purely private property and in the direction of collective use of expensive consumption goods.

Effects of these economic developments on mobility

The adjustment or steering of moral considerations cannot be analyzed without the incorporation of economic aspects. For the automotive industry this means that morally justified developments such as alternative drive concepts must be economically viable and thus affordable. The economic analysis must take two different perspectives. Both the perspective of the manufacturer, which implies a production process that remains profitable and the economic considerations of the buyer are relevant.

---

[467] See van Suntum, U. (2005), p. 3.
[468] See Röpke, W. (2009).

In an environment characterized by a free market economy and shareholder value, the assurance of an economically meaningful production process remains of major importance, especially for big companies such as the automobile manufacturers. Factors such as increasing wage demands, accelerating resource costs, government surcharges, social security contributions and the demands for higher returns exert enormous cost pressures that must be countered. Even minor changes in the serial production process can lead to cost savings in the millions. At the same time, the competitive pressure among the manufacturers continues to intensify. Elaborate logistics enable globally active manufacturers to supply their vehicles efficiently. Especially cheap Eastern European or Asian production sites are a major competition for the German manufacturers, mainly in the sector of midsized vehicles. Brands such as Dacia, but also Toyota or Mitsubishi promise reasonably priced quality automobiles. Numerous automobile manufacturers are also facing the problem of many years of significant excess capacities – economically optimal company management and production are almost impossible in that case. The industry continues to attempt additional diversification measures, especially by investing in promising technologies of the future. The sales market for the current vehicle types is increasingly destabilizing, not least because of the major financial crisis of the past years. As an example, the Japanese automobile group of Toyota, Daihatsu and Hino was unable in 2009 to reach its sales target which was set above 10 million vehicles. In fact, only 8.24 million vehicles, 700,000 fewer than in the previous year, were sold. But the anxious automotive industry suspects more than just crisis-induced consumer restraint behind the declines in demand.[469]

This illustrates how moral, ecological or specific economic influences not only have an effect on the general buying behavior of customers, but immediately become relevant for the automotive industry. They are forced to develop alternative mobility solutions and mobility concepts if they do not want to lose touch with changing customer preferences. In an environment characterized by a global economic crisis, weak banks and states, customers are increasingly trying to obtain financial protection for their retirement, to spend less or to obtain alternative products at lower costs. At the same time, customers consider whether the investment needed to purchase a vehicle continues to make sense or whether new mobility concepts based on urban trends or alternative mobility concepts such as leasing or car sharing are more promising.

Alternative mobility concepts and drive technologies can ultimately only succeed if they are economically feasible. The area of electromobility depends mainly on the development of new storage technologies. The current lithium-ion generation is still too expensive. Apparently only renting and leasing are feasible options in this market at the moment. As an example, battery cells for use in vehicles are estimated at 500–600 EUR/kWh. However, the value needed for effective serial production stands at around 300 EUR/kWh.[470]

In summary, it is of enormous relevance for the automotive industry to recognize the changing mobility demands of its customers early on and at the same time implement developments that make it possible to react to fundamental changes in society. Emission-free automobiles still have not reached the stage of mass production. New storage solutions are required to reach the efficiency of combustion engines. At the same time strategies must be developed to counter the trend of abandoning individual possession of a vehicle. The chal-

---

[469] See Cancler, W., Knie, A. (2009), p. 3.
[470] See Buller, U., Hanselka, H. (2009), p. 2.

lenge lies in the development of solutions that can be seamlessly integrated into the automobile value chain of the manufacturers, so that the market for alternative usage concepts is not occupied by other suppliers.

7.3.4 Demographic Developments

Demographic developments today

The number of inhabitants in Germany has increased steadily for a long time. Figure 88 shows that the peak was reached in the year 2002 at about 82.54 million. Since then, the population has declined slightly.

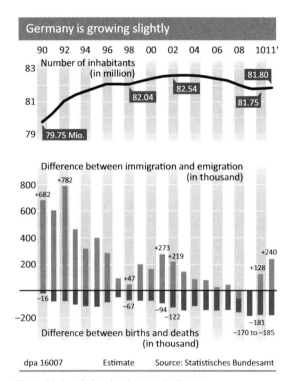

Figure 88: Population development in Germany
Source: dpa, Statistisches Bundesamt (2009)

Based on its own estimates, the statistical office in Wiesbaden announced that the population increased slightly for the first time in eight years in 2011. The reason for this is identified by the statistical office as a positive migration balance, as Figure 91 makes clear.[471]

With currently about 81.8 million inhabitants, on 357,114 km², Germany is one of the most densely populated countries on this planet. While there have been more deaths than births in Germany since 1972, the total population remained relatively stable since the migration balance tended to be positive. In addition to this development, Germany has been in a process of

---

[471] See Zeit (2011).

7.3 Determinants of Future Mobility Needs

demographic ageing for some time, which is caused by decades of declining birth rates and continuous improvements in life expectancy, as can be seen in Figure 89.

Population development and age structure
Population in absolute numbers. shares of the age groups in percent. 1960 until 2060. as of end of 2010

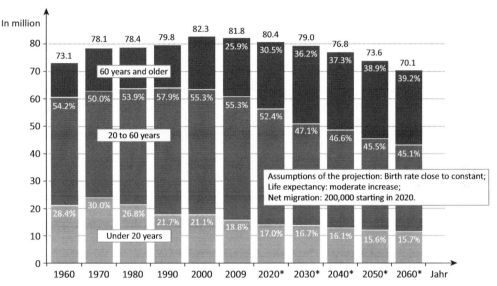

Figure 89: Population development and age structure
Source: Bundeszentrale für politische Bildung (2011)

Demographic developments tomorrow

As already discussed, a decisive success factor for the automobile manufacturers is targeting the customer demands respectively the mobility demands of the future. A realistic deduction of these demands also requires the inclusion and analysis of future demographic trends as important drivers of demand. A close relationship exists between key figures for passenger car mobility and population developments.[472]

Once the likely development of the population and its structures has been assessed, the resulting mobility demands must be anticipated. This enables the automotive industry to take timely measures and to meet anticipated customer demands in the future.

It can be expected that the future demographic development in Germany is characterized by an ongoing and accelerating population decline which is caused by further declines in birth rates and increased deaths as a result of the ageing population. According to the estimates of the statistical office, the widening birth deficit cannot be compensated by net migration. This leads to a decline of the population to approximately 65 to 70 million by the year 2060 (depending on the values used in the simulation)[473]. This decline goes hand in hand with strong changes in the age structure, as shown in Figure 90.

---

[472] See Shell Deutschland Oil GmbH (2009), p. 8.
[473] See Statistisches Bundesamt (2009), p. 3.

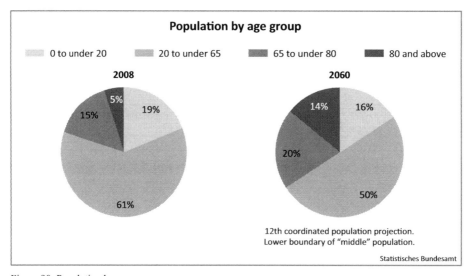

Figure 90: Population by age group
Source: Statistisches Bundesamt (2009), p. 17

By the year 2060, every third inhabitant (34% of the population) will at least be 65 years old, while about 14% will be 80 years or older. Of particular relevance is the segment of the population of working age (here: from age 20 to age 65). This segment of the population, which is most dependent on mobility, will decline and get older. The numbers will go down from currently close to 45 million to 37 million in the year 2030, respectively 32 million in the year 2060.[474]

In addition, demographic change in Germany will also affect the number and structure of private households, which are considered to be particularly important consumers as well as buyers of long-lived consumption goods such as automobiles. 50 years ago the average household size was approximately three persons. Today the average household size is two persons. A continuation of this trend towards smaller households is expected. This means that one-person and two-person households will continue to gain in relevance.[475]

Effects of these demographic developments on mobility

Starting with the anticipated population trends for Germany presented above, namely an ageing society and an increasing share of inhabitants in higher age groups, the question must be asked whether this automatically implies a future decline of motorization (ratio of passenger cars to population) and mobility.[476] After all, the increasing share of older citizens in society will mean a higher average age of mobility participants (motorists, pedestrians, cyclists, users of busses and trains). According to forecasts, the increase of the number of older citizens and the increase of the share of older citizens who hold a driver's license is supposed to lead to an increase in the share of the drivers that are sixty and older in the overall population (from about 12% in the year 1950 to 24% in the year 2025).[477] The Innovation Center for

---

[474] See Statistisches Bundesamt (2009), pp. 5ff.
[475] See Shell Deutschland Oil GmbH (2009), pp.15–16.
[476] See Shell Deutschland Oil GmbH (2009), p. 4.
[477] See Reiter (1997), pp. 218–219.

7.3 Determinants of Future Mobility Needs

Mobility and Societal Change also considers the older generation of the future to be more mobile than previous generations.[478]

Also relevant is the age structure effect, since spending on transportation differs by age group. Young and middle-aged groups spend above average amounts on mobility. By comparison, these expenses go down considerable at an advanced age. This implies that the ageing of the population will also lead to lower spending on mobility and thus also on the automobile. This development is offset somewhat by the cohort effect. It means that later birth years (cohorts) are more mobile compared to earlier generations and thus spend comparably more money on mobility. Even though this cohort effect is expected to continue, it will not completely compensate for the age structure effect, which states that older citizens are characterized by below average spending on mobility.[479]

In its passenger car study, the oil company Shell considered the possible consequences of demographic change on automotive mobility in Germany. Key questions were: How is it possible that passenger car motorization and mobility continue to grow against the backdrop of a stable economy, society and population and how will automotive mobility, expressed as passenger car motorization rates and distance traveled, develop until the year 2030, given the anticipated demographic change. With the study Shell developed important insights for traffic research. It is expected that passenger car motorization rates will continue to increase significantly among women (from the current figure of about 340 to about 430 passenger cars per 1,000 women), while the increase for men will only be marginal (from the current figure of close to 700 to about 715 in the year 2030).

As Figure 91 shows, the forecast assumes an increase of the overall volume of passenger cars from currently 47 million vehicles to 49.5 million vehicles in the year 2030. The average "statistical" motorization rate across all groups of owners would thus go up from approximately 630 passenger cars per inhabitant – compared to approximately 570 at present. For newly registered passenger cars a volume between 3 and close to 3.5 million per annum was assumed.

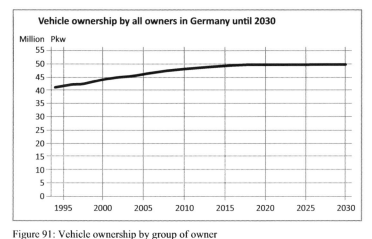

Figure 91: Vehicle ownership by group of owner
Source: Shell Deutschland Oil GmbH (2009), p.25

---

[478] See Canzler et al. (2009), p. 1.
[479] See Shell Deutschland Oil GmbH (2009), p. 17.

On balance, strong demand for automotive mobility can be assumed until the end of the period under consideration in the year 2030, despite the demographic change. With regard to the increasing relevance of women and older drivers, smaller households, fewer children and fewer young persons, mobility demands will witness change. Most noticeable will be changes of the automobile with regard to use and handling, equipment, safety and comfort, but also in everyday traffic.[480]

The demographic tendencies will lead to changes in mobility behavior and to new mobility demands. When describing future mobility demands of older citizens it is not sufficient to simply refer to previous older generations. Instead the changes in the conditions of one senior generation to the next must be taken into consideration. Today's older citizens are more experienced in mobility than previous generations. Consequently each new senior generation has its own specific mobility problems and requirements. In general the mobility demands of an ageing society are determined by age-related changes of the physical and psychological capabilities. These include deteriorating eyesight, reduced motor skills and agility, slower speed when processing information, making decisions and implementing a planned activity, lower endurance and earlier fatigue. For that reason, demands for an age-appropriate equipment of motor vehicles with a greater weight on safety features and comfort, combined with simplicity, are likely to go up.[481] Automobiles with features such as ergonomic entry, loading and seating solutions, visual aids for a superior view at night and in the rain, simple handling also for complex functions and devices, timeless design or side-view and rear-view cameras, automatic transmission, cruise control, electronic aids and mirror systems for parking are likely to gain in relevance.[482] These technological innovations may enable the automobile manufacturers to expand their sales potential, especially among older citizens.

7.3.5 Urban Developments

Urban developments today

Urban development is also relevant, since a major part of mobility takes place in cities. The increasing urbanization is a global phenomenon. It refers to the increase, expansion or enlargement of cities by number, size or inhabitants, both in absolute terms and also in relation to the rural population or those settlements that are not cities.[483] Meanwhile more than half of the entire population lives in cities. Of particular relevance for alternative mobility concepts are the so-called megacities with more than 10 million inhabitants. Its number has quadrupled over the past 20 years and a further doubling is assumed during the next two decades.[484]

Urban developments tomorrow

The expansion and the growth of cities are among the megatrends of the twenty-first century. Already in the year 2015, 40% of the entire world population will live in cities that have more

---

[480] See Shell Deutschland Oil GmbH (2009), p. 42.
[481] See Limbourg, M. (1999).
[482] See study by Oliver Wyman (2010).
[483] See Bähr, J. (2008).
[484] See Shell Deutschland Oil GmbH (2009), p. 11.

7.3 Determinants of Future Mobility Needs

than one million inhabitants and 17% will even live in cities with more than five million inhabitants.[485] The topic of megacities is particularly relevant for growth regions in South America and Asia, were the movement of large segments of the population into urban regions is advancing quickly and were about two thirds of the global megacities are located.[486]

Effects of these urban developments on mobility

The expected future increase of agglomerations and megacities will lead to new mobility concepts which will affect all forms of mobility globally, and the automobile in particular. With the urbanization, the demand for local transport of merchandise and goods, but also the flow of people will go up. This will force major cities to contemplate new mobility solutions. Otherwise they are threatened with chronic congestion of streets and an increase in the rate of accidents. Higher traffic volumes or traffic density could lead to reduced average speeds for automobiles, especially in megacities with a weak infrastructure. Already today the working population in cities such as Sao Paulo, Lagos, Bangkok or Peking is forced to accept extremely long commutes to work. It is not uncommon that people spend more than two hours commuting each day. In addition to large distances from the periphery to the center, the continuous congestion of downtown areas further limits urban mobility and is responsible for extremely low average speeds in city traffic.[487] The creation of sufficient parking spaces will also become a major infrastructural challenge for the megacities.

The increased traffic volume also puts a greater strain on the environment. It is possible that stricter environmental regulations, especially in megacities, will mean that automobiles which emit exhaust fumes are no longer allowed. For a number of years now, several German cities are already requiring emissions stickers, which have the purpose of limiting the emission of particulate matter and to keep cars that exceed certain emission thresholds away from the city centers. The replacement of the combustion engine with alternative drive technologies appears unavoidable, especially in city centers.

For the automobile manufacturers it will be decisive to see how people organize their mobility in the daily routine of major cities and which demands they have with regard to mobility. The demands on an automobile will be different tomorrow than they are today, given the above requirements.

A possible reaction of the road users to the increased traffic volume is the switch to alternative means of transportation such as rail vehicles (metro, subway, train and others), which are not affected by traffic congestion. Cities could make public transport more attractive and thus lure more people away from their own vehicle and into city busses and other means of public transport. Road users who value individual mobility are more likely to develop a preference for smaller and more flexible motor vehicles. This will reduce energy consumption and facilitate the search for parking spaces. Possible new mobility demands could also be the simple switch between driving position and relaxation, a focus on entertainment and communications functions, infotainment & networking, automation of stop-and-go situations and the protection from smog.[488]

---

[485] See study by Oliver Wyman (2010).
[486] See Kauschke, P., Reuter, J. (2009).
[487] See Ribbeck, E. (2003).
[488] See study by Oliver Wyman (2010).

7.3.6 Ecological Developments

Ecological developments today

Oil disasters, the breaching of threshold values for ozone levels, fruits and vegetables that contain high levels of pesticides, poisonous phenol in toys for children or the discussion about limits for particulate matter have led to a feeling of insecurity, but also to a heightened awareness of the population in the major industrial nations for the topic of "ecology and sustainability." Sustainable agriculture, fair trade as well as guarantees about the origin and the manufacturing of merchandise have gained in relevance as purchase criteria of consumers. The willingness in the population to take social responsibility and the awareness that changes in individual behavior can have a positive ecological effect are clearly on the rise. Since climate change is now directly observable everywhere on the planet, a global reassessment is under way.

The effects of the ecological changes are felt in Germany as well. The number of natural disasters such as flooding, storms or heat periods has increased by a factor of three since 1970.[489] Climate researchers by and large agree that extreme weather developments will be more frequent in the future and point to the increased emission of climate gases such as CO_2 as the main reason for that development. The awareness that the industrial nations are among the major producers of these damaging gases has especially in Germany caused a major rethinking among the population and particularly among politicians. The introduction of emission certificates, subsidies provided for heat insulation or renewable energies are only a few examples that demonstrate the political will to counter climate change.[490] Even though the awareness for the climate exists among a majority of the population, it must be pointed out that the willingness to change personal behavior or to adopt technologies that are environmentally friendly usually requires some economic advantages or financial incentives as well.[491] Not least because of increasing crude oil prices, the automobile has been identified by many citizens as a possibility to make a contribution towards improving the carbon footprint, and also to generate economic advantages. By now, the mileage of an automobile is just as important in the purchasing decision as other attributes such as price, brand and design. As a consequence of this change in demand, which for the most part has already happened in the industrial countries as well as regulatory measures by politicians such as stricter limits for CO_2 emissions, the automobile manufacturers are forced to optimize their products with regard to efficiency and ecology. Over the past years this has happened by advancing the development of hybrids, modern bio fuels, fuel cells, hydrogen drives as well as electromobility and by increasing the efficiency of existing combustion engines.

Ecological developments tomorrow

Forecasts of growth rates in the automobile sector generally provide a positive outlook for the automobile manufacturers. The global demand for individual mobility will continue to increase. It is predicted that the passenger car density in China, one of the major growth markets, will increase threefold by 2030 (to about 115 vehicles per 1000 inhabitants). In Germany meanwhile, which is representative for other industrial nations, will only witness slight increases in the demand for passenger cars until 2020, followed by stagnation. In order to be successful in the global realization of the targeted climate goals, the emerging markets must be

---

[489] See Schmitt, T. (2009).
[490] See Bode, S. et al. (2007), pp. 29–30.
[491] See Schöller, O. et al. (2007), p. 568.

more fully integrated into the innovative process of "green technologies" and the general awareness for the environment must be strengthened. At present the demand structure in the automotive industry of the fast growing emerging markets is different from that of the industrial nations. Automobiles with strong engines are primarily in demand in these markets.[492] But here as well, also driven by political forces, change is both inevitable and needed.

Effects of these ecological developments on mobility

The automobile will increasingly be caught in a conflict between attractive individual mobility and problematic environmental damages. It is not imaginable that large parts of the population will abandon individual mobility and thus the tension must be released by integrating the environmental aspect with the help of new technologies. For the citizen and his mobility needs, not only the question "whether" he wants to get from A to B but also "how" he does it, will be relevant in the future. The demand for novel mobility concepts will increase. Established automobile manufacturers will find that they are in a completely new ball game. New suppliers are able, without major barriers to entry, to join the market for electric automobiles. Previous competitive advantages which are due to many years of experience in optimizing engines and drive systems are not very relevant in this completely new field. In addition, new image fields for the positioning of existing brands will have to be found and occupied. This is due to the fact that features previously used to differentiate a vehicle such as engine power or driving characteristics will no longer play a primary role in the future. To use the example of electromobility one more time, it will be almost impossible to achieve differentiation in these areas. Established manufacturers face the challenge of supplying sufficient research and development capacities for the new areas without neglecting the optimization of existing concepts and the current demand. In general it can be stated that the ecological aspect, considering the need of the society to be mobile, will increasingly gain in relevance, is already among the most important drivers at present and needs to be taken very seriously by the automotive industry. But considering the ecological demands of consumers, green drive technologies such as the electric engine must be considered in their entirety. Potential buyers will only fully accept this technology if the electrical power needed is also obtained from regenerative energy sources. In that regard, cooperation between utilities and automobile manufacturers seems possible in the long term. Considering climate change and the increasing pollution of the environment and the air, it is also possible that the thinking about resource conservation which currently appears limited to individual mobility is extended to other areas such as air travel and trucking. This would again give rise to new definitions of needs. If unexpectedly consumers are unwilling to accept the green technologies at present, they will likely have no choice in the long term, given the growing global environmental burden.

7.3.7 Technological Developments

Technological developments today

None of the issues listed above have changed the social life and the demands of citizens in the past decades as much as technological developments. The development of the internet and the networking among participants make it possible to exchange information at any time and at any place within seconds. "Social" and "Business Networking" increasingly replace personal contacts and make it possible to maintain a large number of contacts simultaneously. E-Busi-

---

[492] See Katzensteiner, T. (2008), p. 66.

ness is gaining in importance. Travel, medicine or clothing, all can be bought simply, quickly and independent of store opening hours via the internet. Company networks enable employees to work from home in the context of a "Home Office Concept" and to save money and time. Music, movies, books or the current newspaper; the entertainment segment of the internet also offers many possibilities for organizing leisure time. Internet access in most industrial nations – especially for the population between 12 to 54 years – constitutes a fundamental need and is becoming increasingly relevant in social life.[493] It is thus not surprising that the number of "Offliners," those who do not use the internet, is declining year after year. This number only stood at about 28% in Germany in 2009.[494] A major catalyst for the rapid ascent of the internet is the development in communications technologies. The networking and integration of the newest technologies in the so-called "smartphones" has turned them into mobile information centers. Fundamental pillars for the development of mobile information technologies are the advances in the areas of storage technologies both for data and for energy.

The lithium-ion technology and its continuous improvement make it possible to store energy in a compact fashion in lightweight batteries. And in the automotive industry as well, this is the engine for new developments. Electric vehicles which previously were thought to be unfit for the future, because of extremely heavy batteries with low capacities are now considered to be ready for mass production. Electric engines with an efficiency of up to 99% are very attractive compared to conventional combustion engines (efficiency 25–35%). But until the technology has fully matured, the automobile manufacturers continue to work in parallel on the further development of the combustion engine. Its efficiency was enhanced considerably (about 15%) via electronic fuel injection and downsizing (reduction of the engine size while keeping performance constant).[495] Engineers at the company Bosch estimate that there is further potential to enhance the efficiency of the combustion engines by an additional 25–30% by 2015.[496]

Other technical developments in the automotive industry such as mobile navigation can certainly be considered standard by now, just like integrated Bluetooth speaker phones, which make it possible to make phone calls while on the road. Intelligent systems that allow communication between vehicles, for example to avert accidents, or systems that use cameras to scan the surroundings in order to avoid dangerous situations or to park independently are already part of the offering of many automobile manufacturers, especially in the premium segment. Their aim is to improve the security and simplicity of individual mobility. In order to meet future customer demands and to achieve differentiation from the competition, technological innovations of this kind are indispensable.

Technological developments tomorrow

The Massachusetts Institute of Technology (MIT) in its "Technological Review 2010" compiled the 10 most important technological developments of the future across all industries. Among them are search engines that search in real time. They make it possible to check when and how many entries are produced for a topic in real time. Other technological mega-

---

[493] See Czajka, S., Mohr, S. (2009).
[494] See Statista (2010).
[495] The following served as a basis for comparison: Standard engines, used in a typical European automobile with a weight of 1,400 kilogram, with multipoint injection, performance of about 100 kilowatt, four cylinders and two liter engine, 7.7 liters of gasoline per 100 kilometers and CO_2 emissions of 182 grams per kilometer.
[496] See Leonhard, R. (2009).

trends that the experts identify are "Green Concrete" that can absorb CO_2, "Social TV", a combination of TV and social network, as well as the further development of smartphones in the third dimension. Certainly of biggest interest for the automobile manufacturers is the development of "Solar Fuels," where microorganisms produce diesel or ethanol with the help of sunlight. All these developments will surely influence our social life and shape the future. The technological components of future mobility concepts will be considered in more detail in the following paragraphs.

Effects of these technological developments on mobility

For society as a whole, certain technological megatrends such as the increasing interconnectedness via the internet have become fully established in social life and must be taken into consideration as pioneering customer demands when looking at developments in the area of individual mobility. Electric vehicles of certain manufacturers already include voice-controlled communication and navigation systems as well as internet access (for example Kia UVO). Overall two different development paths for automobile manufacturers are apparent. First there are developments which aim at making driving more secure, simpler, more spectacular and interactive. Second, there are developments aimed at increasing efficiency and advancing new drive technologies. Both developments determine the future potential for success of the automobile manufacturers and it needs to be stressed that both paths must truly be covered. While an unbalanced positioning may lead to short-term success, in the long run "green technologies" cannot be successful without technological innovations and vice versa. The mobility of the future needs to become both greener and more sophisticated technologically.

It is hard to assess which directions future technological developments will precisely take. In the following section a few innovative mobility concepts are presented, which provide insights into current trends and developments.

7.4 Concepts in the Mobility Area

7.4.1 Mobility Concept – Mu by Peugeot

What is "Mu by Peugeot?"

The automobile manufacturer Peugeot started a novel mobile user concept with "Mu" in five French cities (Paris, Lyon, Brest, Nantes and Rennes) and the German capital Berlin in February, respectively May 2010. Following the online registration and payment of a registration fee of € 10, the customer receives a prepaid card which can be loaded online with so-called "Mu points." One point has a value of about 20 Cents. These points can be exchanged for various mobility solutions or the rental of accessories at selected Peugeot dealerships. The aim is to provide a solution from the company portfolio that is suitable for the individual mobility demand of the customer. The product range comprises 18 different automobiles, two scooters, two bicycles and eight different accessories such as snow tires, a ski box or a GPS system. No matter whether a cabriolet for a road trip, a bicycle for a weekend trip, a scooter for city traffic or a van for moving is rented, the costs only depend on the usage time. Already included are a comprehensive insurance coverage and unlimited mileage. Costs for fuel are extra. But in order to also take this cost factor and the heightened environmental awareness into consideration, the concept was expanded to include the electric vehicle I-on, the electric bike e-City and the electroscooter e-Vivacity. The aim is to also integrate so-called partner offerings. Similar to the Miles & More model of the Star Alliance Group for air travel, bonus points can be collected when using certain offerings of cooperating partners, which can be redeemed in the context of the Mu concept. Meanwhile the project is continuously expanded to the cities Brussels, London, Munich, Hamburg, Madrid and Milan and the network of dealerships is also growing.

Which challenges are addressed by "Mu by Peugeot?"

The concept is based on the idea that customers should be offered a greater degree of flexibility. This is related to the societal trend that ownership of an automobile is losing its relevance as a status symbol.[497] At the same time, the need for individual mobility continues to be intact. Life in a big city increasingly turns automobile ownership into a burden. Parking spaces are either lacking or expensive and traffic jams during rush hour or car vandalism in the open street are common. All this can be ignored with the appropriate mobility solution "Mu by Peugeot." It makes sense for example to switch to a scooter for city traffic and to pick a comfortable limousine for traveling greater distances. Upon arrival, parking in the lot of the dealership is easy. Mu thus provides solutions for the increasing urbanization, the resulting mobility challenges and the ongoing value change. And the system also takes economic criteria into consideration. An automobile on demand for longer trips outside the city, for vacation travel or for evening entertainment combined with the use of public transportation not only allows for maximum flexibility, it also avoids the expensive purchase of a vehicle while the same level of mobility is maintained. The concept is further enhanced by the inclusion of an electric vehicle, which satisfies the ecological considerations of society and at the same time avoids expensive purchases. Peugeot almost achieves complete coverage with "Mu" and addresses a large part of future challenges with the concept.

What are advantages of "Mu by Peugeot?"

The concept addresses the problem that many citizens do not have the necessary financial means or are unwilling to purchase an automobile for themselves. The user has the opportunity to always utilize the most recent models without having to accept the disadvantage of a high loss of value of the new vehicle. When choosing cooperating dealerships it was assured that these can be reached easily via public transportation in order to contain the costs of using a taxi. The settlement, which takes place via the internet is simple and provides quick implementation. Existing Peugeot customers also benefit from the accessories, which can be used independently of a vehicle rental. With its planned cooperations, regional expansions and the integration of environmental aspects, the concept demonstrates its variable construction and its adaptability to changing needs.

What are disadvantages of "Mu by Peugeot?"

The disadvantages quite clearly follow from the fact that only certain dealerships are cooperating and the rented object always has to be returned to the dealership were it was rented. Pure rental stations, for example at airports or train stations, which are customary for related approaches do not exist and are not planned. Rental and return is thus only possible during the regular opening hours of the partners. An additional disadvantage for the user is the fact that the concept is limited to Peugeot products. Thus only a certain group of users is reached and cost advantages, which would result from targeting larger audiences, are not being gen-

---

[497] See Kilimann, S. (2010).

erated and thus cannot be passed along to consumers. The project also suffers from the weakness that its use across countries is not possible at current and thus customers with the German "Mu Prepaid Card" cannot use the French offering. In addition, partner offerings are discussed on the webpage, but do not yet exist.

Summary for "Mu by Peugeot"

Peugeot is marketing "Mu" as a completely new mobility concept, which, if looked at more closely, does not offer anything novel, at least at the moment, apart from the prepaid card and the possibility to check out accessories. Renting a vehicle has always been possible and with regard to pricing the offering of Peugeot is similar to that of conventional rental car companies. Certainly also due to the sophisticated marketing concept, the start in Paris was very successful and Peugeot was able to acquire more than 1,000 new customers within 3 months. It is certainly gratifying for Peugeot that this number also included users of other brands.[498] Peugeot now has the opportunity to convince them of the advantages of its own product range. On balance it appears that customers are looking for new ways to satisfy their demand for mobility and are thankful for the concept with all its limitations, if only due to a lack of alternatives. But the concept will only achieve a breakthrough if it continues to gain in flexibility, acquires strong cooperating partners, offers more attractive prices and allows use across countries.

7.4.2 Mobility Concept – "Better Place"

What is "Better Place?"

At the end of 2007, the founder and former SAP manager Shai Agassi started with the implementation of his idea, the establishment of a comprehensive infrastructure for the operation of electric vehicles in the mass market. This mobility concept is entirely based on the electric motor technology. It is the aim of "Better Place" that the customer purchases an electric vehicle of any manufacturer without a battery and that the battery is provided by Better Place. In its business model, Better Place only charges for the distance actually traveled by the user. In order to counter the problem of the low range of electric vehicles, Better Place is establishing a comprehensive network of charging stations and cooperates with gas stations. It is the responsibility of the gas stations to store and to charge a large number of batteries for automobiles. If the battery charge in an automobile is approaching empty, the customer drives to the next gas station. There he can either recharge the battery via high voltage charging or replace the battery in a fully automated switching station. This only takes a few minutes. First pilot projects started in 2011 in the countries Denmark, Israel and Australia.[499]

Which challenges are addressed by "Better Place?"

According to the philosophy of "Better Place,"[500] the concept mainly tackles the problems of finite oil reserves, very volatile prices of crude oil, air pollution and climate change. These are the ecological and moral labels used to convince customers of a "clean automobile" and the advantages for the environment. But here it must be argued again that the ecological

---

[498] See Kilimann, S. (2010).
[499] See Better Place (2010a).
[500] See Better Place (2010b).

argument of environmental protection is weakened as long as the energy production is not completely switched over to renewable procedures that are low in emissions. However, it is a fact that crude oil reserves are finite. Ultimately the concept is also dealing with additional challenges. Especially the fields of e-mobility and storage cell technology suffer from the problem that charging a battery can take a long time (depending in the voltage of the charging station it can take up to 13.5 hours – however, even in the high voltage sector of 370 Volt it still takes about 3.5 hours before the average battery is completely charged). In addition the excessive charging times are associated with the problem of insufficient range. In this regard only a slight behavioral modification is needed by customers of "Better Place." Even when using a combustion engine, drivers must utilize a gas station before the tank is empty. The same is true for customers of "Better Place." Only the frequency is higher due to the range limitations. But the charging or switching process only takes a few minutes. Then the customer can continue the journey with a new battery.

What are advantages of "Better Place?"

The concept tackles the two features that are currently seen as the biggest disadvantages of electric vehicles: low range and long charging times. To avoid or better to redistribute these problems would provide electric vehicles with a convincing sales argument, which would lend further support to the ecological reasons. An additional advantage of this concept is its relative ease of implementation. The more technological advances are made in the field of batteries and electromobility, the more attractive the concept will be in daily use.

What are disadvantages of "Better Place?"

The disadvantages of "Better Place" relate among others to the high costs during the implementation stage. In addition, the electric power needed for the batteries is momentarily not produced in an environmentally conscious fashion and does not satisfy the demand for zero emissions. And the need to store batteries could cause problems for the owners of gas stations. Providing a constant supply and sufficient availability of batteries will become increasingly difficult, expensive and challenging as the concept matures and enters the mainstream.

Summary for "Better Place"

Among the concepts for new types of mobility that are currently under way or under consideration, the approach of "Better Place" appears to be among the most easily implementable ones. It can rely on technologies in the field of e-mobility that already exist, benefit from the accelerating technical progress and especially make use of the already existing infrastructure of gas stations. With the help of statistics of seasonal gasoline use, providers of batteries and gas stations can be well prepared for peaks in demand. As the production of energy is increasingly switched towards technologies that are low in emissions, the attractiveness and likelihood of project implementation go up.

7.4.3 Mobility Concept – PRT 2getthere

What is "PRT 2getthere?"

"Personal Rapid Transit" (PRT) is an urban transport system for persons that is energy efficient. It consists of small and very light cabins which provide room for up to three persons. With these cabins, passengers are taken to their individually chosen destination within the

7.4 Concepts in the Mobility Area 161

PRT network. The cabins are directed by a computer and do not have a driver. They move on guideways which are either below ground, on the ground or above ground. Acceleration and braking is done electronically via magnetic fields on the guideways. The PRT can reach maximum speeds of up to 60 km/h. The computer assures that the quickest route is taken and that collisions with other cabins are prevented. The system assures safety margins between cabins and directs cabins into tracks in different heights. Loading and unloading does not take place on the main track, but rather on sidetracks. This allows uninterrupted travel to the destination. Empty cabins are waiting in the stations until passenger get on and not the other way around. The main idea is to let the passengers decide when and where they want to travel and to provide them with a cabin immediately and without a wait. Thus the concept does not work with a fixed schedule and there are no predetermined routes.

Which challenges are addressed by "PRT 2getthere?"

Against the backdrop of increasing traffic volumes and related emissions, mainly in major cities, PRT is a suitable transport system for persons. Travel is emission-free and use of the flexible network system does not add to road traffic and congestion. This mobility concept is suitable especially for persons that need to travel relatively short distances, for example between other means of public transport or major traffic intersections, and that value time as well as privacy during their travel.

What are advantages of "PRT 2getthere?"

The passenger travels in small cabins and reaches the destination which he determines independently. He does not have to worry about a schedule, which provides a certain individuality of travel. He is not required to pay attention to the road situation or other drivers. Since the vehicles are small and not heavy, the required infrastructure (tracks and stations) is inexpensive. The light-weight cabins use relatively little energy compared to heavy passenger cars. This is supplemented by the central operating system, which optimizes the flow of traffic. The energy-efficient drive technology is also an environmentally conscious alternative to the passenger car. A final advantage is the comprehensive computer control of the system, which leads to a lower risk of collisions, accidents or traffic jams compared to automobile traffic.

What are disadvantages of "PRT2getthere?"

The distance which can be traveled depends on the dimension of the PRT infrastructure. Long distances can only be traveled within major systems. A further disadvantage is the relatively low passenger volume that can be transported compared to existing public transport systems.

Summary for "PRT 2getthere"

It cannot be expected that the PRT concept will replace the automobile. It is rather an alternative to the existing and "overstrained" traffic systems in major cities and agglomerations. Overcrowded busses, subways or traffic jams can be avoided. The system can be a meaningful alternative to the automobile in big cities, since it provides a certain level of privacy. This means of transportation can be utilized especially in office parks, suburbs or densely developed city centers.

7.5 Outlook – Novel Mobility Concepts

The presentation of the various aspects that influence general mobility has made it clear that their evolution leads to a number of new needs, which must be addressed by the automobile manufacturers. It appears to be very difficult to combine all the potential needs in one novel mobility concept. Different aspects can lead to the same need and thus a specific need may appear particularly relevant. In the following sections, two novel mobility concepts are presented, which have the potential to address the needs summarized in Figure 92.

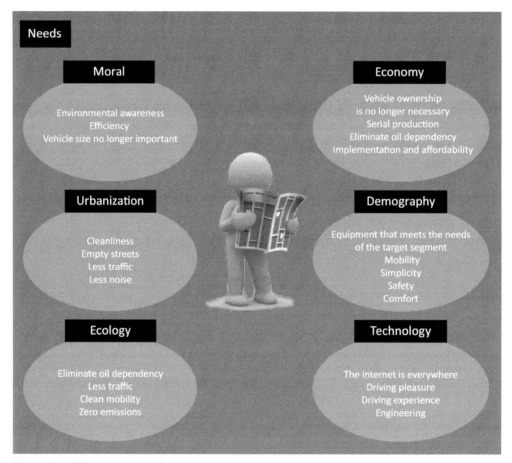

Figure 92: Mobility aspects and derived needs
Source: Authors' presentation

7.5.1 "Car Packaging and Pooling" – a Mobile Usage Concept

What is "Car Packaging and Pooling?"

The concept "Car Packaging and Pooling" is basically made up of two components, which can both be considered to be separate mobile usage concepts. In the following paragraphs, "Car Pooling" is derived from "Car Packaging." For that reason, "Car Packaging" is pre-

7.5 Outlook – Novel Mobility Concepts

sented first and then "Car Pooling" is discussed. The concept of "Car Packaging" constitutes a mobile usage concept, which can be provided by automobile manufacturers as well as by dealerships with direct customer contact. The customer is given the opportunity to purchase a combination of different automobiles as a package, instead of a single vehicle. The price of this package should be significantly below the individual prices of the two vehicles. Depending on the structure of needs and their ideas about usage, customers can choose among a number of versions, such as the summer-winter combination. The basic idea is the switch from the summer vehicle (for example a convertible) to the winter vehicle (for example a SUV). The customer has some flexibility in combining the two vehicles or can use them for a defined period of time. The combinations can be extended without limit and ultimately determine the price of the offering. Possible other versions include working days versus holidays, where the user gets an efficient small car during normal workdays and a roomy and powerful station wagon for his vacation. A global version could also be integrated. If a customer stays abroad for a certain time period, he could get his own vehicle in that location, which is already registered in his name, while the vehicle at home is returned to the automobile manufacturer during that time period. Exiting that model should be possible at any time by getting a refund for the less expensive vehicle or by making an additional payment for the more expensive one. It is acquired by the user and can either be used or resold.

In order to assure the optimal utilization of the unused second vehicle, "Car Pooling" is employed. The customer can choose between two versions for his second vehicle, either exclusive use (more expensive package) or leaving the second vehicle to the automobile manufacturer for further use. The advantage for the customer is a reduced price for his package and the participation in any rental income. Unused passenger cars from car packages could for example be provided at train stations or other highly frequented places that can be reached by public transportation. Only pooling customers of the automobile manufacturer have access to these pooling vehicles. They are equipped with a mobility card issued by the automobile manufacturer, which gives them access. The customer registers at a check-in terminal and selects one of the available vehicles for rental. He gets the key and can now use the parked vehicle. While parked, the vehicle is connected to a device that diagnoses errors. When returned, it must again be connected to that device. If an error is detected, a notice is send to the closest automobile dealership and the vehicle is taken in for repairs. The vehicles must be refueled by the user whenever the fuel level falls below one third. Payment is done via the card of the automobile manufacturer and does not require cash. Charges for the exact usage are determined via an electronic connection of the vehicle in the park position. Ultimate charges for the user depend on usage time and exact expenditures incurred. The usage fee is credited proportionately either to the package customer, the automobile manufacturer or the responsible dealership. The pooling customer as mobility user can choose among the passenger cars provided at the pooling site. Via internet the availability of vehicles at the different locations can be checked continuously and vehicles can also be reserved. To increase the popularity of pooling, a cooperation with other providers is also possible. As an example, the mobility card could also be used as a credit card and similar to the Miles & More model, points could be awarded for purchases, which can be redeemed for global mobility services.

Which challenges are addressed by "Car Packaging and Pooling?"

The concept is flexible and can thus provide answers to a number of future needs. The individual structuring of the various mobility concepts makes them attractive for specific target groups and a quick and timely reaction to societal trends is possible. If the user has a desire for efficiency and ecology, he can choose a combination of electroscooter and electric vehicle for the daily use in the city and a hybrid limousine for longer journeys, for example for his vacation travel. An adjustment of the packages would also allow adequate reactions to demographic shifts. Vehicle packages with specific equipment such as boarding aids could be offered. In sum, the concept would follow the trend of an increasing focus on the use of individual mobility, while the image of the automobile as status symbol is losing its appeal. If the ecological aspect needs to be stressed further, the pooling sites could also be equipped with solar charging stations. If electric vehicles are not part of the package, they could be provided for rental by the automobile manufacturer. The concept tackles the urban challenges of the future. Parking spaces downtown are no longer blocked by unneeded vehicles. In town it may be possible to do completely without mobility or to use small vehicles. The efficiency of the use of fossil fuels could be increased and the strain from noise and smog could be reduced.

What are the advantages of "Car Packaging and Pooling?"

With regard to the advantages it must be distinguished whether they relate to society, the customer of the manufacturer. The packaging customer certainly has the advantage that he can use mobility in a way that fits his needs without having to acquire several vehicles. The system is theoretically unlimited and can react immediately to customer demands and trends in society. Thanks to the flexibility of the system, it would be possible to access the global distribution network of the automobile manufacturer in the context of globalization. Instead of getting a rental car during vacations, a locally available pooling car could be used instead. Suitable networks and specific smartphone applications could be used to determine the closest pooling locations and their availability via public transport. Mobility would be available everywhere as a flexible short-term service. For society, the advantage would be a reduced number of vehicles downtown with their associated negative effects. Advantages for the manufacturer would be a more efficient use of its global distribution network, the generation of additional sales from selling packages, the brand-specific advertising in cities via the pooling locations, the establishment of brand loyalty and the generation of additional revenues via vertical differentiation in the rental car market.

What are the disadvantages of "Car Packaging and Pooling?"

The major disadvantage of "Car Packaging und Pooling" are its complex and cost-intensive individualization and the efficient management of the vehicle fleet. Further disadvantages are the number of cooperating dealerships needed, availability of attractive pooling locations as well as the infrastructure investment required for the concept.

Summary for "Car Packaging and Pooling"

In order to obtain differentiation from the competition and to provide answers to future mobility needs, it is absolutely essential for the automobile manufacturers to develop new concepts. Every concept also entails risks and is associated with costs. Due to its many advantages, "Car Packaging and Pooling" can be considered a viable investment which secures the continuation of the company in selected customer segments. Advantages in the implementation certainly are obtained by providers with a wide selection, since they can fall back on a broad base with respect to choice and opportunities to contact customers. The concept is visualized in Figure 93. Nonetheless, a comprehensive implementation of the concepts does not appear likely at present.

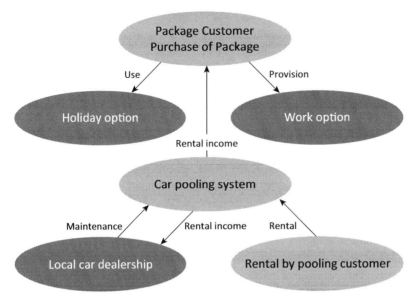

Figure 93: Car Package to combine several classes of automobiles as needed
Source: Authors' presentation

7.5.2 Combination of "Better Place" & "PRT" – a Novel Mobility Concept

The final mobility concept deals with a novel approach that appears possible in the future. It requires new technologies and infrastructure, which still need to be established. However, given the current state of technological knowledge, this would theoretically be possible. If the needs collected in the previous sections are once again scrutinized carefully, a few major needs of our current society can be identified. These are:

- **Avoid dependency on crude oil**: Sooner or later, society must move away from this dependency and choose new, renewable or constantly available forms of energy for transportation. Crude oil and other non-regenerative raw materials are finite.
- **Ecological awareness**: Society must deal with the necessity to answer ecological questions concerning climate change, stop the greenhouse effect and avoid pollution. For the automotive industry, this implies the end of the combustion engine as we know it today and the need for a zero-emissions vehicle.
- **Increasing urbanization**: The trend towards megacities appears unstoppable. The rural exodus is continuing, population density as well as traffic density in major cities is increasing, while available space is dwindling. It seems unavoidable to provide for cities were traffic is reduced, while mobility is maintained.
- **Demographic development**: The average life expectancy of the population is increasing steadily and at the same time, family size in the major industrial nations goes down. This implies that mobility must become simpler for the older generation in order to satisfy age-adequate requirements.

An optimal mobility concept would thus combine these four main elements of the evolving needs. If the already existing concepts are considered, it appears that there are already theoretical alternatives, which can cover a majority of these needs. Especially the ecological aspect with the awareness that we need to move away from the use of crude oil and towards zero-emissions is already taken up in numerous studies. An optimal solution could be the combination of the advantages of existing ideas in a new self-supporting concept.

What is the combined mobility concept?

The mobility concept presented here is a combination of two existing mobility concepts that were already discussed in this chapter. They were preselected since they meet many of the needs described above. The combination of the two concepts is supposed to cover the four main elements listed above and is explained in more detail in the following.

The concept "Better Place" which was outlined above especially tackles the first two factors, avoidance of oil dependency and ecological awareness. The combination of electric vehicles with a recharging infrastructure and its technology, namely the automatic switching of the fundamentally important storage units, addresses two problems. First, it eliminates the dependency on oil and second, it meets the need to be ecologically conscious and be mobile with zero emissions. An absolute requirement for this approach is the meaningful and ecological production of electric power. But this problem is not addressed further at this point.

The concept "PRT 2getthere" mainly tackles the remaining two needs and at the same time constitutes the visionary part of the mobility concepts and thus also of this chapter. On the one hand the issue of increased urbanization is tackled, namely the fact that downtown areas of major megacities are becoming narrower, denser and also more dangerous as a result of the high traffic volumes. On the other hand, this form of transportation is particularly suitable for older citizens. By combining individual mobility with a system of mass transit, which directs cabins or vehicles automatically in subway tunnels or on the road, the simplicity of mobility cannot be improved. Humans need not take any action, the cabin moves on its own and takes the user to the desired destination. This would prevent dangers in road traffic caused by demographic developments. Especially with regard to the megacity trend, this concept provides a vision for the future where mobility takes place in the remaining unused spaces of the cities, namely the air and the underground. At the same time, humans are eliminated as risk factors, since they are no longer in charge of the vehicle.

Which challenges are addressed by the mobility concept?

The combination of both concepts makes use of their major features. On the one hand, a major charging infrastructure is established. Existing networks of gas stations can be used or modernized. The technology of "Better Place" helps to overcome the current problems and weaknesses in using electronic engines, mainly the battery cells. The fully automated and quick exchange of batteries at the switching stations replaces the need for long interruptions of the journey in order to charge the battery. Figure 94 shows the switching stations for batteries which are used in the concept of "Better Place."

At home it will of course still be possible to charge batteries via cable. Alternatively, an additional product could be established to deepen the offering, namely the placement of these switching stations in private garages. This would also facilitate the charging process at home. Currently unused batteries can be loaded and are fully charged when needed. The visionary

7.5 Outlook – Novel Mobility Concepts

component of the concept is the combination with the philosophy of the urban mobility concept. Automobiles are reconfigured in a way that they can drive autonomously in cities. Two solutions appear possible:

- Fully automated urban traffic system that is supported by a software
- New and automated infrastructure networks for general movement (for example below ground)

The two suggested solutions address the challenge of improving or solving the traffic situation and the connected problems arising in big cities. At this point we will deal with the first version, which is considered most likely to be implementable and which already has some of the needed technology in place. A number of models of automobile manufacturers are equipped for fully automated driving even today; aids such as a fully automated parking pilot are already implemented in mass production.

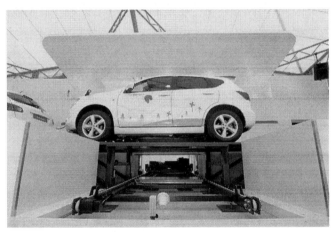

Figure 94: Switching station of "Better Place" for quick switching of batteries
Source: cleantechblog (2009)

The problems of overcrowded streets, poor traffic flow, accidents and resulting traffic congestion pose enormous problems in major cities. With the help of fully automated urban traffic systems that are supported by software, the human factor could be eliminated. Instead an automated system would be used that reacts to current street and traffic conditions. Its functioning could be as follows: automobiles are supplied with a unified software system. At the same time a very comprehensive and highly technological system is developed, which can be used to direct an urban traffic system. Once the driver approaches a major city, the vehicle is taken over by an autopilot and guided by the traffic system. At that point, the driver is no longer required to take any action. He simply needs to supply the destination or vicinity where he would like to park. He and all the other traffic participants will be guided on the streets and other traffic options by the fully automated system. The system can plan, determine and implement all the factors that are likely to influence the flow of traffic such as speed, traffic lights and navigation in order to provide the optimal route.

Important in implementing this combined concept is the need for a major harmonization. Automobile manufacturers and mobility providers must engage in intense cooperation in order to establish a supraregional and functioning urban concept. Needed are unified hardware solutions for the battery switching technology, a unified charging technology as well as a unified and adaptable software solution. This would enable the automobile manufacturers to continue with their different brands and product versions, while they would be forced to cooperate with regard to features such as battery switching technology or software equipment. The use of standardized technologies and parts would lead to savings during the production process and other synergies, since features such as chassis and battery suspension would be developed and produced in an identical fashion for the entire automotive industry.

Advantages of the mobility concept

The advantages of the combined concept cover a wide range. The customer is no longer dependent on fluctuating oil prices, oil supplies or the oil industry in general. He can use inexpensive electrical power and thus realize a major cost advantage. Short switching times for the batteries provide unlimited range without waiting times. Dependency on charging stations is not seen as a direct disadvantage, since stops to get fuel in order to maintain mobility are also required today. An additional advantage of the concept is the availability of an existing infrastructure of gas stations. They just need to be upgraded and the switching technology must be installed. Combinations with solar cells or similar technologies to generate electric power are also possible in order to first, support the charging of batteries and second, to combine it with the "smart grid" technology of the future. The storage units are combined with the power grid in this approach and can be used to facilitate the quick absorption of peak demand. General advantages of the concept are avoidance of smog and pollution in cities, reduction of noise, prevention of traffic jams as a result of sophisticated traffic planning and maintenance of a steady traffic flow.

Disadvantages of the mobility concept

As with other concepts as well, the requirements needed for implementation must be considered as disadvantages. The establishment of the charging infrastructure, the standardization of all relevant vehicle components across the entire automotive industry as well as the cost and complexity associated with an independent urban traffic system are major obstacles. They are likely to hinder any development for a long time. The requirement to produce electric power in a way that is ecological and sustainable in order to satisfy the condition of zero emissions not only for the vehicle, but also at a macroeconomic level, will continue to pose great challenges for society. The unified integration of the charging and switching systems for batteries into the production cycle of all manufacturers as well as the integration of a unified software system are not optimally supported by the current principle of a free market economy and free competition.

Summary for the mobility concept

The development of an adequate system to direct city traffic and to avoid traffic jams, accidents and high emissions appears to be without an alternative in light of the accelerating urbanization. The advantages of the "Better Place" approach which entails the ecological use of clean mobility and quiet traffic can be easily understood. The need for cleaner cities manifests itself for example also in the new emissions stickers and environmental (city) zones. With the first steps in the direction of this concept, both the idea of a green city can be strengthened and our responsibility towards the environment demonstrated. Automobile manufacturers can save costs via synergies and benefit from the global or national revaluation of conventional automobiles and satisfy the growing demand of the market for electromobility and thus generate additional sales.

7.5.3   Future Potential Competitors of the Automobile Manufacturers

As was pointed out repeatedly, the development of new mobility concepts will also imply completely new conditions in the automobile market. Currently specialized niche providers from related industries such as battery production could witness a stellar ascent as the market balance shifts towards electric vehicles. As experts in their fields with the potential for vertical differentiation, they should not be ignored. Already today they can use their entire resources to serve future business fields, while the automobile manufacturers are required to utilize the majority of their resources to satisfy the current market demand. Competitive advantages and market barriers that have been built over many years are likely to be weakened with the establishment of completely new concepts. For that reason, automobile manufacturers must give top priority to the analysis of markets, trends and the competitive situation, also with regard to potential future fields of competition. Should usage concepts such as "Car Packaging and Pooling" be implemented, the industry must be in a leading position and erect barriers to market entry early on.

Potentially serious competition in this field is likely to come from car rental companies. First of all, the concept is threatening their market and secondly, car rental companies have already established global distribution networks across brands, which provide value to their customers. If mobility continues to gain in relevance and the importance of ownership of an automobile continues to lose in importance, rental companies could be first to cover the market with flexible and efficient usage concepts. Automobile manufacturers thus face the challenge to quickly counteract such developments.

8 Strategic Currency Management for Automotive Manufacturers

8.1 Executive Summary

One of the major risk factors for internationally active automobile manufacturers is the exchange rate risk. For automobile manufacturers with a high share of exports, currency management has become essential. The effect of an exchange rate which is used by a manufacturer to convert holdings of foreign currency into domestic currency – the so-called transfer rate – on company earnings is very large: the better the transfer rate for the company, the better the result of the company. The second aim of currency management is the hedging of a transfer rate in order to minimize the effects of currency fluctuations on the company. Low volatility of the transfer rate is important for the company, because it increases the reliability of planning. In order to reduce the risk of currency fluctuations, automobile manufacturers must identify their currency risks in a first step. Currency risk mostly results from:

- **Invoicing in foreign currency**
- **Issuing of debt capital**
- **Currency conversion when consolidating the corporate accounts**

These risks can be lowered with the help of **natural hedging**. Natural hedging can be implemented via adjustments of the cost structure in line with revenues or vice versa. The adjustment of the cost structure to revenues can be implemented with regard to the procurement policy via **local suppliers**, with regard to the choice of location by setting up production facilities in the country in question or via **Completely Knocked Down (CKD)** manufacturing as well as via contract design.

But currency management also plays an integral role for **cash management** and for international **investment planning**. Relevant for cash management are strategies for:

- **Pooling**
- **Netting**
- **Blocked Funds**

In the case of investment planning especially **political risks** need to be considered, which have an effect on currency management.

With the help of these strategies a **net exposure** is determined for each currency, which can be hedged by the company.

For this residual risk, the automobile manufacturer must define an appropriate strategy, which depends on the degree of **risk aversion** of the company. Automobile manufacturers with a bigger margin are often willing to accept higher risks concerning exchange rate fluctuations. This is reflected in the choice of financial instrument used for currency hedging. Most frequently used financial instruments are:

- **Forwards**
- **Options**
- **Range options**
- **Swaps**

The use of these instruments to reduce exchange rate risks is called **financial hedging**. The currency manager must determine the appropriate hedging strategies. The strategies differ with regard to the **hedging instruments**, the **recommendations for action** and other requirements such as the minimum number of months that should be hedged.[501]

8.2 Fundamentals

8.2.1 Definition of Terms

8.2.1.1 Currency

A **currency** defines and orders the entire financial affairs of a state. It determines the system of coins and bills in a currency area. The currency area defines the regions where the currency is valid. A currency facilitates the transfer of goods and services, since the provision of other goods or services in exchange is not required. The currency describes a certain type of money. Most currencies are traded in international currency markets. The exchange rate is the price which is quoted in these markets.[502] Exchange rates have a major effect on the current account and are therefore among the most important prices in an open economy. Currency fluctuations have an effect on imports and exports of a nation. This in turn has an effect on the value creation of a nation and the related growth and prosperity. The demand for imports and exports, which is of particular importance for automobile manufacturers, is affected by relative prices. These prices are made comparable with the help of exchange rates.

An important role in international currency trading is played by the liberalization of the exchange rate of the US-Dollar in the year 1973 in most Western European countries and in Japan. Exchange rates became flexible with this development. At this time the term "free floating" was created which is the opposite of a fixed exchange rate. Smaller nations attempted to maintain fixed exchange rates for a long time. This turned out to be increasingly difficult over time, as the speed of international capital movements accelerated and controlling the exchange rate became more and more difficult.[503]

8.2.1.2 Currency Management

The term **currency management** is defined as the managing, quantifying, forecasting and controlling of transaction and translation risks as part of general exchange rate or currency risks of a company. Exchange rate risks can be distinguished in transaction exposure and

---

[501] We thank Felix Nunninger for his support in the topic area of "Currency Management." His work has made the success of this book possible.
[502] See Schricker W., Rubin E. (2001), p. 134.
[503] See Eichengreen, B., Rennert, U., Rhiel, W. (2000), pp. 183ff.

translation exposure. Transaction exposure results from relationships with suppliers and customers in different currency areas. It is also called operative exchange rate risk. Translation exposure results from currency conversion, for example for individual subsidiaries.[504]

The term currency management thus describes the entire management of foreign currencies in a company. Currency management is of particular relevance for companies with a high share of exports in countries with different currencies. The automotive industry and especially the German automobile manufacturers are among this category. 75.9% of the entire German passenger car production in 2010 went abroad. This is the highest export share for passenger cars globally.[505] In order to manage, quantify, forecast and control exchange rate risks, volatility, correlations and open currency positions are considered. The open currency position is also called exposure and is determined for every foreign currency by taking into consideration all claims for delivery and obligations to deliver on and off the balance sheet. The term structure of the existing foreign exchange positions is taken into consideration to determine the swap rate risk.

8.2.2 Chapter Focus

This chapter aims at providing an overview of strategic currency management for automobile manufacturers. The setup of currency management operations at an automobile manufacturer, the instruments used for hedging and the currency management strategies of an internationally active automobile manufacturer are described. On the basis of the literature, a connection is made between the instruments that are available for currency hedging and the strategies in the areas of natural hedging, financial hedging, international cash management and international investment planning. The aim is to demonstrate the relevance of currency management in all areas of international financial management. In the areas of cash management and investment planning, parameters are listed which influence the strategic currency management of automobile manufacturers. In the areas of natural and financial hedging, strategies and solutions for the reduction of exchange rate risk are presented. The link is displayed in Figure 95.

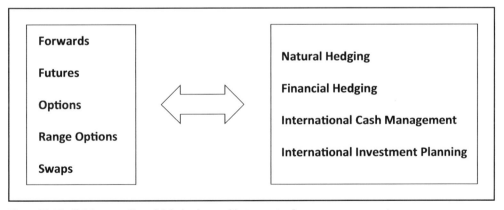

Figure 95: The link between financial derivatives and instruments of currency management
        Source: Authors' presentation

---

[504] See Breuer (2000), pp. 93ff.
[505] See Verband der Automobilindustrie (2011).

8.3 Currency Management: Reasons and Current Challenges

8.3.1 Uses of Currency Management

Initially the question arises why an automobile manufacturer should be concerned with currency management. The main reason to conduct currency management is the reduction of risk. An automobile manufacturer for example wants to reduce the risk that the exchange rate of a country which he supplies with automobiles moves against him. This can be illustrated with reference to a simple example. BMW AG sells an automobile in the USA for US$ 50,000. It wants to exchange this amount in Euro since most if its costs of personnel and materials are in Euro. For an exchange rate between Euro and US$ of 1.20 (as of: June 2010) BMW AG receives an amount of € 41,666.67. If instead the exchange rate stands at 1.40 US$ per Euro (as of: March 2011), BMW AG only receives € 35,714.28 for the same automobile. That is a difference of almost 15%, which could have drastic effects given tight pricing and small margins in the automotive industry.

Reasons for the currency management of automobile manufacturers are in particular the high exchange rate risks caused by:

a. High export shares
b. Invoicing in foreign currency
c. Issuing of foreign currency debt
d. Currency conversion when consolidating the corporate accounts

High export shares:

Since exports are the dominant growth drivers of the German economy, exchange rate fluctuations play an important role for companies, and especially for the automotive industry. With the help of currency management, the automobile manufacturers want to reduce or control exactly that risk. For that purpose a company needs to identify the different sources of its currency risk. These can be different even within the automotive industry and depend on the specific strategy of the company.

Invoicing in foreign currency:

One risk arises from invoicing in a currency that is different from the one used for conducting business operations. This is the case, for example, if an invoice for a delivery or a service is written in a foreign currency. The risk for the party writing the invoice – in this case the automobile manufacturer – is a negative development of the exchange rate between invoicing date and payment date, which means that the company does not obtain as much money as anticipated. The most straightforward example for this is the sale of an automobile in a country with a different currency.

Issuing of debt:

An additional risk arises if debt is issued in Euro, but used for investments outside the Euro area. If, for example, Daimler AG takes out a loan in Euro for an investment in China, there is a risk that the EUR/CNY exchange rate develops unfavorably and not enough Remnimbi are obtained for the original Euro amount.

Currency conversion when consolidating the corporate accounts:

The currency conversion when consolidating the corporate accounts and translating all revenues and costs into the reporting currency also involves currency risk.[506] If for example Volkswagen AG consolidates all its revenues and costs of Volkswagen Australia, it is subject to fluctuations in the EUR/AUD exchange rate.

8.3.2 Current Challenges in Currency Management of Automobile Manufacturers

Hedge accounting: Case studies reveal that the hedging of foreign currencies as part of the currency management is merely used to cover certain risky positions and not to speculate.[507] Partly responsible for this are certainly the international accounting standards IFRS and the relevant standard IAS 39. Derivatives can be classified as so-called "Hedge Accounting" if they actually serve to cover an open risk position. If an amount was hedged that exceeds what is actually needed, the surplus cannot be classified as "Hedge Accounting", but must be assessed at fair value. This in turn can lead to strong volatility. But the major aim of currency management is exactly the avoidance of such risks and fluctuations in order to put planning on a sounder base. If the volumes of the hedging transactions are analyzed, the high importance of the use of currency derivatives for internationally active companies becomes clear. Volkswagen AG for example showed a volume of hedging transactions in the amount of € 34 billion in 2007.

Globalization: The topic of "foreign currency risk" and the hedging of this risk will continue to increase in importance for internationally active companies as globalization is advancing. Especially the boom in China is a major challenge for the currency management of automobile manufacturers. On the one hand this is caused by the large volumes that are subject to hedging and on the other hand by the political and cultural situation in China. Strict regulations for dealing with the Chinese currency Renminbi are in place. But not only in China, but also in countries such as Brazil or Argentina an increasing number of vehicles are sold and this leads to an increase in currency risk. While the introduction of the Euro has led to a reduction in the number of currencies in Europe which is expected to continue in the future, new sales markets for the automotive industry are appearing all over the world. A company such as BMW AG must now also conduct hedging transactions for the Thai Baht. And the low liquidity of currencies of smaller economies such as the Norwegian Crown constitutes a challenge for currency management. Here the demand from a single company can lead to a change in the quoted price for a derivatives transaction. In such a case it is important to trade only small volumes. Especially with the outbreak of the sovereign debt crisis and the large market volatility, currency management is facing new challenges.

Natural hedging: Currently the automobile manufacturers attempt to expand their "natural hedging" activities. Currency risks are to be covered in a natural fashion. This is done for example by paying raw materials in foreign currency such as US-Dollar or Swiss Franc. Moving the production into countries with high sales figures also contributes to "natural hedging." In that case, personnel costs and other expenses can be paid in the respective cur-

---

[506] See Bloss, M. et al. (2009), pp. 12ff.
[507] See Bloss, M. et al. (2009), p. 27.

rency. The so-called "netting," the subtraction of costs from revenues in the foreign currency leads to a decline in the currency exposure. The balance is called net exposure and describes the amount that must be hedged by the currency manager with the help of derivatives.

8.4 Setup and Execution of Currency Management

8.4.1 Setup of Currency Management at an Automobile Manufacturer

Currency management at an automobile manufacturer is usually part of the treasury department. Figure 96 shows the simplified and generalized organization of the currency management operations of an automobile manufacturer.

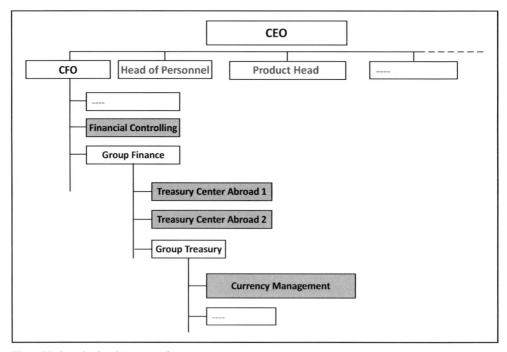

Figure 96: Organizational structure of currency management
　　　　　Source: Authors' presentation

In this example Currency Management is a part of Group Treasury. Group Treasury in turn belongs to Group Finance which reports to the CFO. Additional departments that work with Currency Management are for example foreign treasury centers. For European automobile manufacturers these are usually located in Singapore and New York at current. These centers should allow trading around the clock and watch the markets for 24 hours. In addition it is important in certain markets to establish a physical presence to facilitate direct negotiations with the local banks. An additional and important department in the process of currency management is Financial Controlling. It supervises the currency management group, assesses and analyzes the transactions conducted and their results.

8.4.2 Operational Structure of Currency Management at an Automobile Manufacturer

To begin the operational structuring of the hedging process, the **exposure** must be determined. The exposure is the amount of foreign currency that needs to be hedged by the currency management group in line with the strategy.[508] This amount is calculated by the financial controlling group usually for the next five years and then expressed as an annual or monthly exposure. For this purpose, data at the highest possible level of precision about the expected receipts and outflows of foreign currency in the different currency areas is collected.

For the calculation of these **forecasts** the entire value chain of the automobile manufacturer is considered. This includes research and development, procurement, production and distribution. This gives rise to an amount in US$ that the manufacturer must exchange into home currency at the end of each month.

This amount can be reduced with the help of "**natural hedging**," for example by flexibly adjusting the utilization rates of global production capacities.[509] "Natural hedging" is hedging that does not require the use of derivatives transactions. A company can also attempt to pay for a share of its raw materials in foreign currency in order to reduce the amount that needs to be hedged and thus also to reduce foreign currency risk.

Once the exposure is determined, a **committee** usually decides which share of the exposure should be hedged up to which point in time. The company strategy plays a decisive role when these decisions are reached. If the strategy of the purchasing power parity approach is chosen, the percentage of the exposure that needs to be hedged depends on the deviation of the spot price from its equilibrium value.[510]

Two versions of currency trading are possible: "Trading via an electronic trading platform" and "Telephone trading."

- **Electronic trading:** When trading via this platform, the trader of the automobile manufacturer enters the desired value, the desired currency and the due date online into the software of the platform and within seconds he obtains a quote from the banks which he preselected. He can select a quote and complete the derivatives transaction. For smaller amounts below € 10 million the banks frequently utilize automatic dealers. This means that the system automatically generates a quote for the customer.
  Examples for electronic trading platforms are: FXall, 360T and HTUB-Bloomberg-FX-Trading.
- **Telephone trading:** Works similar to electronic trading, but here the company treasurer calls the individual banks personally and asks for a quote for the desired derivatives transaction. A disadvantage of telephone trading is the timing component, since it usually takes several minutes before a price quote is obtained. Meanwhile in electronic trading it only takes a few seconds to close a transaction. In addition, several banks can be asked simultaneously. In electronic trading it can also be prevented that the banks immediately share the information about the desired trade and thus drive up the price.
  Trading via electronic platforms is likely to gain in importance in the future and will account for an increasing percentage of overall trading volume.

---

[508] See Rudolph, B. Schäfer, K. (2010), p. 152.
[509] See Bloss, M. et al. (2009), p. 21.
[510] See Coyle, B. (2000), p. 33.

Once a derivatives transaction is completed, it will be registered in the internal system of the automobile manufacturer und in that way become visible for controlling and accounting. The analysis, surveillance and assessment of the complete derivatives transaction is done by the financial controlling department.

The current situation or the hedged volume can also be stated in months covered. To do that, the number of months in the future which is covered from a current perspective is calculated. Months covered is calculated by dividing the overall volume of hedges divided by the monthly exposure for a currency.

$$\frac{Overall\ volume\ of\ hedges}{Monthly\ exposure} = Months\ covered$$

$$Example: \frac{\$252\ million}{\$14\ million} = 18\ months$$

This result would mean that the automobile manufacturer is covered for the next 18 months for a monthly exposure of US$ 145 million and a current exchange rate of 1.42 USD per EUR, since he has entered into currency derivatives valued at US$ 252 million. Figure 97 presents the months covered strategy graphically.

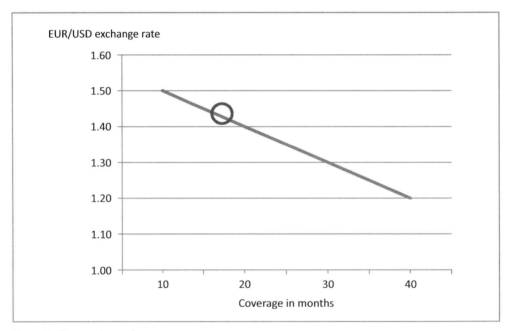

Figure 97: Coverage in months
Source: Authors' presentation

The line displays the current EUR/USD rate of 1.42. The red circle shows the current level of coverage of about 18 months at the current exchange rate. It can be concluded from the graph that a decline of the EUR/USD exchange rate to 1.30 leads to an extension of the coverage to 30 months.

Normally the volume of currency hedges goes down in the future and the exposure goes up, since increasing sales figures are expected. The exposure can also change within a year, if there are changes in the sales figures in the relevant currency area. Should there be excess hedging in one year, the possibility exists of swapping – or moving forward – excessive derivatives transactions into the next year. But this should be avoided if possible because it may create accounting problems. Only the portion of the derivatives used for hedging is covered by the so-called "hedge accounting."

8.4.3 Banking Policy

An important point in the context of currency management of automobile manufacturers is the banking policy. It deals with contacts and relationships with the individual banks. Two different strategies with regard to banking policy can be distinguished: the policy of core banking or the policy of significant diversification.

- **Core banking:**
  In the core banking model the company usually identifies between three and five banks and develops very close relations with them. Selection criteria for a core bank are for example the knowledge in the currency area or the liquidity in rarer currencies as well as the research provided by the bank. The advantage of this strategy is the existence of very good relations with the chosen banks and the possibility to obtain better prices from these banks due to the large number of transactions and a better understanding of the bank for the processes and needs of the company. A disadvantage is the dependency on a small number of banks.
- **Diversification of the banks:**
  The model of a maximum degree of diversification goes exactly against that dependency. By distributing the business among a maximum number of banks, the risk of a default is reduced. A further advantage of this strategy is the limited insight of an individual bank into the business of the company and thus into the exact volumes that need to be hedged.

The responsibilities of the banks with regard to currency management are trading with the companies and providing information about currency market developments. Traders at banks and at the companies are in daily contact to exchange information. Before trading with banks can be initiated, a so-called **ISDA** must be negotiated with every bank. It is a contract which specifies the exact conditions of the derivatives transactions. It is standardized and is called the ISDA master agreement. The International Swaps and Derivatives Association (ISDA) is a trading organization of the participants in the market for OTC derivatives.[511]

8.5 Instruments Used in Currency Management by Automobile Manufacturers

8.5.1 Overview of Available Financial Instruments

The choice of instrument depends on the degree of risk aversion, the type of risk and the legal regulations in the country where the currency needs to be hedged. Figure 98 provides an overview of the six most important financial instruments and their advantages in the cur-

---

[511] See ISDA.

rency management of automobile manufacturers. It helps the currency manager to select the appropriate instrument.

Financial instrument	Advantage 1	Advantage 2	Advantage 3
Forwards	Increased flexibility due to OTC trading	Unconditional derivatives transaction	No fees
NDF	Hedging of currencies that are not convertible	No physical delivery	No fees
Futures	Greater liquidity compared to forward	Unconditional derivatives transaction	No fees
Options	Choice concerning exercise	Participation in favorable development	
Range options	Risk reduced to a range	Participation in favorable development	
Swaps	Reduces interest rate and currency risk	No additional risk	

Figure 98: Advantages of the most important financial instruments for currency management
Source: Authors' presentation

The automobile manufacturers differ significantly in their choice of instrument.

Porsche AG for example prefers to use **options** in order to maintain the possibility of benefitting from advantageous price movements. One disadvantage of this instrument is the option premium.

BMW and **Daimler** preferred the use of **forwards**. With the help of forwards, BMW and Daimler were able to secure a fixed exchange rate without having to pay a fee. Their preference of forwards over futures is explained by the higher flexibility provided by OTC trading. Forwards offer the possibility to enter into a derivatives transaction that specifically meets the needs of the automotive company. This is particularly important with regard to the choice of maturity and volume. For the automobile manufacturers these factors differ significantly from transaction to transaction, since the exposure which needs to be hedged can change on a weekly basis and currency managers need to react to these developments.

Volkswagen AG particularly favors "natural hedging" as a reaction to its Renminbi currency risk. Its two joint ventures in China employ a total of 22,000 people, who are paid in Renminbi. These payments in local currency help to reduce Renminbi risk in a "natural" fashion.[512]

8.5.2 Forwards and Futures

In currency management, a distinction is made between spot and forward transactions. Compared to spot transactions, forward transactions are characterized by differences in timing of contract conclusion and contract fulfillment. Derivatives are utilized to secure a current rate for a future point in time. Derivatives contracts can be used by a company to hedge against the risks which arise from foreign currency liabilities. The volume, the future payment date and especially the exchange rate used in derivatives transactions are predetermined by the contracting parties when they enter into the contract.[513] The forward rate is determined by the spot

---

[512] See German.China.Org.CN (2011).
[513] See Keown, A. et al. (2010), p. 789.

rate and the interest rate differential between the two currencies. A forward contract – as opposed to a futures contract – is an unconditional derivatives transaction that is not traded on an exchange. The lack of standardization of the forward contract offers the parties higher flexibility, but at the same time also lower liquidity compared to a futures contract. In the automotive industry, forwards are preferred to futures thanks to the greater flexibility. The ability of a company to enter into forward transactions also depends on the contract volume.[514]

A specific form of a forward contract is the Non-Deliverable Forward (NDF). These currency derivatives can be used to hedge currencies that are not convertible. An NDF can thus be defined as a type of futures contract that is not standardized and that is not traded at an exchange. In an NDF, a currency that is not freely convertible, such as the Argentine Peso, the Chinese Renminbi or the Korean Won is specified against a freely convertible currency. Normally this is the USD, but the use of EUR is also possible. NDFs are used if the economic strength of a country supports international transactions, but restrictions or the lack of a futures market prevent the use of deliverable currency derivatives. NDFs are so-called "offshore" financial instruments, where no physical settlement takes place, but where instead a cash payment is made at maturity. A transaction consists of a fixed amount (of the currency that is not convertible), a predefined due date and a predetermined forward rate. At maturity the current spot rate (reference value) is compared to the NDF rate.[515] The difference must be paid on the settlement day. This is done in the convertible currency. No payments are made and no accounts are affected in the currency that cannot be converted.

When entering into the Non-Deliverable Forward, the two parties agree on a way to determine the reference value (at maturity). It can either be the daily value which is published by the central bank or an average value derived from the quotations of several banks. NDFs require a specific contract, which is in line with the specifications of the internationally accepted International Swap and Derivatives Association ISDA. Non-Deliverable Forwards are suitable especially for customers that operate in countries with a currency that is not freely convertible and that want to repatriate profits which are obtained in these countries. The relevance of NDFs is increasing steadily, mainly because of the enormous increase in sales numbers of the automotive industry in China. As an alternative to the NDFs, foreign automobile manufacturers can also implement Renminbi hedges via their local Chinese subsidiaries. However, prices tend to be inferior compared to the ones that the parent company can obtain.

8.5.3 Options

8.5.3.1 An Overview of Options

When entering into an options transaction, the buyer of the option (long) has the right and the seller of the option (short) has the obligation to buy or to sell an amount at a predefined point in time and at a previously determined price. The buyer explicitly has the right, but not the obligation to exercise the option. To obtain that right, the buyer of the option is obliged to pay a premium to the seller.[516] Thus entering into an option transaction is more expensive

---

[514] See Wöhe, G. (2010), p. 705.
[515] See Bloss, M. et al. (2009), p. 68.
[516] See Bloss, M. et al. (2009), p. 99.

than entering into a forward, which normally does not involve a fee. But in certain situations or for a specific type of manufacturer, an option may be the preferred instrument. As an example, an automobile manufacturer such as Porsche AG, which has a significantly higher margin than Daimler AG, may prefer the purchase of options and thus assume increased currency risk.

A distinction is made between two types of options: the **call option** and the **put option**. The call option gives the buyer the right of purchasing the currency in question at the agreed price, while the put option gives the right to sell that currency.[517]

8.5.3.2 Range Options

A range option is a specific type of option. It is established as the combination of standard options. By simultaneously purchasing a call (put) option and selling a put (call) option, it is possible to limit price opportunities and risks to a certain range. With regard to its riskiness, this type of financial instrument can be classified between a forward and a standard option, since the risk is reduced to a specific bandwidth.

8.5.4 Swaps

Swaps are exchange transactions which make it possible to utilize comparative cost advantages on international financial markets, which are caused by different assessments of default risk and differences in market access of the contract parties. Both interest payments and principal payment are exchanged in a cross currency swap. At the beginning of the transaction fixed capital amounts in different currencies are exchanged at the current spot rate. During the duration of the swap, the interest payments on the principal are also exchanged among the contract parties. At the end of the maturity, the fixed capital amounts are repaid on the basis of the initially agreed exchange rate.

Currency swaps are used for example to hedge in the case of loans issued in foreign currency to international companies. They also facilitate cost savings compared to a direct loan provided in the relevant foreign currency.[518]

8.6 International Strategies for Automobile Manufacturers

Internationally active automobile manufacturers are facing a number of challenges:[519]
- Differences in taxation
- Tariffs
- Quotas
- Lack of mobility of workers
- Cultural differences
- Differences in external accounting

---

[517] See Keown, A. et al. (2010), p. 790.
[518] See Wöhe, G. (2010), p. 706.
[519] This section draws on Madura, J. (2012) and Keown, A.J., Martin, J.D., Petty, J., Williams, S., David, F. jr. (2010).

- Costs of communication
- Currency risks

But these challenges can also be considered opportunities for international investors.

In order to handle these challenges optimally, the following international strategies should be considered:

- Natural hedging
- Financial hedging
- Netting and pooling in cooperation with cash management
- As well as several parameters in investment planning

They affect all strategic currency management activities.

8.6.1 Natural Hedging

Natural hedging is an attempt to reduce the gap between revenues and expenditures in a given currency. This leads to a reduction in transaction risk, since the amount in foreign currency that needs to be exchanged is diminished. Natural hedging relies on changes in real economic parameters of a company, while financial hedging works with financial instruments to implement a hedge.

Natural hedging can be done in two different ways. Either by

1) **Adjusting the cost structure to the revenue structure** or by
2) **Adjusting the revenue structure to the cost structure.**

These adjustments are done individually for each currency.

1) Adjusting the cost structure to the revenue structure

- **Procurement policy:**
  With the help of the procurement policy, the cost structure can be adjusted to the revenue structure. This can be done, for example, by relying on **local suppliers**, which generate costs in the local currency. This in turn will cause a decline in the exposure. If Porsche AG obtains its raw materials from the USA, its US-Dollar expenses will go up.

- **Choice of location:**
  An adjustment of the cost structure to the revenue structure can also take place by appropriately choosing locations. The company moves production capacities to countries where they sell vehicles in order to reduce the effect of exchange rate fluctuations. This approach was chosen by BMW AG, which established its production site in the USA among other reasons, because they wanted to increase their US-Dollar expenses in order to reduce currency risk. Personnel, material and distribution costs in US-Dollar go up, the US-Dollar exposure goes down and thus the currency risk of BMW AG with regard to the US-Dollar has been reduced.

  The strategy of the **Completely Knocked Down** (CKD) factory is another possibility to lower the currency exposure by choosing an appropriate location. This strategy, which has its origin in the production of automobiles, involves the export, especially by Western manufacturers, of completely disassembled kits into markets with high import duties. These duties are also the main reason for a CKD factory, since the duties are frequently much lower for partly or completely disassembled final products. An example is the

MAN Lion's Coach, where the body is produced in a plant in Ankara (Turkey) and then exported to Santiago de Querétaro (Mexico). For the local distribution, the body is combined with a locally produced CKD chassis.

In addition, the versions Semi Knocked Down (SKD) or Partly Knocked Down (PKD) also exist. In these versions the vehicles are only partly disassembled.

- **Choice of invoicing currency:**
An export oriented company also has the option of involving suppliers and other contract partners in its currency risk. As an example, a manufacturer can agree with its supplier to pay the goods in the currency which is generated with the help of exports. In that way, the business partners also assume parts of the currency risk. In some countries this concept can even be extended to personnel costs.

Figure 99 once again summarizes the options for aligning the cost structure with the revenue structure.

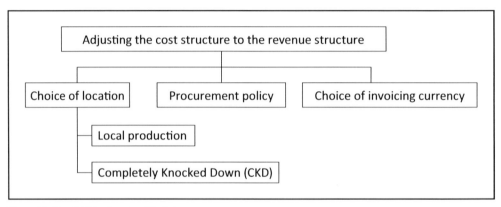

Figure 99: Possibilities for natural hedging
Source: Authors' presentation

2) Adjusting the revenue structure to the cost structure

The second possibility of natural hedging is the adjustment of the revenue structure in line with the cost structure. One example is billing of the export customer in the home currency, since the majority of costs will be in that currency. However, this method requires the granting of additional rebates as the domestic currency appreciates. Otherwise customers are forced to accept higher prices. This in turn should be avoided, given the intense competition in foreign currency areas. While no direct exchange rate losses are reported, the profit margins are under pressure due to the increased use of rebates.

8.6.2 International Cash Management

The currency strategy also plays an important role with regard to cash management operations. Cash management in this context refers to **optimizing cash flows** and **investing cash reserves**.[520]

---

[520] See Keown, A. et al. (2010), p. 792.

8.6.2.1 Techniques to Optimize Cash Flows

Netting: A central element in optimizing cash flows is "netting." The netting of all transactions in a currency (for example on a monthly basis) can lead to a reduction of the administrative and transaction costs involved in the conversion of that currency. A clear advantage of netting is the reduction of general transaction costs, since fewer transactions must be conducted. Netting additionally improves control over the information concerning transactions between subsidiaries. This also facilitates forecasts of the cash flow, since cash transfers only take place at the end of a period.

A distinction is made between the following netting systems:

- Bilateral netting system
- Multilateral netting system

In the case of bilateral netting, netting only takes place between the parent company and a subsidiary or between two subsidiaries. In the case of multilateral netting, the parent company is in touch with several subsidiaries. International automobile manufacturers usually utilize a multilateral netting system, in which all important pieces of information are consolidated and centralized. Since netting is prohibited in a few countries, not all subsidiaries can always be included in the multilateral netting system.[521]

Blocked funds: A further complication that arises in the international trading relations of an automobile manufacturer and its use of foreign currencies is the issue of blocked funds. Blocked funds are liquid assets that cannot be transferred outside a country for legal reasons. These funds are also called trapped cash. Several possible solutions for this problem exist:

1) *Establishment of a Research and Development department, for example in the country with blocked funds:* This department causes costs and thus lowers the blocked funds. At the same time the work of this department helps other subsidiaries to generate new revenues.

2) *Transfer price agreements with the parent company:* Expenses at the subsidiary can be increased with the help of these transfer prices.

3) *Financing of the subsidiary via local banks:* By financing the subsidiary via a local bank instead of the parent company, revenues can be used to repay earlier loans.

8.6.2.2 Investing Excessive Cash Levels

The investment in foreign short-term securities can be rewarding if interest rates are higher than at home. But exchange rate fluctuations also play a central role in this regard. Which instruments of central cash management deserve to be mentioned?

Eurodollar deposits and Treasury Bills: Eurodollar deposits are a frequently used instrument. These are bank deposits denominated in US-Dollar with a term to maturity of up to six months, which are placed with banks outside the USA. Since these deposits are not subject to the minimum reserve requirements of the Federal Reserve Bank, interest payments to depositors can be higher. But the relevance of other currencies has increased in previous years.[522] A further possibility to invest excess cash reserves are Treasury Bills and commercial paper.

---

[521] See Madura, J. (2012), p. 615.
[522] See Madura, J. (2012), p. 618.

Pooling: Pooling can be used to centralize cash management operations and to manage foreign currency exposure. The excess cash reserves of all subsidiaries are combined until needed by one of the subsidiaries.[523]

If all subsidiaries hold the same currency, pooling of these reserves can lead to higher interest rates for the company, since banks are frequently willing to pay more for larger amounts. If, for example, two subsidiaries have excess cash reserves of € 500,000, they would obtain an interest rate of 2.5% per annum from the bank. If instead they chose to pool their reserves and invest € 1 million, the interest rate might go up to 3.5%.

If the subsidiaries hold different currencies, it makes sense to combine the surplus and to convert it into one currency. These pooled funds can once again be invested jointly and thus obtain higher interest rates. The pooling of different currencies can also be done for individual regions. The Asian region for example can be consolidated in Singapore. This means that all Asian surplus funds are converted into Singapore-Dollar (SGD) and are then invested for the short term. For an American automobile manufacturer it would make sense for example to pool all the surplus funds from the Euro zone and to invest them jointly. In that way a subsidiary in the Euro area could also be supplied quickly with a larger amount of money. This strategy is particularly effective if all liquid funds are invested at one globally active bank. In that case transfers are quicker and less expensive.

In addition to pooling, the parent company of the automobile manufacturer can also invest the liquid assets in a currency which is needed by a subsidiary at a later point in time. The due date of the investment should ideally match the point in time when the funds are needed.

Requirements for an effective central cash management: The automobile manufacturers need a well-developed information network. Needed is the timely information about cash positions in every currency at every subsidiary and the relevant interest rates in each currency. With the help of this information, the central cash management operation can determine the liquidity need of each subsidiary and cover it with excess funds from another subsidiary. The improvements in online technologies over the past years have significantly facilitated the task of establishing a multinational communications network for internationally active automobile manufacturers.[524]

Calculating effective interest rates is also a task of the cash management unit. If an automobile manufacturer invests in foreign currencies, not the interest rate per se matters, but rather the effective rate, which also takes into consideration any appreciation or depreciation of the foreign currency in addition to the interest rate. Here again, exchange rate fluctuations play a dominant role.

The theory of interest rate parity implies that the domestic return is equal to the foreign return. Thus it is impossible to obtain an arbitrage profit by investing in foreign currencies. A higher interest rate in one country will be offset by a depreciation of the currency relative to the currency with lower interest rates. The explanation for this effect is provided by the Fisher effect, which describes the relationship between inflation rates, nominal and real interest rates. It states that an increase in the inflation rate will be reflected in proportional increases of nominal interest rates. High nominal interest rates are a reflection of high inflation rates,

---

[523] See Madura, J. (2012), p. 619.
[524] See Madura, J. (2012), p. 620.

which are likely to weaken the currency.[525] Forward rates can be used in an attempt to forecast these developments.

8.6.3 International Investment Planning of Automobile Manufacturers

8.6.3.1 Investment Planning from Different Perspectives

Investment planning depends very much on the perspective. Investment planning from the perspective of the subsidiary can lead to a different result than planning from the perspective of the parent company. The subsidiary of an automobile manufacturer will for example – in contrast to the parent company – not take into consideration the possible effects of exchange rate fluctuations and taxes on the payment streams between parent company and subsidiary. The most important factors which can lead to differences in investment planning between subsidiary and parent company are the following:

- **Differences in taxation:**
  If, for example, the parent company faces a higher tax rate than the subsidiary, an international investment may still be profitable for the subsidiary, while it is already causing a loss for the parent company, since the transfer of profits to the parent company has a negative effect due to the higher tax rate.

- **Limitations on cash transfers:**
  If legal restrictions in the country chosen for the direct investment prevent the transfer of parts of the profit, this negatively influences the assessment of the project from the perspective of the parent company. At the same time, this fact is not relevant for the assessment by the subsidiary. A possible solution for such a problem is to finance these operations via a local bank. In this case, the profits which cannot be transferred abroad can be used to cover the financing costs.

- **High administrative costs:**
  Should a parent company charge high administrative costs for the centrally located management services to its subsidiary, an expense is charged to the subsidiary, while the parent company generates additional revenues. This in turn has an effect on the assessment of an individual project, since the profits are higher for the parent company than for the subsidiary.

- **Exchange rate fluctuations:**
  If profits from an investment are transferred from the subsidiary of an automobile manufacturer to the parent company, they are usually converted into the currency of the parent company. This not only involves transaction costs, but net profits also depend on the current exchange rate. This merely affects the assessment by the parent company. Exchange rate fluctuations are not relevant for the assessment by the subsidiary.

An assessment of international investments in the automotive industry should always be conducted from the perspective of the parent company. This perspective is suitable to determine whether a project increases the company value. An exception is the situation where the subsidiary is not fully owned by one parent company. In this case, the assessment of the

---

[525] See Madura, J. (2012), p. 625.

project should incorporate both perspectives and a compromise should be reached, which makes it possible to increase the value of both companies.[526]

8.6.3.2 Parameters for the Investment Planning of Automobile Manufacturers

Before automobile manufacturers reach a decision in favor of an investment project, a number of important parameters must be assessed. The most important one is the **capital employed.** Capital from the parent company is the biggest source of funds available to support a certain activity. This includes the capital needed to start an activity, the working capital and the financing of inventories, wages and other expenses. At a minimum, this capital is needed until the investment starts to generate sales. Since the capital required for an international direct investment in most cases is needed in foreign currency, it is strongly influenced by the exchange rate. Additional parameters are:

- **Consumer demand**
- **Price**
- **Variable costs**
- **Fixed costs**
- **Project life**
- **Residual value**
- **Expected return**
- **Exchange rates**

Also considered must be political risks such as:

- **Blocking of funds:**
  In some instances local governments prohibit the complete transfer of profits generated from an investment to the parent company which is located abroad. These restrictions affect the net cash flow of a project to the parent company and for that reason should be taken into consideration during investment planning. Since governments frequently change these types of restrictions, only a forecast can be included in the planning process.

- **Tax law:**
  Tax laws vary from country to country and thus the treatment of sales generated by foreign subsidiaries can vary. In some countries a credit for taxes paid abroad is allowed, in other countries it is not. For that reason it is important to incorporate tax effects in the investment planning for an international direct investment.

- **Expropriation:**
  In extreme cases an expropriation of factories and plants is also possible. Either no compensation is paid or the compensation is considerably below the current market value.

- **Additional legal rules:**
  Legislation concerning sales prices, wages and salaries, personnel structures or financing is a risk factor that must be considered before a decision to expand abroad is reached. In that sense it also has an effect on strategic currency management.[527]

---

[526] See Madura, J. (2012), p. 416.
[527] See Keown, A. et al. (2010), p. 795.

8.6.4 Financial Hedging

Financial hedging deals with the management of currency risk. Based on information about current and expected economic developments in the different countries and with reference to historical exchange rate movements, forecasts of future expected exchange rates are generated. On the basis of information about existing and expected payment flows in every currency and for every subsidiary, the exposure concerning exchange rate fluctuations is calculated. The task of currency risk management is the management of that exposure. The following sections deal with the most important issues that must be considered.

8.6.4.1 Exchange Rate Forecasting

International companies need to generate an exchange rate forecast in order to reach decisions concerning the hedging of their receivables and liabilities, their short-term financing and investment needs and their investment planning. The most frequently used techniques are

- **technical**
- **fundamental**
- **market based and**
- **mixed**

approaches. Due to the high volatility of exchange rates it is very hard to generate adequate exchange rate forecasts. In order to assess a forecasting method, it is possible to compare the forecasted value with the current exchange rate. In order to obtain a meaningful assessment, it should be conducted over long time periods. The criteria for such an assessment are precision and tendency and the existence of a systematic bias. When comparing the precision of the forecast for two currencies, relative values must be calculated.[528]

8.6.4.2 Calculating the Exposure

Currency risks can have a negative effect on the financing costs of a company. Financing costs increase with the riskiness of a company. Three types of risk or exposure can be distinguished:

- Transaction exposure
- Economic exposure
- Translation exposure

Transaction exposure: Transaction exposure describes the effect of exchange rate movements on future cash transactions. By capturing all future receivables and liabilities in the different currencies together with the volatilities and correlations among these currencies, the transaction exposure can be calculated. With the help of these data points, the effects of exchange rate fluctuations on sales and costs can be simulated.

Economic exposure: Economic exposure measures the effect of exchange rate movements on all cash flows. A company can calculate that risk by determining the effects of exchange rate fluctuations of all currencies on the cash flows.[529]

---

[528] See Madura, J. (2012), p. 293.
[529] See Madura, J. (2012), p. 324.

Translation exposure: Translation exposure captures the effect of exchange rate fluctuations on the consolidation of balance sheets. In order to determine the translation exposure, profits in every currency must be predicted and then potential exchange rate fluctuations of every currency relative to the home currency must be determined.[530]

8.6.4.3 Exposure Management

Management of transaction exposure: The techniques of futures hedges, forward hedges, money market hedges and currency option hedges are predominantly used in order to manage transaction exposure.

Forwards and futures usually provide the same result, but forwards are more flexible due to their individual contract features and are therefore preferred by major international automobile manufacturers. If interest rate parity is observed, the money market hedge leads to the same result as a forward or a futures contract. The option hedge has the advantage that the option does not have to be exercised in the case of a favorable price development. However, a premium must be paid to obtain that right.

Should the four hedging methods described above be unavailable, additional techniques can be employed to reduce transaction exposure. These are leading, lagging, cross-hedging and currency diversification.[531]

Hedging of liabilities in a foreign currency: Either a futures contract or a forward contract can be utilized for hedging liabilities in a foreign currency. Alternatively it is also possible to use a money market hedge. To do so, the present value of the liability is calculated and converted at the current spot rate. The amount is invested in the money market of the foreign currency. The maturity date of the short-term investment and the liability should correspond. A fourth possibility for the hedging of liabilities is a currency option.

Hedging of receivables in a foreign currency: Forwards, futures and options can also be used to hedge receivables. When using a money market hedge, the company borrows the net present value of the receivable in the relevant foreign currency and converts it at the current spot rate. The due date of the loan and the receivable should be identical so that the money obtained from payment of the receivable can be used to repay the loan. In that way currency risk has been eliminated.

Management of economic exposure:

The economic exposure to exchange rate fluctuations can be reduced by equating the occurrence of receipts and expenditures. To do so, a company needs to determine the dependency of its receipts and expenditures from exchange rate fluctuations. If the receipts relative to the expenditures are more susceptible to exchange rate fluctuations, the company must protect against an appreciation of the home currency, since the unfavorable earnings-related effects exceed the favorable expenditure-related effects. If on the other hand expenditures react more strongly to exchange rate fluctuations than receipts, the company needs to be protected against a devaluation of the home currency.

---

[530] See Keown, A. et al. (2010), p. 787.
[531] See Keown, A. et al. (2010), p. 788.

8.6 International Strategies for Automobile Manufacturers

Management of translation exposure:

Translation exposure can be reduced by selling a forward in the relevant currency. The volume of the forward must be equal in this case to the expected profit of the subsidiary. In case the foreign currency loses in value relative to the home currency, the negative effect on the consolidated profit and loss statement can be compensated via the profit on the forward contract. If the foreign currency appreciates relative to the home currency, selling the forward involves a loss, which is offset by the positive effect on consolidated profits.[532]

---

[532] See Madura, J. (2012), page 381.

9 Maximizing Shareholder Value in the Automotive Sector

9.1 Executive Summary

In the year 2020 maximizing shareholder value will still be the main goal of the strategic financial management of the automobile manufacturers. But our understanding of shareholder value will be revised and a long-term maximization of shareholder value will be sought. These changes are supported by a value change in society, which is reflected already today in the strategies of numerous automobile manufacturers.

The term shareholder value witnessed significant change over time. While Rappaport initially developed a long-term concept, current interpretations focus on the short term. This chapter shows that changes in society in addition to the regulatory framework conditions will be the most important determinants for our future understanding of shareholder value.

As a consequence, shareholder value maximization can also be expected to remain the dominant goal of strategic financial management in the automotive industry in the future. However, this maximization will be subject to the important binding constraint that the value creation is sustainable.[533]

9.2 Definition of Terms

9.2.1 Shareholder Value and Stakeholder Value

Shareholder value in an absolute sense is defined as the "economic value of the equity capital."[534] In addition to this absolute magnitude of shareholder value it is also possible to look at changes in the shareholder value. To do so, the predicted value change during a future period is measured. Value is created with the help of investments that exceed the required cost of capital of the capital market. Shareholder value is thus turned into a measure for planning and assessing the economic value of different lines of business. It is a model for the valuation of investments, as it demonstrates how much cash can be generated during a period of time. All cash flows must be associated with their respective risk levels.

---

[533] We thank Astrid Wagner and Karina Requardt for their support in the topic area of "Shareholder Value." Their work has made the success of this book possible.
[534] See Rappaport, A. (1999), p. 60.

> **Shareholder value following Rappaport**
> is the economic value of the equity of a company. Most important are long-term cash flows of the company. Shareholder value is calculated as follows:
> Shareholder Value = Company value − Debt capital

To determine the company value, the entire market value of the entity must be assessed with the help of one of the available total capital approaches. Closest to the definition of Rappaport is the discounted cash flow method for the determination of company value.[535] Also suitable are the multiplier method (trading and transaction multiples), the trade buyer's approach, the real options approach, the intrinsic value method (based on reproduction or liquidation values) or the book value. The market value must be used for the debt capital.

In the following, the market capitalization of a company at the stock exchange is used to determine the company value. It is calculated as the current market value of a share multiplied by the number of shares outstanding. In contrast to the methods presented above, the market capitalization is not a total capital approach, but rather an equity capital approach. It thus follows:

> The shareholder value of a company is equal to the market capitalization of that company at the stock exchange with the stipulation that long-term cash flows are paramount.

A distinction must be made between the terms shareholder value and stakeholder value. Stakeholders are all groups that have a stake in a company. The stakeholder model has the aim of balancing the interests of the various groups who all contribute to the existence of the company.[536] The most important stakeholders are employees, government, suppliers and customers as well as the public.

> **Stakeholders**
> are persons, "who bear some form of risk as a result of having invested some form of capital, human or financial, something of value, in a firm."[537]

Thus the stakeholder value is the share of the various groups in the total capital value.

9.2.2 Automobile Manufacturers and Automotive Industry

For the following considerations the geographic focus will be on the automobile manufacturers from the traditional markets in the triad. Only one automobile manufacturer – in this case Tata Motors – will be included as a representative from the emerging markets. The automobile manufacturers which are included in the following considerations are summarized graphically in Figure 100.

---

[535] See Rappaport, A. (1999), pp. 8ff.
[536] See Rappaport, A. (1999), p. 8.
[537] See Clarkson, M. (1994), p. 5.

Figure 100: Automobile manufacturers of the triad & Tata as examples for newcomers in the emerging markets
Source: Authors' presentation

9.2.3 Strategic Financial Management

Company financial management has undergone significant change over the past decades. While it initially had a largely administrative function, present day financial management makes a much greater contribution towards shaping the company results. Financial management can be seen as the counterpart to the operative units in a company. It can be broken down into the fields of investments (use of the financial funds) and financing (provision of the financial funds). It coordinates the payment streams and assures the solvency of the company, which is crucial for its existence. In line with general management principles, financial management also consists of the modules planning, organization and controlling of the financial aspects of the company.[538]

Within financial management, a distinction is made between operative financial management and strategic financial management with responsibility for fundamental strategic decisions. The strategic field also includes long-term management. Especially decisions about the capital structure of a company and the allocation of capital are reached here.

The task of the financial management unit of a company is the management of all payment streams. It is responsible for the targeted procurement and use of the financial means of the company, while considering the assurance of sufficient liquidity and the interests of the providers of capital, especially of equity capital.[539]

9.2.4 Sustainability and Sustainable Development

The term "sustainability" and the related term "sustainable development" are based on "The Report of the Brundtland Commission" of the UN World Commission on Environment and Development (WCED).

> Sustainable development "meets the needs of the present without compromising the ability of future generations to meet their own needs."[540]

Sustainability thus has an ecological, economic and social dimension. The foundations for these dimensions are the economic activities of people, social structures in a society, and the global natural resources.[541]

---

[538] See Egger, U.-P. (1995), p. 75; Eilenberger, G. (2003), p. 62; Tebroke, H.-J. and Laurer, T. (2005), p. 20; Wöhe, G. and Döring, U. (2005), pp. 583ff.; Häfner, M. and Hiendlmeier, A. (2008), pp. 174ff.
[539] See Drukarczyk, J., Lobe, S., Schüler, A. (2006), p. 1765; Tebroke, H.-J., Laurer, T. (2005), p. 15.
[540] WCED (1987), p. 54.
[541] See WCED (1987), p. 54; von Hauff, M., Kleine, A. (2009), pp. 17ff.; Grunwald, A., Kopfmüller, J. (2006), p. 11.

These three pillars are also reflected in the mission statement for shaping the future in a sustainable manner of the Study Commission of the 13th German Bundestag. Sustainable development has an ecological, economic and social dimension and all three dimensions must be considered in an integrated and equitable manner. Due to the complex interrelationships between these three dimensions, sustainability policy can be considered to be an aspect of social policy.[542]

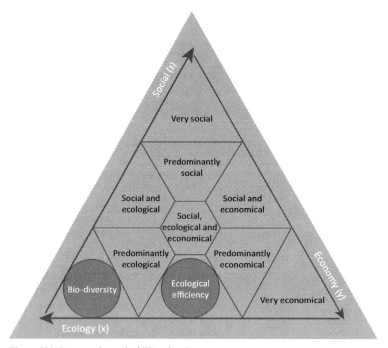

Figure 101: Integrated sustainability triangle
Source: von Hauff, M., Kleine, A. (2009), p. 125

As presented in Figure 101, the completely equal treatment of the three dimensions, which are labeled "social," "ecological" and "economic," leads to the middle of the sustainability triangle. The areas near the middle can be considered as approximations of this state, whereas the corners are extreme positions where one dimension dominates. While "ecological efficiency" for example gives equal weight to the two dimensions ecology and economy, "bio diversity" only stands for the ecological dimension.[543]

In line with this understanding of sustainability, mutually dependent targets can be formulated. One example is equal opportunity, which is initially a social goal. But this social goal immediately has an economic dimension, since it affects economic efficiency.[544] In summary it can be stated that the overarching goal of sustainable development is "the assurance and improvement of ecological, economic and social effectiveness."

---

[542] See Deutscher Bundestag 13th legislative period (1998), pp. 18ff.
[543] See von Hauff, M. and Kleine, A. (2009), pp. 125ff.
[544] See Deutscher Bundestag 13th legislative period (1998), pp. 19ff.

9.2.5 Expectations

The second half of the 20th century was characterized by a strong tendency towards short-term increases of the shareholder value. This is measured with the help of the market capitalization of the company or the dividend yield of the shares. The strategy was reflected in the company goals, the management remuneration and in the behavior of investors. The trend was further supported by external framework conditions such as technological developments and the legal requirements on capital markets.

In this context the term shareholder value maximization was frequently used as a synonym for ruthless and short-sighted behavior of management. However, chasing quick price increases or short-term profits was not a convincing strategy. It resulted in instability in the form of crashes and mass layoffs.[545]

For that reason, a significant trend reversal can be expected in the future. Several current attempts and goals of the automobile manufacturers already show that the long-term and sustainable maximization of the shareholder value has moved up higher on the agenda.

Companies can only be successful over the long term if they cater to the interests of all involved parties and if stakeholder value is generated as well. The fuller consideration of stakeholder value will also enhance value for shareholders in the long run.[546]

> It can be expected that maximizing shareholder value will continue to be the main goal of the strategic financial management of the automobile manufacturers in the year 2020. But our understanding of shareholder value will be revised and a long-term maximization of shareholder value will be sought. These changes are supported by a value change in society, which is reflected already today in the company strategies of numerous automobile manufacturers.

9.3 Maximizing Shareholder Value in the Automotive Industry to Date

For many industrial companies including the automobile manufacturers, the end of World War II constitutes a turning point in their orientation. The focus on the production of military vehicles could be abandoned and the development of civilian vehicles gained in relevance. But the specific focus of the analysis is the more recent past, since it is particularly useful for drawing conclusions about future developments. Both external factors, which can be seen as framework conditions, and company-specific factors, which can be influenced by each automobile manufacturer, must be included in the considerations.

Particularly important external factors are the changes in the framework conditions on the capital markets, which coincided with the spread of digital media towards the close of the 20th century, and the modernization of accounting standards. Both points are analyzed concerning their effects on German automobile manufacturers as well as the German automobile market. Since Germany, because of the size of its sales market and the number of premium and volume manufacturers that are present in this market, can be considered to be representa-

---

[545] See Krüger, W., von Schubert B., Wittberg, V. (2010), pp. 89ff.
[546] See Krüger, W., von Schubert B., Wittberg, V. (2010), pp. 89ff.

tive for the global automotive industry, this market is used as an example. With BMW and Mercedes, two of the most valuable brands globally are from Germany. Five German brands are among the Top-10 of the most valuable automotive brands according to the BrandZ study from 2011 (see Chapter 2).[547]

The company-specific factors are determined by the various aspects of the company strategy. Especially the aspects company targets, growth strategy, management remuneration and corporate social responsibility are analyzed, since they are major determinants of the shareholder value of a company.

9.3.1 Capital Markets

For a company from the automotive industry, the capital market is of particular relevance, since the industry is usually made up of globally active and listed companies, which obtain the majority of their financing from that market. The interaction of the companies with the capital market participants also influences the value of the company and thus directly its shareholder value. A violation of current standards, for example, will lead to a damaged reputation and a loss of investor confidence. Also considered must be fines, even though they may only be of secondary importance.[548]

9.3.1.1 Stock Market Listing

A stock market listing assures the continuous valuation during the trading hours of the exchange. With their buy and sell orders at the various exchanges, the investors provide an assessment of the current and future value of the company. These opinions are in turn available to all other investors via open order books, which are used by electronic trading platforms and lead to very high market transparency.

It is characteristic for the automotive industry that the major producers are publicly listed stock companies with different levels of free float. Figure 102 provides an overview of the free float as well as the dates of the IPO of the automobile manufacturers considered. Only Fiat and BMW were already traded at an exchange prior to World War II. The remaining automobile manufacturers went public in the second half of the 20th century while GM was listed in the year 2010.

In 1949 the longest bull market phase commenced at the New York Stock Exchange (NYSE). It lasted for eight years and drove up quotations in the USA without any major setbacks. Since the turn of the century, however, several global crises have developed. They caused enormous turbulences and price declines at the stock exchanges. Examples are the bursting of the internet bubble in the spring of 2000, the financial and economic crisis in the year 2008 and the sovereign debt crisis in 2011.

These increasing fluctuations also affected the shares of the automobile manufacturers as can be seen in Figure 103. The graph makes it clear that the shares witnessed growing volatility during increasingly shorter time intervals. This represents short-term value creation from higher prices, which is followed in the next step by value destruction in the form of lower prices. The price development allows the conclusion that increases in company value over

---

[547] See WPP BrandZ (2011).
[548] See PwC (2010/2011).

9.3 Maximizing Shareholder Value in the Automotive Industry to Date

the past years were primarily short lived. The price development from 1990 until June 2011 also reveals that the value increases over the entire period as measured by the share price were below 100%. The only exceptions are BMW, Tata and VW. Thus the shareholder value has not even doubled since the year 1990, despite the fact that numerous acquisitions took place in the automotive industry during this period.

Year of initial listing	Company	Home exchange	Free float
1903	Fiat	Borsa Italiana	52.8%
1926	BMW	Germany	50.29%
1949	Toyota	Japan	93.75%
1956	Ford	NYSE	60%
1961	VW	Germany	9.87%
1998	Daimler	Germany	81%
1994	Renault	Paris	58.25%
2004[549]	Tata	Bombay, NSE of India	65.17%
2010	GM	NYSE, Toronto	45.27%
1989	Peugeot	Paris	60.77%

Figure 102: Stock market listing and free float of the automobile manufacturers
Source: Authors' presentation, Data from Bloomberg, Deutsche Börse AG, Fiat S.p.A., NYSE, Renault S.A., Toyota Motors Corporation

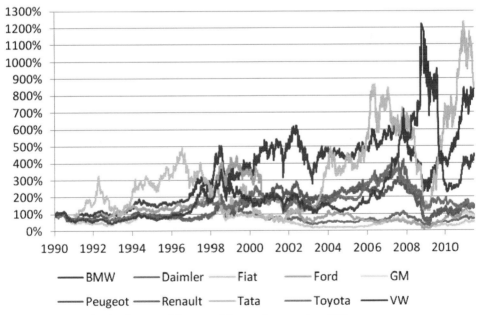

Figure 103: Share price development of the automobile manufacturers since 1990
Source: Authors' presentation, Data from Bloomberg

---

[549] Tata was listed in the USA in 2004. It was already listed in India prior to that date.

9.3.1.2 Availability of Information

The availability of company information changed rapidly with the spread of the internet. If there were still restrictions for investors with regard to relevant information about companies, the internet eliminated these barriers for all publicly available information. Institutional investors can use the standard information systems Bloomberg and Reuters to obtain continuous updates about market developments. Private investors have access to company news via the internet, specialized TV channels and mobile apps in a very transparent and timely fashion.

The need for investor information was also realized by the individual stock exchanges. Diverse systems are on offer, which provide their customers with information about market developments. Several stock exchange operators founded additional company units that deal with data provision and its optimization. An example is "Market Data & Analytics" of Deutsche Börse AG.[550]

In addition to the availability of market information, insights about trading prices and volumes of the individual securities also play a major role. An example which demonstrates the plurality of information about prices and market volumes is the open order book for Xetra at the Frankfurt Stock Exchange. Every investor can obtain free information via the internet. The information contained in the open order book is shown in Figure 104, using the example of ordinary shares of BMW. Interested investors can access the latest prices as well as number, volume and limits of all existing buy and sell orders. Access to the real time transmission of the data and additional details are available for a charge. This information can also be used to derive expectations of market participants.[551]

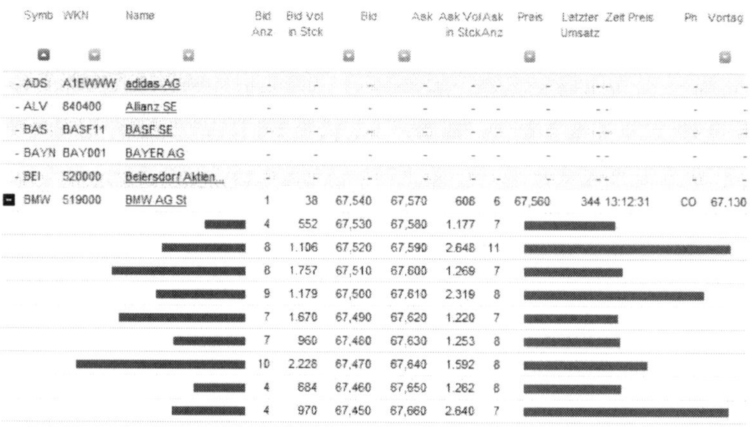

Symb	WKN	Name	Bid Anz	Bid Vol in Stck	Bid	Ask	Ask Vol in Stck	Ask Anz	Preis	Letzter Umsatz	Zeit Preis	Ph	Vortag
- ADS	A1EWWW	adidas AG	-	-	-	-	-	-	-	-	-	-	-
- ALV	840400	Allianz SE	-	-	-	-	-	-	-	-	-	-	-
- BAS	BASF11	BASF SE	-	-	-	-	-	-	-	-	-	-	-
- BAYN	BAY001	BAYER AG	-	-	-	-	-	-	-	-	-	-	-
- BEI	520000	Beiersdorf Aktien...	-	-	-	-	-	-	-	-	-	-	-
BMW	519000	BMW AG St	1	38	67,540	67,570	608	6	67,560	344	13:12:31	CO	67,130
			4	552	67,530	67,580	1.177	7					
			8	1.106	67,520	67,590	2.648	11					
			8	1.757	67,510	67,600	1.269	7					
			9	1.179	67,500	67,610	2.319	8					
			7	1.670	67,490	67,620	1.220	7					
			7	960	67,480	67,630	1.253	8					
			10	2.228	67,470	67,640	1.592	8					
			4	684	67,460	67,650	1.262	8					
			4	970	67,450	67,660	2.640	7					

Figure 104: Open Xetra order book for BMW ordinary shares (ISIN DE0005190003) on June 27, 2011, at 01:29 pm
Source: Deutsche Börse AG

With the complete elimination of floor trading in Frankfurt in May 2011, the electronic trading platform Xetra is now mainly responsible for providing prices based on supply and de-

550 See Deutsche Börse AG.

551 See Xetra Deutsche Börse Group.

mand. It even publishes real time prices free of charge in the internet.[552] And the NYSE as well developed instruments for the speedier dissemination of information. In the sixties the focus was on optimizing the automated transmission of trade and price data. In the following, the NYSE introduced a system which linked other American exchanges in order to improve the dissemination of information.[553] Towards the end of the 20th century it developed a real time ticker and a wireless data system.[554]

As these two examples demonstrate, investors have at their disposal an increasing volume of data about price developments and expectations at increasing speed and timeliness. This enables them to react to new information without delay. It is even possible to immediately cause major price changes by trading large volumes.

These developments also force the listed companies to react. The automobile manufacturers must also react to the increased transparency requirements formulated by investors, lawmakers and supervisory authorities. For the premium segment of an exchange, such as the Prime Standard at the Frankfurt Stock Exchange, companies are required to publish annual and semi-annual financial reports according to IFRS, quarterly financial reports and ad-hoc disclosures both in the local language and in English. Conferences for analysts must be held regularly, a current corporate calendar must be available in the internet and other reporting requirements as defined by securities law must be fulfilled.[555]

In addition to these required publications, the companies also have the opportunity to publish additional items and to enter into an intensive dialogue with their investors. The entire external company communication of the globally active companies of the automotive industry is coordinated these days by so-called investor relations departments. At the same time it has also become easier for advocacy groups to publish their views in different media, especially the internet.

The improved availability of information puts investors and shareholders in the position to better assess the value of a share and to draw conclusions for their own activities. In the case of negative news or an unfavorable outlook, there is a risk that investors quickly turn away from a company. With these reactions they influence the shareholder value of companies. To increase the shareholder value, companies are therefore asked to quickly disseminate positive news and successes in order to increase investor interest in the company.

9.3.1.3 Securities Transactions

Securities trading used to take place in the past via the different stock exchanges which were established after World War II. Traders and brokers met in floor trading and personally conducted their business at the exchange. Over time trading over the telephone and the computer was added. For brokers and traders this offered the additional advantage of communications and the transfer of securities outside the premises of the exchange. Later on, fully automated trading platforms were added. Examples of this global development are the introduction of

---

[552] See Xetra Deutsche Börse Group.
[553] See NYSE.
[554] See NYSE.
[555] See Deutsche Börse AG (2008).

SETS at the London Stock Exchange in 1986,[556] of Xetra at the Frankfurt Stock Exchange in 1997[557] and NYSE Direct+® at the NYSE.[558] Today these fully automated trading platforms manage almost all securities transactions. Further changes in securities trading were ushered in by the accelerating spread of internet platforms, which facilitate off-market trading. As a result of these technological developments, orders are presently executed within seconds and the overall trading volume has gone up significantly.

9.3.2 Accounting Standards

Caused by the increasing connectedness of markets and the ascent of national companies to the status of global players, it is also attempted to standardize the principles of accounting standards. The aim is to facilitate the comparison of published information by companies with headquarters in different countries.

The following comparison of two different accounting standards is used to demonstrate the different effects on the company value. The comparison deals with the German commercial code HGB as a national regulation and IFRS as an international accounting standard for Europe.

The German commercial code HGB represents cautious accounting rules which focus on the protection of the creditor, while IFRS stresses the current market value. Thus the HGB is closer to a stakeholder orientation, while IFRS puts a focus on the interests of the owners. The main valuation regulations of HGB and IFRS are compared in Figure 105.

	HGB	IFRS
Valuation principle	Principle of prudence	Fair value
Principle for subsequent measurement	(Amortized) acquisition costs/cost of production as maximum value	Choice between (amortized) acquisition cost/cost of production model and re-valuation method[559]
Impairments	Lowest value principle[560]	Obtainable amount for fixed assets, lowest value principle for current assets
Maximum amount of value increase	(Amortized) acquisition costs/cost of production [561]	(Amortized) acquisition costs/cost of production or the fair value[562]
Depreciation schedule	Frequently tax law is used as guidance	Period of economic use as guidance

Figure 105: Central differences in the valuation of assets according to HGB and IFRS
Source: Authors' presentation, based on the legal texts

---

[556] See London Stock Exchange.
[557] See Deutsche Börse AG (2008).
[558] See NYSE.
[559] This only holds for fixed assets. For current assets the lower value of acquisition costs/costs of production and net selling value must be used.
[560] For current assets the strict lowest value principle is in effect. An impairment loss on fixed assets is only required if the value impairment is permanent. (§253 (III and IV), HGB).
[561] An exception is acquired goodwill (§253, (Vii), HGB).
[562] Depending on the principle chosen for subsequent measurement.

9.3.2.1 National Accounting Standards – The Example HGB

Concerning the effects of accounting standards on the shareholder value, the valuation principles of §252 and §253 HGB are particularly relevant. The following statements only refer to the current version (2011) of the HGB. The situation prior to the introduction of the Accounting Modernization Act BilMoG is not analyzed.

The principle of prudence is a central regulation of the HGB which is found in §252 (IV). It is of major importance and consists of the realization principle and the imparity principle.

Expected losses and gains are not treated equally in the HGB. Based on the realization principle profits can only be shown once they have been realized. Expected profits are not included in the balance sheet. However, expected losses must be quantified and included in the annual accounts as soon as they are known.

An additional pillar of the HGB is the upper limit for acquisition and production costs. According to §253 (I) of the HGB, the amortized acquisition or production costs constitute the maximum value for the valuation of assets in later periods. Increases in value are not taken into consideration in the accounting standards of the HGB. At the same time, reductions in value must be captured via the scheduled depreciation if they are of a permanent nature (§253(III) HGB) or if they relate to current assets (§253 (IV) HGB). These approaches support the setting up of hidden reserves, which can serve as a buffer in times of declining market values.

The balance sheet according to HGB thus does not reveal the true value of the assets on the balance sheet date, but a value development that has been smoothed to the upside. This means that value increases that are short-term and temporary are not shown on the balance sheet. Under the assumption that the shareholder value is also linked to the balance sheet, for example the development of the equity capital of a company, these principles imply a lower volatility of the shareholder value. They counter attempts at short-term maximization.

However, for the automobile manufacturers in Germany accounting according to HGB is relevant predominantly for the assessment of the tax burden. As companies with a capital market orientation, which also attract international investors, they focus more on international accounting standards. Since the financial year 2005, companies are required to provide financial statements in line with IFRS, if they are companies with a capital market orientation domiciled in the EU.[563]

9.3.2.2 International Accounting Standards – The Example IFRS

The valuation of assets according to IFRS depends on the type of asset. IFRS, unlike the HGB, does not formulate general rules which can be used to subsume various issues. Instead rules for specific cases are formulated. As an example, inventories must be valued according to IAS 2, tangible assets according to IAS 16, intangible assets according to IAS 38, financial instruments according to IAS 39 and real estate held as investment property according to IAS 40. For the treatment of impairments a separate standard exists, namely IAS 36.[564] In the following the valuation of inventories, tangible assets and intangible assets will be considered in more detail.

---

[563] See regulation (EC) No. 1606/2002 of the European Parliament and the des European Council, (2002), pp. 1–2.
[564] See regulation (EC) No. 1126/2008 of the European Commission (2008).

For inventories as the most important component of current assets, the strict lowest value principle is applicable as in the case of the HGB. The lower of cost and net realizable value must be used (IAS 2.9).

In contrast there are significant differences to the HGB with regard to the subsequent valuation of tangible assets. IAS 16.29 provides a choice between the cost model (IAS 16.30) and the revaluation model (IAS 16.31). First, the HGB does not offer a choice at this point and second, the HGB does not provide the option of a similar revaluation model. A central component of the revaluation model is the possibility to take into account valuation increases that have not yet been realized. For the accounting figures of a company this may mean increased volatility of asset values as a result of current market developments. As a consequence of the revaluation, unrealized gains in value are included on the balance sheet and with it the risk that these are only temporary.

According to IAS 38, intangible assets must be reported at acquisition/production costs. This is true both for acquired as well as for internally generated intangible assets which fulfill the definitions of IAS 38.10 and following. According to IFRS, recognition as an expense in the period in which it was incurred is only required if the assets do not fulfill these criteria (IAS 38.10). In comparison, the HGB does not allow capitalization of internally generated intangible assets (§255 (2a) HGB). As a consequence, profits for the IFRS financial statements and asset values can be higher in comparison to financial statements which are based on the HGB. Over the long term, these differences are equilibrated via depreciation of the assets. The brand value in addition to patents and licenses is a major immaterial asset for automobile manufacturers (also see Chapter 2).

9.3.3 Company Strategy

The shareholder value orientation of management is reflected in the company strategy, which includes the company goals, the growth strategy, the remuneration of management and the corporate social responsibility of the company.

9.3.3.1 Company Goals

The goals pursued by a company can be economic, ethical, social and political in nature. The goal of self-preservation is considered to be the most important company goal in the automotive industry as well. To reach this goal, liquidity must be maintained, business must be profitable and growth must be generated. Thus the goal of self-preservation can be broken down in financial targets, performance targets and operative targets as shown in Figure 106. Among the performance targets is also the creation of shareholder value. Additionally qualitative company goals can be considered in the context of the shareholder value approach.[565]

Almost all automobile manufacturers analyzed in this chapter added social considerations in addition to economic targets to their company goals already at the beginning of this millennium. Figure 107 provides an overview of the economic and social goals of the automobile manufacturers.[566]

---

[565] See Düsterlho von, J.-E. (2003), pp. 14ff.; Brunner, M. (2006), p. 138; Haunerdinger, M., Probst, H.-J. (2008), pp. 17–18.

[566] For Fiat, Peugeot and Tata this information has not been made public to date.

9.3 Maximizing Shareholder Value in the Automotive Industry to Date

Figure 106: Goal of self preservation
Source: Authors' presentation, based on Haunerdinger, M. (2008), pp. 17ff.

Automobile manufacturer	Economic goals	Social goals
BMW	- Increase sales in order to obtain economies of scale (1 million vehicles) - Increase return on sales - Increase company value for the shareholders	- Save resources (environmentally conscious products and materials, recycling)
DaimlerChrysler	- Become the number one in the world of automobile manufacturing - Increase profitability (make use of synergies among the various group brands)	- Sustainable environmental protection (relates to all segments of the group and the complete product life cycle) - Increase attractiveness for employees - Improve training opportunities
Ford	- Strengthening of the group brands (higher capacity utilization) - Above average performance of the share price	- Strengthen ties with related parties (with employees, suppliers, dealerships, customers, investors, society in general)
GM	- Increase company value (increase sales figures and market share, increase profitability) - Minimum return on the capital employed of 12%	- Integrity vis-à-vis employees, business partners and society - Protection of natural resources and the environment

Renault	- By 2010: Global player (world market share of 10%) by
	   - Lowering cost
	   - Speeding up of processes
	   - Improvements of quality
	   - Increased flexibility
	- Meet expectations of shareholders
	- Return on shareholder capital of 11%
		- Assume ecological responsibility (production process and entire product life cycle, keep impact on environment from production sites as low as possible)

Automobile manufacturer	Economic goals	Social goals
Toyota	- Increased competitiveness (cost positions, increase sales) - Internationalization (global distribution, gaining of market share outside the home market of Eastern Asia)	- Company activities in line with the demands of society - Ecological responsibility - Meet customer demands - Good relations with employees (trust and respect)
VW	- Until 2006: automobile sales of 6 million units - By 2018: World market leader - Return on equity of 9% - Increase of company value (via increase of operative result)	- Corporate social responsibility (Responsibility for sustainable social and ecological viability of the actions of the company and its representatives, namely ecological compatibility of products and services, environmental protection in all company activities)

Figure 107: Economic and social goals of the automobile manufacturers
Source: Authors' presentation, based on Intveen, C. (2004), pp. 76ff.

Maximizing shareholder value is stressed among the company goals in addition to first social and ecological targets.

9.3.3.2 Growth Strategy

Innovative and suitable products and services are the basis for value enhancement.[567] Companies can achieve growth by either adapting their offering of existing and new products or by tackling existing and new markets. The four different growth strategies are listed again in Figure 108.[568]

Markets \ Products	Existing	New
Existing	Market penetration	Product expansion
New	Market expansion	Diversification

Figure 108: Product market matrix
Source: Macharzina, K., Wolf, J. (2010), p. 339

In the context of the *market penetration strategy*, traditional markets are served with existing products. This strategy is for the most part unavailable in the triad countries, since the sales markets for automobiles are already saturated. A relevant indication is the number of new registrations of passenger cars, which has been stagnant at a low level over the past years. Until the end of the seventies, the automobile market in Germany was still a classical seller market. Demand in some cases exceeded the production capacity of the companies.[569] But for many years now, automobile manufacturers have only been able to increase their market share in the major sales markets by luring away customers from the competition.

---

[567] See Rappaport, A. (1999), p. 12.
[568] See Macharzina, K., Wolf, J. (2010), p. 339.
[569] See Becker, H. (2007), pp. 13–14.

The aim of the *product expansion strategy* is to sell products on already existing markets. In the past, the automobile manufacturers improved the technological performance and the safety of the vehicles, exclusive features were introduced on the market and the design of the body was adapted. With these product innovations it was possible to increase the market share in the industrialized countries. Today the focus is on more efficient engines and vehicles that are as light as possible, in order to reduce fuel consumption and at the same time satisfy the need for safety and comfort of the customers.

With the *market expansion strategy* the automobile manufacturers aim at selling their existing products in new markets. As an example, German automobile manufacturers have expanded their distribution networks in the past to include a large number of foreign markets.

The *diversification strategy* meanwhile aims at the introduction of new products in new markets. Examples are specific long versions of selected vehicle types for the Chinese market.[570]

The *volume strategy* supplements the product market matrix. It aims at generating value by making use of economies of scale and generating cost synergies. As in the case of the product market matrix it is important to obtain a market share that is as high as possible in the old and new sales markets, since only mass production assures economies of scale.[571] Figure 109 lists M&A transactions as the third possible approach to achieve economies of scale.

Figure 109: Volume strategy
Source: Becker, H. (2007), pp. 194ff.

Especially in the automotive industry there are numerous examples from the past where shareholder value was destroyed as a result of acquisitions. The failed merger between Daimler and Chrysler as well as the takeover of Rover by BMW can be considered as prominent examples of company takeovers, which ultimately did not have a positive effect on shareholder value.

9.3.3.3 Management Remuneration

In the opinion of Rappaport, members of the management board and other executives at the company level are responsible for maximizing the return for the owners in the form of dividends and share price advances. To reach this goal, remuneration systems must be tied to

---

[570] See Focus online (2010).
[571] See Becker, H. (2007), pp. 194ff.

performance standards. The aim is to provide financial incentives to management at the group level and to managers with operative responsibility. The difficult part is the performance assessment. Rappaport suggests a combination of short-term performance assessment and long-term value from a transaction.[572]

The remuneration systems of many companies have included the component "long term incentives" for a number of years, for example in the form of equity options. The minimum holding period for equity options used to be two years in Germany. But during the financial crisis the holding period was extended to obtain an assessment basis that covers several years and an element of sustainability in variable compensation.[573] The effects of the regulation on the remuneration policies of the automobile manufacturers is clarified by a comparison of the annual reports of Volkswagen AG from the years 2008 and 2010 as presented in Figure 110.

Annual report 2008 (prior to the regulation)	Annual report 2010 (following the regulation)
- **Additional annual variable amount paid:** Based on the result obtained and the economic situation of the company as well as *annually recurring* components that are tied to the business success of the company. - **Variable remuneration components with long-term incentive:** Issue of convertible bonds. Can be converted *for the first time following a holding period of 24 months*	- **Bonus:** Based on the results achieved and the economic situation of the company *with regard to the last two years* - **Long Term Incentives:** Since 2010 reaching the goals of the Strategy 2018 including *a consideration of the past four business years* is the relevant standard

Figure 110: Annual reports of VW AG following the regulation of management remuneration
Source: Authors' presentation based on the annual reports of Volkswagen AG 2008/2010

9.3.3.4 Corporate Social Responsibility

Corporate social responsibility refers to the willingness of corporations to assume responsibility for societal developments in the areas of ecology and social development. Corporate responsibility meanwhile comprises the four elements capital, employees, society and environment. An internal and an external dimension can be distinguished in corporate social responsibility. The internal aspect focuses on employees. Examples are additional training for employees or the introduction of a corporate health management plan. The external dimension combines all other stakeholders, including the local community, suppliers, customers and public authorities.[574] Corporate social responsibility is thus closely linked to the creation of shareholder value. Efficient market mechanisms are in place, which assure that decisions made by top management with the aim of increasing shareholder value also have effects that are desirable for society.[575] By now the automobile manufacturers also publish corporate social responsibility reports on their homepages in order to raise awareness for their activities.

---

[572] See Rappaport, A. (1999), pp. 133–134.
[573] See Koch, R., Raible, K.-F., Stadtmann, G. (2011), pp. 10ff.
[574] See Jonker, J., Stark, W., Tewes, S. (2011), p. 5.
[575] See Rappaport, A. (1999), p. 6.

Figure 111 provides examples of specific corporate social responsibility projects of selected automobile manufacturers in the triad.

Automobile manufacturer	CSR reports on homepage	Examples for specific corporate social responsibility projects and initiatives
BMW	✓	Age-adequate workplace (production), Educational activities for children and youth
Daimler	✓	Traffic education, Art initiatives, Corporate volunteering initiatives, CO_2-emissions in production
Fiat	✓	Training for young persons, Investment in local communities, Donations, Water use
Ford	✓	Donations, Volunteering, Purchasing from minorities/women-owned businesses, Clean-up of contaminated sites
GM	✓	Donations (natural disasters, deserving organizations), Diversity of workforce
Peugeot	✓	Support of nonprofit organizations, Equal opportunity (career)
Renault	✓	Traffic education and training for children, teenagers and young drivers, Diversity of workforce, Support of young talent from all countries.
Tata	✓	Charity runs, Encouraging staff to participate in various social activities, Support of societal causes (help for the homeless, for example)
Toyota	✓	AIDS package of measures for employees, Support of suppliers, Environmental protection
VW	✓	Nature projects, Water management, Local school program, Drug prevention

Figure 111: Examples of specific CSR projects
Source: Authors' presentation, information taken from the homepages of the respective companies

9.4 Maximizing Shareholder Value in the Automotive Industry in the Year 2020

9.4.1 Capital Markets

The increasing globalization, company networks in the form of global strategic alliances as well as comprehensive investments in the entire value chain mean that automobile manufacturers will continue to depend on the capital market as a major source of financing in the year 2020. But some of the existing framework conditions on the capital markets must be overcome in order to support the aim of maximizing the shareholder value over the long term and in a sustainable fashion. The increasing connectedness of the markets also offers new opportunities for the companies as globally accepted values and norms are established and as a consequence competitive advantages are obtained.

9.4.1.1 Stock Market Listing

The listing on a stock exchange will continue to constitute a decisive source of financing in the year 2020 for all globally active automobile manufacturers. Therefore an increased delisting of the automobile manufacturers should not be expected. Instead it is more likely that new automobile manufacturers and mobility providers will also make use of a stock market listing.

A stock market listing can also have an image function in addition to providing sources of financing. The stock market listing gives companies the opportunity to be included in an index and to benefit from its image. In addition to traditional industry and country indexes, sustainability indexes have been in existence for a number of years. These indexes list companies that act in a sustainable fashion according to defined criteria.

The inclusion in a sustainability index can lead to an improved reputation of the company among stakeholders and have a positive effect on competitiveness. This can be used to present evidence in support of sustainable company goals, which may enable a long-term increase in shareholder value. At the same time there is a risk that halfhearted actions hurt the credibility and authenticity of the company.[576]

In the Dow Jones Sustainability Index (DJSI) World, which was introduced in 1999, BMW, Fiat and Volkswagen were listed as examples from the automotive industry in the year 2011.[577] As long as the idea of alternative mobility concepts continues to gain in importance, the introduction of a stock market index for the sector of "sustainable mobility" appears possible as well.

In addition to the automobile manufacturers, investors also focus on the topic of sustainable development. At the moment this type of investor is still in the minority and active in a niche market. But it is likely that this group will grow in the future. The driving force is the ongoing value change in society. An example is the changed energy policy in Germany as a result of increasing demands from society.

9.4.1.2 Information Management

The plurality and availability of information will continue to increase in the future. This trend was picked up, for example, by the data provider Bloomberg with the introduction of a smartphone application which supplies the user with company data around the clock via the mobile internet.

Future challenges will relate to the management and selection of available information. Numerous investors are already using so-called business intelligence solutions in order to identify information which is relevant for decision making among the vast amount of available data. These software packages help among other uses in the process of data selection, data presentation and preparation of decisions. For the automobile manufacturers as providers of information the biggest challenge is to find new approaches in the competitive process and to find the relevant recipients for their messages. The topic of social media will be of increasing

---

[576] See Hofmann, M. (2011).
[577] See Dow Jones Sustainability Indices (2011) for the listed companies.

relevance in this regard. This trend is observable already today with the increase of company pages in social networks.

9.4.1.3 Securities Transactions

The automation of securities transactions will continue to increase in the coming years. Intelligent computer-aided programs will automatically trigger buy or sell orders when observing certain price movements. A simple example for this development that exists already today is the limit order. For example stop-buy limits, stop-loss limits or "One Cancels the Other Orders" can be placed. When the listed trigger is reached, the (limit) orders are executed.

The trading hours of the exchange will witness further changes. Caused by the increased links among the stock market companies and the increasing globalization, a development towards longer trading hours appears very likely. First indications are given by post- and pre-trading phases at the Frankfurt Stock Exchange.

9.4.2 Accounting Standards

International accounting standards already dominate in the automotive industry with its strong ties to the capital markets. As a result of the increasing globalization, this trend will continue and national regulations will lose further ground.

By the year 2020 it cannot be expected that the fair value approach, which is dominant in the Anglo-American regions, will be abandoned. This development can be seen for example in the changes of the HGB which were introduced by the German Act to Modernize Accounting Law. It reflects convergence with the IFRS and the fair value principle.[578] Whether such a development supports the sustainable maximization of shareholder value will depend on the future interpretation of the balance sheet with regard to shareholder value expectations. Under the assumption that the short-term appreciation of asset values gives rise to demands for shareholder value increases, there is a danger that the pursuit of short-term shareholder value maximization will continue.

9.4.3 Company Strategy

9.4.3.1 Company Targets

Company targets will increasingly include major societal factors in addition to purely economic considerations.[579] In the future, this development can have a positive influence on a long-term and sustainable approach for the maximization of the shareholder value. In the current company targets of the automobile manufacturers, an orientation along the three dimensions of sustainability is already apparent. Figure 112 provides an overview of the company targets of the automobile manufacturers from the year 2011.[580]

---

[578] See KPMG (2011).
[579] See Jonker, J., Stark, W., Tewes, S. (2011), p. 27.
[580] No public information is provided by GM on this issue.

| Automobile manufacturer | Company goals | Orientation along the three dimensions of sustainability |||
		Ecology	Economy	Social
BMW	✓ Leading provider of premium products and premium services for individual mobility	✓ Responsibility for the product ✓ Group-wide environmental protection	✓ Sustainability as an element to create value ✓ Risk management ✓ Corporate governance and compliance	✓ Commitment for society ✓ Responsibility for workforce ✓ Sustainability as an element of company responsibility
Daimler	✓ Continued profitable growth and increased company value ✓ To be among the leading automobile companies globally	✓ Become the leader in sustainable drive technologies with pioneering technologies	✓ Continued profitable growth and increases in company value	✓ Support of education, science, environment, culture, sports and health ✓ Support of charitable projects ✓ Support during natural disasters ✓ Support diversity of the workforce in a sustainable manner
Fiat	✓ Best-in-class performance	✓ Responsibility for the environment (leading position with regard to the lowest CO_2 emissions)	✓ Become a global player ✓ Optimize capacity utilization and investments ✓ Create synergies	✓ Leadership as a noble cause to enrich the life of others
Ford	✓ Be the global leader for products and services in the automotive sector	✓ Develop environmentally friendly products and processes	✓ Maximum profitability ✓ Improving the balance sheet ✓ Innovative products that are in demand and valued by customers	✓ Cooperation in global teams

9.4 Maximizing Shareholder Value in the Automotive Industry in the Year 2020

Automobile manufacturer	Company goals	Orientation along the three dimensions of sustainability		
		Ecology	Economy	Social
Peugeot	✓ Be one step ahead with products and services ✓ Become a global player ✓ Become the benchmark for efficiency ✓ Act responsibly	✓ Produce automobiles with an environmental conscience	✓ Growth/increase market share ✓ Capacity utilization	✓ Role in society as a responsible company ✓ Personal development and growth
Renault	✓ Renault – 2016 – Drive the Change	✓ Provide access to sustainable mobility for everybody	✓ Assure growth ✓ Generate free cash flow (minimum of € 2 billion cumulative) ✓ Sales of more than 3 million vehicles in 2013	✓ Not apparent
Tata	✓ To be the best in India – with regard to operations, products, our value system – and in the future also outside India	✓ To preserve and regenerate the environment	✓ International growth via excellency and innovation	✓ Maintain balance with civil society
Toyota	✓ Zero emissions	✓ Sustainable models, trend-setting technologies (hybrids) ✓ Adjust product life cycle to the environmental effects (sustainable production, recycling)	✓ Continuous improvement (Kaizen) ✓ Continue growth in harmony with global society	✓ Respect for humans, health and safety of the employees ✓ Responsibility towards society (projects from the social sphere, education, research and science as well as charitable projects)

Automobile manufacturer	Company goals	Orientation along the three dimensions of sustainability		
		Ecology	Economy	Social
VW	✓ Global economic and ecological lead among automobile companies ✓ By 2018 become the most successful and fascinating automobile company globally	✓ Innovation and technologies with environmentally conscious direction	✓ Return on sales before taxes of at least 8% ✓ Sales in excess of 10 million vehicles annually ✓ Above average participation in the development of the growth markets	✓ Be a top employer

Figure 112: Comparison of the company goals with a focus on the sustainability dimensions
Source: Authors' presentation, information taken from the homepages of the respective companies

The fact that the topic of sustainability is currently given more weight by both companies and investors is also confirmed by a study of *Dachverband der kritischen Aktionärinnen und Aktionäre*, an association that takes a critical look at capital markets. At the same time, the study identifies enormous future challenges for the companies. As an example, the association demands that BMW needs to show a greater awareness for the topic of sustainability in the future.[581]

9.4.3.2 Growth Strategy

The *market penetration strategy* will be of little relevance for the automobile manufacturers since the market is largely saturated. Some companies will be squeezed out of the market and the concentration among manufacturers will increase. As a consequence, the market shares are redistributed among the remaining companies, which would witness growth as a result.[582] By focusing on innovations, the automobile manufacturers will achieve growth via the *product expansion strategy*. Sustainable technologies to save energy such as electric vehicles, light vehicles or automobiles with hybrid drive will play a larger role.[583] The new business fields for services in the area of sustainable mobility concepts – such as comprehensive car sharing offerings – will gain in relevance not only in large cities.

The *market expansion* will continue to focus on the booming emerging markets, where the biggest opportunities for automobile sales are seen. Growth rates will continue to be high especially in the BRIC countries. The focus will continue to be on China. For the next three

---

[581] See Hofielen, G. (2010), pp. 1ff.
[582] See Becker, H. (2007), pp. 139ff.
[583] See Rick, H., McGuckin, T., Kuhnert, F., Breen, D., McCarthy, P. (2011), pp. 1ff.

9.4 Maximizing Shareholder Value in the Automotive Industry in the Year 2020

years until 2015, a continuation of double digit growth can be expected. The basis for this can be seen in the established growth regions in the East, but also in the developing regions of the West and in the central parts of the country. With the further development of the infrastructure in these parts of the country, the demand for automobiles will also grow.[584] In these markets, which have not been fully captured yet, additional opportunities for *diversification* will also be available (see Chapter 5).

9.4.3.3 Management Remuneration

Effective incentive systems must be aligned with the long-term success of the company and reward sustainable leadership. Managers should be required to bear some of the losses in the case of unfavorable developments and liability insurance for managers should include an obligatory deductible.[585]

There are several possibilities to establish sustainable incentive systems:

- Bonus payments
- Long term incentives[586]
- Pre-control variables

Bonus payments
According to Rappaport, annual bonus payments could be based on the performance over the past three to five years. A different approach would be to move the bonus payments back in time. In that case they would be based on long-term value creation, because they depend on the future performance. A general limitation of bonus payments should not be considered, since it could negatively affect the motivation of high performers.[587]

Long term incentives
Equity options reward top management for a superior performance. Their exercise price is based on the index of a comparable company or the market. Owners of equity options are given an opportunity, but a negative performance does not have consequences. Equity options are issued at the company level, since managers with operative responsibilities are not in a position to influence the share price. The minimum holding period for equity options before they can be exercised usually amounts to several years.

Pre-control variables
Pre-control variables allow an assessment of every business transaction. Pre-control variables are determined for the sustainable value of an investment and then assessed. Examples of pre-control variables are key figures about customer satisfaction, customer loyalty or productivity improvements.[588]

---

[584] See Rick, H., McGuckin, T., Kuhnert, F., Breen, D., McCarthy, P. (2011), pp. 1ff.
[585] See stern.de (2009).
[586] At this point we are only concerned with equity options.
[587] See Rappaport, A. (1999), pp. 157–158.
[588] See Rappaport, A. (1999), pp. 134ff.

9.4.3.4 Corporate Social Responsibility

The future shareholder value of the individual automobile manufacturers will largely depend on the ability of the companies to realize their goals with regard to sustainability. One reason for that could be a general value change towards more sustainability, which is caused among others by environmental catastrophes. Stakeholders have several possibilities to evaluate the implementation.

Measuring the ecological performance can be done with the help of the average CO_2 emission of the fleet. In the first half of 2010, Fiat, Toyota and Peugeot were at the top with the lowest CO_2 emissions of their vehicles.[589] Further sustainable development key performance indicators in the automotive industry are the group-wide use of energy and emissions of greenhouse gases in production.[590] In the carbon disclosure project, emissions of greenhouse gases of organizations are recorded and published.[591]

Rating agencies in the segment of sustainable investing can provide additional information about the sense of responsibility of companies.

---

[589] See Haynes, P., Hale, P.(2010), pp. 1ff.
[590] See Bundesministerium für Umwelt, Naturschutz und Reaktorsicherheit (2009).
[591] See Carbon Disclosure Project (2011).

10 Automotive Industry or Mobility Industry in the Year 2020

The automotive industry has witnessed dramatic change over the past years.[592] The speed of the expected monumental challenges will accelerate considerably until the year 2020 and the complexity, especially for the automobile manufacturers, will increase significantly. The heightened environmental awareness and changing customer needs constitute the main pillars. The question "What is the state of the automotive industry in the year 2020?" must be rephrased in our opinion as follows: "What is the state of the mobility industry in the year 2020?"

What will be the development of the global economies and thus of the automobile markets? Which reactions of the manufacturers are possible or required in anticipation of these changes? What are the products of the future? Which changes in the business models, the automotive value chain and the business processes are necessary preconditions for the successful positioning in the year 2020?

The unique challenge for the automobile manufacturers lies in the fact that their longstanding and strong relationships with suppliers and dealerships are now under attack from new market participants, who are active across industries in the fields of electric mobility, networked vehicles and novel mobility concepts.

For the companies it is essential to realize the upcoming trends and to react flexibly and in an innovative fashion. This is the only way to cope with the new challenges and at the same time capture the opportunities which are provided by the transformation towards the new mobility industry in the year 2020. Based on the previous chapters, we have derived the following ten trends for the year 2020:

1. Traditional brands will disappear – Local brands will be established
2. Regulations for ecology and sustainability provide the framework conditions
3. New mobility demands of the customers gain in importance
4. New mobility providers are successful on the market
5. The networked vehicle will become an information and communication instrument
6. Strategic alliances are key to obtaining a competitive advantage
7. Triad was yesterday, BRIC is today and emerging markets will be tomorrow
8. Tier-2 and tier-3 automotive suppliers will look for a new orientation
9. Electromobility – there is more than one way forward
10. The automobile manufacturers create a global brand image

---

[592] We follow Ernst & Young and F.A.Z.-Institut für Management-, Markt- und Medieninformationen with the megatrends in the automobile industry listed below. (See Ernst & Young and F.A.Z.-Institut für Management-, Markt- und Medieninformationen (2011): Acht Megatrends in der Automobilbranche).

10.1 Traditional Brands will Disappear – Local Brands will be Established

Over the past 40 years the market for automobile manufacturers has been characterized by an ongoing trend towards consolidation. Since the structural problems in the automobile sector especially in Europa, the US and Japan are severe, a further reduction in traditional brands can be expected over the long term. With regard to individual market participants, this will certainly mean that brands such as Saab, Vauxhall or Volvo are likely to disappear from the market. It cannot be ruled out that in a few years three or four global volume manufacturers will dominate the mass market. Volkswagen, Toyota, Ford and GM are currently in the best position to achieve this domination. The premium segment will continue to offer considerable potential for the two German manufacturers BMW and Daimler. Thanks to the strength of their brand and the newly found financial strength, they are in an excellent position.

New and possibly also local manufacturers see the biggest potential for brand positioning in the field of electromobility as well as in the up and coming emerging markets in Latin America, Asia and Eastern Europe.

10.2 Regulations in Support of Ecology and Sustainability Provide the Framework Conditions

Three factors are relevant for the mobility of the future: resource conservation, environmental compatibility and safety. Under pressure from legislators, the automobile manufacturers will be forced to focus on vehicles that are environmentally friendly and safe both in manufacturing and during their use. They will also be required to sell vehicles that are free of emissions.

Restrictions and incentives will play an important role for customers in the decision which automobile to buy and how to use it. It is possible that a toll will be charged for downtown areas or for road use in general. But it is also conceivable that the purchase of a zero-emissions vehicle is made more attractive via discounts.

10.3 New Mobility Demands of the Customers Gain in Importance

The global trend towards urbanization will likely convince people in industrialized countries to look for alternatives to the automobile. The demands on mobility from people who live in industrialized countries are very different from the ones made by people in emerging markets. In the emerging markets people want to own a vehicle and use it for transportation. But it is unlikely that the development of the infrastructure will keep pace with the rapid increase in the number of vehicles.

As different as the mobility demands in the industrialized countries and in emerging economies may be, they result in a *common* conclusion for the automobile manufacturers: They must expand their presence in the various vehicle segments and at the same time develop integrated mobility concepts and car sharing programs.

10.4 New Mobility Providers are Successful on the Market

New customer needs coupled with technological progress imply that new providers will enter the market. Their offerings include car sharing and integrated mobility services, use-based "black box" insurance policies, which are priced according to the actual vehicle use determined in real time and new entertainment systems for the automobile.

With these new business models, previous industry outsiders will obtain access to the traditional value chain in the automotive industry. For the established manufacturers, this requires a fresh strategic orientation. This is the only way to successfully meet the new challenges and at the same time utilize the opportunities that present itself with the changed situation.

10.5 The Networked Vehicle will Become an Information and Communication Instrument

The use of the internet in almost all aspects of daily life will further accelerate the transformation towards a global information and communication society. The exchange with other people, with networks and with information and service providers will witness a further boom in the years to come, also inside the vehicle. The major focus of the information and communication technology will continue to be on the topics of vehicle safety and driving assistance. But it can be expected that specialized service providers for mobility solutions will capitalize on the market opportunities provided by connecting with mail accounts and other traffic participants.

A first application of such a mobility service could be the fee-based provision of information about the next available parking space. In a second expansion stage, the further development of band widths to transport and exchange large amounts of data can provide a major push, especially with regard to entertainment on board. The provision of comprehensive connectivity on board is an exciting challenge for the automobile manufacturers and the communications industry. It is likely that companies will soon cooperate across industries along the new value chain.

10.6 Strategic Alliances are Key to Obtaining a Competitive Advantage

In the future, the automobile manufacturers will aim at an even more intense cooperation with their most important suppliers. This cooperation will also include companies in the technology and telecommunications sector. The development of standards for new technologies is likely to be done jointly, especially when unified regulations for automobile networks or the charging infrastructure for electric vehicles are at stake. The automobile manufacturers furthermore show an increasing willingness to share their own platforms with competitors and to focus on flexible production. This will lower costs for research and development, lower risks and reduce the time to market.

10.7 Triad was Yesterday, BRIC is Today and Emerging Markets will be Tomorrow

The grave repercussions of the financial and economic crisis in combination with the sovereign debt crisis in Europe have left a lasting mark on the triad countries. In the years 2010 and 2011, the global automotive industry was able to compensate stagnating sales of new vehicles in the traditional markets thanks to enormous growth rates in the BRIC countries and especially in China and India. The automotive industry, which is accustomed to increases in the sales volume, absolutely depends on accelerating dynamics in new economies and the possibility to open up further sales potential for their automobiles.

For that reason, the market expansion into the emerging economies must be a mandatory component of the company strategy of the automobile manufacturers. Taking into consideration overall economic perspectives and the pent-up demand for individual mobility, the countries Argentina, Brazil, Chile, Indonesia, Malaysia, Mexico, South Africa, South Korea, Thailand, Turkey and Vietnam are among the most promising automobile markets until 2020.

10.8 Tier-2 and Tier-3 Automotive Suppliers will Look for a New Orientation

The relationship between manufacturers and suppliers is particularly tight within the automotive value chain. From the perspective of the suppliers, the link between the value chain and the logistics chain is frequently inseparable, both from a technical and a business perspective.

The strenuous savings attempts which were undertaken by the automobile manufacturers as well as the tier-1 suppliers in the context of the automotive crises since 2008 made the weaknesses among the tier-2 and tier-3 suppliers apparent. Most notable are the relatively high financial instability as well as the missing product, market and customer diversification.

In order to cope with these difficulties, simple restructuring measures are not enough. Tier-2 and tier-3 suppliers need a strategic reorientation. Successful companies will enhance their return by eliminating business segments that are not part of their core activities. In addition they will establish working relationships with different manufacturers and develop products that also find a market outside the automotive industry. This enables them to spread their risks.

10.9 Electromobility – There is More than One Way Forward

Germany intends to become the leading market for electromobility by 2020. The Federal Government has formed the advisory council "National Platform Electromobility (NPE)" consisting of representatives from industry, politics, science, associations and unions. Despite the fact that only a few years remain, the NPE continues to adhere to the target of one million electric vehicles on German streets by the year 2020.

Even though the leading automobile manufacturers have been thoroughly engaged for more than ten years in research & development on all relevant questions related to electromobility, the topic of which drive technology will dominate in the future is still hotly debated. A one dimensional perspective with a single focus on only one global drive technology of the future is rather short-sighted. Furthermore this would not do justice to individual mobility demands. Depending on the location, the availability of resources and the technological applications, optimal mobility can take many different forms. Comprehensive coverage with only one drive technology is thus not realistic.

For the automobile manufacturers this means that in the medium term they need to continue with the optimization of combustion engines, advance the development of hybrid concepts and at the same time not lose sight of the ultimate goal of electric drives with zero emission. This attempt to square the circle constitutes an enormous challenge for all companies involved, especially against the backdrop of massive development costs in all areas of electromobility.

10.10 The Automobile Manufacturers Create a Global Brand Image

The automobile will continue to be the mobility concept with the highest emotional component. No other means of transportation, be it bus, train or airplane, evokes similar emotions among customers. Faced with a convergence in technology, appearance, haptic and design, the automobile manufacturers need to stress the communication of its brand values.

A brand and its history are particularly suitable to define a set of values for a vehicle. In a world characterized by globalization, the brand provides orientation when acquiring an automobile. The challenge for automobile manufacturers is not only to develop company specific brand values, but also to place them globally using different instruments. Outstanding examples for the global positioning of a brand that involves the use of emotions are certainly FC Barcelona from the area of sports, Apple from the field of communications as well as the brand Red Bull for consumption goods. First promising approaches are observable especially among the German manufacturers. These include building the BMW World or the automotive city by Volkswagen, the activities of Audi at FC Bayern München and in winter sports as well as the involvement with Formula 1 by Mercedes-Benz.

Here at the German Institute of Corporate Finance, we want to continue thinking about future trends in the automotive industry. Certainly new mobility concepts will take hold as mobility needs have changed. We will continue to conduct research in this field. Further information can be found at **www.dicf.de**.

We look forward to your comments and suggestions at

▸ German Institute of Corporate Finance (GICF)
  Mendelssohnstraße 87
  60325 Frankfurt am Main
  info@dicf.de

11 Bibliography

Books and articles:

ADAC Motorwelt (2011): Mobilität der Zukunft, Heft 5. Mai 2011, S. 20

Allgayer F. (2009): Wettrennen um Mobilitätskunden. In: W&V Media 7/2009, S. 34–35

Andrade, G., Mitchell M., Stattford, E. (2001): New Evidence and Perspectives on Mergers, Journal of Economic Perspectives 2001, vol. 15, issue 2, pp. 103–120

Ansoff, H. I. (1988): Corporate Strategy, London, Penguin Books

Avantalion (2012): AUTOMOTIVE OEMs – Emerging Markets Q4/2011 Report

Bähr, J. (1983): Verteilung und Dynamik der Bevölkerung in globaler, nationaler und regionaler Sicht, 1. Auflage, Stuttgart

Bamert, T. (2004): Markenwert, 1. Auflage, Zürich

BBDO Consulting (2002): The Power of Ingredient Branding in the Automotive Industry, Düsseldorf

Becker, H. (2010): Investition und Finanzierung; Grundlagen der betrieblichen Finanzwirtschaft, 4. überarbeitete und erweiterte Auflage, Wiesbaden

Becker, H. (2007): Auf Crashkurs: Automobilindustrie im globalen Verdrängungswettbewerb, 2. Aufl., Springer Verlag/Berlin/Heidelberg

Beike, R., Barckow, A. (2002): Risk-Management mit Finanzderivaten, 3. Aufl., Boston

Bell, T., Gaskill, A., Norris, J. (2009): Mastering the Currency Market: Forex Strategeis for High and Low Volatility Markets, New York

Bernhart, W., Zollenkop, M. (2011): Geschäftsmodellwandel in der Automobilindustrie; Determinanten, zukünftige Optionen, Implikationen. In: Bieger, Thomas (Hrsg.). Innovative Geschäftsmodelle; konzeptionelle Grundlagen, Gestaltungsfelder und unternehmerische Praxis, Berlin, S. 277–298

Bloss M., Ernst, D., Haas, C., Häcker, J., Prexl, S., Röck, B. (2010): Financial Modeling, Stuttgart

Bloss, M., Eil, N., Ernst, D., Fritsche, H., Häcker, J. (2009): Währungsderivate, München

Bloss, M., Ernst, D. (2008): Derivate – Handbuch für Finanzintermediäre und Investoren, 1. Aufl., München

BMI Industry Insights – Automotives, Western Europe (2010): Company News Alert – PSA's Electric Vehicle Leasing Plan Could Keep It Ahead Of Its Rivals, 09. September 2010

Brachat, H., Dietz, W., Reindl, S. (2011): Grundlagen der Automobilwirtschaft, Verlag Autohaus Buch und Formular, 5. Auflage

Breuer, W. (2000): Unternehmerisches Währungsmanagement, 2. Aufl., Wiesbaden

Broese, M. (2010): Kraftfahrzeuge/KFZ-Teile. In: AHK Jahresbericht – Russland 2009, S. 40–44

Brunner, M. (2006): Strategisches Nachhaltigkeitsmanagement in der Automobilindustrie: Eine empirische Untersuchung, 1. Aufl., GWV Fachverlage GmbH/Wiesbaden

Buller U., Hanselka H. (2009): Zukunftstechnologien: Förderung von Elektroautos – wie sinnvoll ist die Unterstützung einzelner Technologien? In: ifo Schnelldienst, 62. Jahrgang 22/2009

Business Monitor International (2011): Germany Autos Report. includes BMI's Forecasts, Q2 2011

Business Wire (2010b): Leo Motors Develops Improved EV Battery Management Technology, 26. Juli 2010

Business Wire (2010c): Nation-E Lauches the First Mobile Charging Station for Electric Cars: Angel Car®, 13. September 2010

Busse, F. (2003): Grundlagen der betrieblichen Finanzwirtschaft, 5. Auflage, München

Canzler, W., Knie, A. (2009): E-Mobility – Chance für intermodale Verkehrsangebote und für eine automobile Abrüstung. In: Ufu Themen und Informationen Heft 66, 2 / 2009

Capgemini (2009): Cars online 09/10 – Understanding consumer buying behavior in a volatile market

Cheung, M. T., Yeung, D. (1998): Pricing foreign exchange options: incorporating purchasing power parity, 2. Aufl., Hong Kong

Clark, I. J. (2011): Foreign Exchange Option Pricing: A Practitioners Guide, Chippenham

Clarke, I. (2002): Symbols for Sale… at Least for Now: Symbolic Consumption in Transition Economies. In: Advances in Consumer Research, Heft 29, S. 25–30

Clarkson, M. (1994): A risk based model of stakeholder theory: Toronto. Proceedings of the Second Toronto Conference on Stakeholder Theory, Centre for Corporate Social Performance and Ethics, University of Toronto/Toronto

Coyle, B. (2000): Hedging Currency Exposures: Currency Risk Management, Canterbury

Czotscher, E. (2010): Geschäftsmodelle auf dem Prüfstand. In: Automotive Now. Hrsg. KPMG Europe LLP, Sommer 2010, S. 5ff

Daimler-Chrysler (2004): Autobanken auf der Überholspur, Präsentation, Universität Ulm

Daimler Group AG (2008): Geschäftsbericht

De Pamphilis, D. (2005): Mergers, Acquisitions, and Other Restructuring Acitvities

Deutsche Bank Equity Research (2008)

DeFilippis, F. (2011): Währungsmanagement in kleinen und mittleren Unternehmen, Wiesbaden

DeRosa, D. (1998): Currency Derivatives, New York

DeRosa, D.F. (2000): Options on Foreign Exchange, 2. Aufl., New York

Diehl, S., Esch, F.-R., Gawlawski, D. (2009): Markenbindung für das ganze Leben. In: absatzwirtschaft, Ausgabe 12/2009, S. 40–41

Diehlmann, J., Häcker, J. (2010): Automobilmanagement – Die Automobilhersteller im Jahre 2020, München, Oldenbourg Wissenschaftsverlag

Drukarczyk, J. (2008): Finanzierung: Eine Einführung mit sechs Fallstudien, 10. Aufl., Lucius & Lucius Verlagsgesellschaft mbH/Stuttgart

Düsterlho von, J.-E. (2003): Das Shareholder-Value-Konzept: Methodik und Anwendung im strategischen Management, 1. Aufl., Deutscher-Universitäts-Verlag/Wiesbaden

Egger, U.-P. (1995): Unternehmensfinanzierung: Wie Sie Liquidität optimal sichern, Betriebswirtschaftlicher Verlag Dr. Th. Gabler GWV Fachverlage GmbH/Wiesbaden

Eichengreen B., Rennert U., Rhiel W. (2000): Vom Goldstandard zum EURO – Die Geschichte des internationalen Währungssystems, Berlin

Eilenberger, G. (2003): Betriebliche Finanzwirtschaft, 7. Auflage, Oldenbourg Verlag

Ernst & Young (2007): The Russian Automotive Market

Ernst & Young (2010): Automotive Market in Russia and the CIS – Industry Overview February 2010

Ernst & Young (2010): Starthilfe – Die Markteinführung der Elektromobilität in einer modernen Welt

Ernst & Young (2011): Mega trends shaping the Chinese light vehicle industry

Ernst & Young und F.A.Z.-Institut für Management-, Markt- und Medieninformationen (2011): Acht Megatrends in der Automobilbranche. Studie des Global Automotive Centers von Ernst & Young unter Mitwirkung von (in alphabetischer Reihenfolge): Regan Byron, Peter Fuß, Michael Hanley, Jeff Henning, Alexa Nassif, Anil Valsan, Sandra Warmbrunn

Ernst & Young (2011): Perspektiven des Automobilstandortes Deutschland – F.A.Z.-Institut

Ernst & Young (2012): Six growing trends in corporate sustainability

Ernst, D., Häcker, J. (2011): Applied International Corporate Finance, 2. Auflage, Vahlen Verlag, München

Esch, F.-R. (2004): Strategie und Technik der Markenführung, Vahlen Franz GmbH, Auflage: 2. A. (Januar 2004)

Esch, F.-R. (2010): Mehrmarkenstrategien für Automobilkonzerne im Zeitalter der Globalisierung. In: ZfAW – Zeitschrift für die gesamte Wertschöpfungskette Automobilwirtschaft, Ausgabe 2/2010, S.6–14

Esch, F.-R., Knörle, C. (2008): Zukunft der Marke? In: Markenartikel, Ausgabe 4/2008, S. 96–101

Feingold, B., Lang, R. (2004): Handeln mit Futures und Optionen, München

Franzen, O., Burkhardt, A. (2006): Marken ganzheitlich bewerten und managen – Ein Beispiel aus der Automobilindustrie. In: Planung & Analyse, Ausgabe 6/2006, S. 59–63

Frost & Sullivan (2011): Throwing Light On the Future: Mega Trends That Will Shape the Future of the World

Fuchs, C.-M. (2006): Mythos Markt, Verlag für Sozialwissenschaften, Wiesbaden

Gegner, M. (2008): Die Brasilianer und ihr Eigenmobil. In: Canzler, W., Schmidt, G. (2008): Zukünfte des Automobils, edition sigma, Berlin

Göller, K. (2008): Kauf, Miete und Leasing nach International Financial Reporting Standards (IFRS), Gabler Verlag, S. 119–149

Göttgens, O., Böhme, T. (2005): Strategische Bedeutung des Markenwertes. In: Zeitschrift für die gesamte Wertschöpfungskette Automobilwirtschaft, Ausgabe 1/2005, S. 44–50

Gottwald, A. von (2009): Antriebstechnik am Scheideweg. In: Automobil-Produktion, Heft 9/2009

Greeno, S. (2010): Are Electric Vehicles A Viable Solution For The Transport Sector CO2 Emissions Problem? S. 36ff

Grunwald, A., Kopfmüller, J. (2006): Nachhaltigkeit, Campus Verlag GmbH/Frankfurt/Main

Grunwald, T. (2007):, Cognitive Mapping von Marken – Sozialpsychologische Grundlagen eines ganzheitlichen Ansatzes

Guilford, D. (2010): California dreaming? It's the EV era, but carmakers see L.A. as test bed for fuel cells, 20. September 2010, Automotive News, S. 2

Guyette, H. (2008): Russian Auto Market open for Business. In: Aftermarket Business, Heft 1/2008, S. 69–71

Habrich-Böcker, C. (2010): China drückt aufs Tempo: Ab 2013 gilt in China ein neues Emissionsgesetz. Darum beschleunigen die Autobauer die Schadstoffsenkung. In: Euro am Sonntag, Nr. 20

Hackhausen J. (2007): Die Summe des Teilens. In: Wirtschaftswoche Nr. 33, S. 86

Häfner, M., Hiendlmeier, A. (2008): Strategien im Finanzbereich. In: Keuper, F. u.a. [Hrsg.]. Die moderne Finanzfunktion. Strategien, Organisation und Prozesse, Betriebswirtschaftlicher Verlag Dr. Th. Gabler GWV Fachverlage GmbH /Wiesbaden, S.147–175

Hartel, D.H. (2009): Consulting im Industrieunternehmen, München

Haslbeck, A. (2006): Vorgehen japanischer Automobilhersteller in der europäischen Union, GRIN Verlag, Norderstedt

von Hauff, M., Kleine, A. (2009): Nachhaltige Entwicklung. Grundlagen und Umsetzung, Oldenbourg Wissenschaftsverlag/München

Haunerdinger, M., Probst, H.-J. (2008): BWL leicht gemacht: Die wichtigsten Instrumente und Methoden der Unternehmensführung, FinanzBuch Verlag/München

Häusler, J., Stucky, N. (2003): Markenmanagement und finanzielle Transaktionen. Auszug aus: Wiedmann, C., P., Heckmüller, C.: Ganzheitliches Corporate Finance Management, Wiesbaden, S. 3.20

Hicks, A. (2000): Managing Currency Risk Using Foreign Exchange Options, Cambridge

Höhn, J. (2009): Chinas Führung erprobt die Elektromobilität. In: VDI NR. 24

Honal, M. (2009): Loss given default von Mobilien-Leasingverträgen, Wiesbaden

Hones, B. (2010): Kfz-Industrie und Kfz-Teile Russland, German Trade and Investment

Hudetz, K., Kaapke A. (2009): Lexikon Handelsmanagement. Deutscher Fachverlag, Frankfurt am Main

Hull, J.C. (2009): Optionen, Futures und andere Derivate, 7. Aufl., München

IBM Global Business Services (2006): Automotive 2020. Clarity beyond the chaos, S. 5

IBM (2009): Customer financing: making it a competitive instrument, Brokerreport

Industrial Minerals (2010): The Lithium Supplement 2010: Electric Vehicles, 27. Juli 2010, S. 2f.

Intveen, C. (2004): Unternehmensstrategien internationaler Automobilhersteller: Auswirkungen verkehrspolitischen Engagements auf die Gesamtunternehmerebene, 1. Aufl., GWV Fachverlage GmbH/Wiesbaden

Janovsky, J., Kashabian, B., Pilarek, D., Pulg, C. (2011): Marktepansion in Schwellenländern – Mit Service-Innovationen zum Geschäftserfolg, 1. Auflage, Gabler

Johnson, G., Scholes, K., Whittington, R. (2006): Exploring Corporate Strategy. Text and Cases, 7. erweiterte Medienauflage, Essex: Pearson Education Limited, S. 9ff

Jonker, J., Stark, W., Tewes, S. (2011): Corporate Social Responsibility und nachhaltige Entwicklung: Einführung, Strategie und Glossar, 1. Aufl., Springer Verlag/Berlin/Heidelberg

Kakar, S., Kakar, K. (2006): Die Inder: Portrait einer Gesellschaft, Verlag C. H. Beck oHG: München

Katzensteiner, T. (2007): Allein gegen alle. In: Wirtschaftswoche, Nr. 042 vom 13.10.2008, S. 66

Keese, S. (2010): The Brazilian Automotive Industry at Crossroads, Roland Berger, Sao Paulo

Keown, A.J., Martin, J.D., Petty, J., William, S., David, F. jr. (2010): Financial Management: Principles and Applications, 11. Aufl., Upper Saddle River

Kotler, P. (2009): Grundlagen des Marketing, Pearson Studium, München

Kotler, P., Armstrong, G. (2010) Principles of Marketing

KPMG (2010a): KPMG's Global Auto Executive Survey, KPMG

Kratzer, J., Kreuzmair, B. (2002): Leasing in Theorie und Praxis; Leitfaden für Anbieter und Anwender, 2. Auflage, Wiesbaden

11 Bibliography

Kristoffersen, S., Ljungber, F. (1999): Mobile Use of IT, Jyväskylä University Printing House, S. 271–284

Krüger, W., von Schubert B., Wittberg, V. (2010): Die Zukunft gibt es nur einmal!: Plädoyer für mehr unternehmerische Nachhaltigkeit, 1. Aufl., Gabler Verlag/Springer/Wiesbaden

Kuhnert, F., Niederdrenk, R., Maser J.C. (2011) Strategie. Umsetzung. Controlling. Autofacts Strategy Group, PricewaterhouseCoopers

Kurylko, D. (2008): VW CEO looks to US, Russia to grow. In: Automotive News Europe, Heft 6/2008, S. 20

LaMonica, M. (2010): How much does cost matter in the first wave of EVs?, 28. Juli 2010, CNET News.com, S. 9

Lange, N. S., Mauerer, S. (2010): Winning the BRIC Auto Markets, Boston Consulting Group

Leschus, L., Stiller, S., Vöpel, H. (2009): Berenberg Bank – HWWI: Strategie 2030 – Mobilität, November 2009, Hamburg: Berenberg Bank, S. 7ff

Li, Z., Ouyang, M. (2011): A win-win marginal rent analysis for operator and consumer under battery leasing mode in China electric vehicle market. In: Energy Policy 39 (2011), p. 3222–3237

Logwin (2009): Indien – Auf Wachstum programmiert. In: Logwin Magazin, Heft 02/2009, S. 5 ff

Lorenz, J. (2001): Wettbewerbsstrategien für Finanzdienstleister in der Automobilwirtschaft, Verlag: Peter Lang GmbH, Frankfurt a. M.

Macharzina, K., Wolf, J. (2010): Unternehmensführung: Das internationale Managementwissen: Konzepte – Methoden – Praxis, 7. Aufl., Springer Fachmedien/Wiesbaden

Madura, J. (2012): International Financial Management, 11. Auflage, High Holborn

Marketwire (2010): Hertz Commits to Electric Vehicle Mobility Platform, 21. September 2010

Meyer, D. (2006): Pressebericht – Brasilien Automobil Zulieferer Synergiebörse, Forum Brasilien, Stuttgart

Montes de Oca, P. (2007): Strategien für eine nachhaltige Mobilität anhand ausgewählter innovativer Beispiele. Studienarbeit, Grin Verlag, Norderstedt

Motavalli, J. (2010): Charging Ahead: The Electric Car Revolution is Coming-But Not Fast Enough., E Magazine, 11: S. 22–28

Münchner Merkur (2011): Wie Elektroautos funktionieren, Nr. 113, 17. Mai 2011. S. 7

Murphy, M. (2010): Forecasting the market for electric vehicles, 21. Juli 2010, Automotive World, S. 1

Olfert/Reichel (2005): Finanzierung, Kiehl Verlag GmbH, 13. Auflage, Ludwigshafen (Rhein)

Pearson, S., Ellinghorst, A., Shah, N. (2010): Equity Research European Auto Makers, Credit Suisse

Pepels, W. (2008): B2B-Handbuch General Management – Unternehmen marktorientiert steuern, 2. Auflage, Symposion Publishing Verlag, Düsseldorf

Perlitz, M. (2004): Internationales Management, 6. Auflage, Stuttgart

Petkovic, M. (2008): Employer Branding – Ein markenpolitischer Ansatz zur Schaffung von Präferenzen bei der Arbeitgeberwahl, 2. Auflage, Rainer Hampp Verlag, München und Mering

Pitour, M. (2010): Der Akku im Abonnement, 03. September 2010, Die Presse

Porter, M. E. (1999): Wettbewerb und Strategie, München: Econ Verlag, S. 9ff

Porter, M.E. (2008): The Five Competitive Forces That Shape Strategy, Harvard business Review, Januar 2008

Prem, M. (2011a): BMW rüstet sich für grüne Zukunft. In: Münchner Merkur Nr. 110, 13. Mai 2011, S. 5

Prem, M. (2011b): Warum die Motoren schrumpfen sollen. In: Münchner Merkur Nr. 79, 05. April 2011, S. 7

Rappaport, A. (1999): Shareholder Value: Ein Handbuch für Manager und Investoren, 2. Aufl., Schäffer-Poeschel Verlag für Wirtschaft/Stuttgart

Reiter, K. (1997): Ältere aktive Kraftfahrer – Möglichkeiten und Grenzen der motorisierten Verkehrsteilnahme im Seniorenalter. Bericht über die Internationale Konferenz „Mobilität und Sicherheit", Wien

Revill, C. (2008): Russia means big profits. In: Automotive News Europe, Heft 13/ 2008, S.1

Rick, H., McGuckin, T., Kuhnert, F., Breen, D., McCarthy, P. (2011): Growth reimagined

Roeder, A. (2009): Wie VW in Indien gewinnen will, In: Absatzwirtschaft, Heft 06/2009, S. 46–48

Roeder, R. (2011): Nachhaltigkeit und Wirtschaftlichkeit: Zauberformel der E-Mobilität. In: FLF – Finanzierung Leasing Factoring 01/2011, S. 25–30

Roland Berger Strategy Consultant, Amrop (2011): Automotive landscape 2025: Opportunities and challenges ahead, February 2011, S. 3ff

Roland Berger Strategy Consultants (2005): Trends in der KFZ-Finanzierung in Deutschland, Brokerreport.

Ross, A. (2010): Plugging in world to electric vehicles. 14. Juli 2010. The San Francisco Chronicle. S. 1

Rudolph, B., Schäfer, K. (2010): Derivative Finanzmarktinstrumente: Eine anwendungsbezogene Einführung in Märkte, Strategien und Bewertung, 2. Aufl., Springer Verlag

Schimansky, A., Stucky, N. (2004): Der Wert der Marke – Markenbewertungsverfahren für ein erfolgreiches Markenmanagement, Vahlen Verlag GmbH, München

Schmid, S. (2004): Der russische Konsument – Lebenswelt – Konsumverhalten – Markenwahrnehmung, OWC-Verlag, Münster

Schneck, O. (2010): Risikomanagement – Grundlagen, Instrumente, Fallbeispiele, Weinheim

Schöller O., Canzler W., Knie A. (2007): Handbuch Verkehrspolitik. VS Verlag für Sozialwissenschaften, Wiesbaden

Schricker W., Rubin E (2001): Geld & Kredit & Währung, 6. Aufl., München

Schubert K., Klein M. (2006): Das Politiklexikon. 4. aktualisierte Auflage, Dietz Verlag, Bonn

Schulze, G. (2009): Wirtschaftstrends Russland. Jahreswechsel 2009/2010. German Trade and Investement.

Seethaler P., Steitz, M. (2007): Praxishandbuch Treasury-Management, Wiesbaden

Sheth, J. N, Parvatiyar, A. (2001): The antecedents and consequences of integrated global marketing, International Marketing Review, Vol. 18, Iss. 1, S. 16–29

Shoup, G. (1998): Currency Risk Management, Chicago

Soellner, F. N., Rattey, F., Stolle, W. (2006): China und Indien auf der Überholspur, Studie der Unternehmensberatung A.T. Kearney

Städler, A. (2009): Deutlich Bremsspuren bei Investitionen und Leasing sichtbar. In: Finanzierung, Leasing, Factoring, Heft 1, 2009, S. 18–26

Stenner, F. (2010): Handbuch Automobilbanken; Finanzdienstleistungen für Mobilität, Berlin

Stephens, J.J. (2001): Managing Currency Risk Using Financial Derivatives, John Wiley & Sons Ltd., London

Stocker, K. (2001): Wechselkursmanagement auf Euro-Basis, Wiesbaden

11 Bibliography

Tebroke, H.-J., Laurer, T. (2005): Betriebliches Finanzmanagement, W. Kohlhammer GmbH/Stuttgart

The Engineer (2010): Electric Vehicles: Driven by design, 06. September 2010, S. 2

Thiele, M. (2010): Global Automotive Transaction Expertise, Angermann M&A, Stuttgart

Tselikov, S. (2007): Automotive Market of Russia – Trends, Prospects and Forecast of Development of Automotive Market until 2012, Autostat

Van Suntum U. (2005): Die unsichtbare Hand. Ökonomisches Denken gestern und heute, 3. verbesserte Auflage, Springer Verlag, Berlin, Heidelberg

Weinreich S. (2003): Nachhaltige Entwicklung im Personenverkehr – eine quantitative Analyse unter Einbezug externer Kosten, Physica Verlag, Flensburg

Winterhoff, M., Kahner, C., Ulrich, C., Sayler, P., Wenzel, E. (2009): Zukunft der Mobilität 2020. Die Automobilindustrie im Umbruch? S. 7ff

Wöhe, G. (2010): Einführung in die Allgemeine Betriebswirtschaftslehre, 24. Aufl., München

Wöhe, G. Bilstein, J. ,Ernst, D., Häcker, J. (2010): Grundlagen der Unternehmensfinanzierung, 10. Auflage, München

Wöhe, G., Döring, U. (2005): Einführung in die Allgemeine Betriebswirtschaftslehre, 22.Aufl., Verlag Franz Vahlen GmbH/München

Xinhua's China Exonomic Information Service (2010): Analysis: top energy firms form electric vehicle industrial union with automaker, 19. August 2010, S. 1

Zantow, R., Dinauer, J. (2011): Finanzwirtschaft des Unternehmens; Die Grundlagen des modernen Finanzmanagements, 3. aktualisierte Auflage, München

Main internet sources:

ABC Carbon (2010): 50,000 Electric Vehicles: France Commits to Infrastructure & Production. 13. April 2010. URL: http://archive.constantcontact.com/fs085/1102918945378/archive/1106217041847.html

ADAC (2011a): ADAC Servicetest in NRW zum Thema „Service und Qualität von Carsharing-Anbietern in NRW", URL: http://www.adac.de/_mm/pdf/Auswertung%20Service-Test%20Carsharing_58307.pdf

ADAC (2011b): Elektroautos: Bestandsaufnahme/Kenndaten, URL: http://www.adac.de/_mm/pdf/ElektroautosBestandsaufnahmeKenndaten_46583.pdf

ADAC (a): Autogas. Technik. Umwelt. URL: http://www.adac.de/infotestrat/tanken-kraftstoffe-und-antrieb/autogas/default.aspx

ADAC (b): Erdgas. Technik und Umwelt. URL: http://www.adac.de/infotestrat/tanken-kraftstoffe-und-antrieb/erdgas/default.aspx?tabid=tab4

ADAC (c): – Strom tanken – Der Elektroantrieb. Hybrid. URL: http://www.adac.de/infotestrat/tanken-kraftstoffe-und-antrieb/elektroantrieb/default.aspx?tabid=tab3

ADAC (d): – Strom tanken – Der Elektroantrieb. Technik. URL: http://www.adac.de/infotestrat/tanken-kraftstoffe-und-antrieb/elektroantrieb/default.aspx

ADAC (e): – Strom tanken – Der Elektroantrieb. Umwelt. URL: http://www.adac.de/infotestrat/tanken-kraftstoffe-und-antrieb/elektroantrieb/default.aspx?tabid=tab2

ADAC (f): Tanken, Kraftstoffe & Antrieb. URL: http://www.adac.de/infotestrat/tanken-kraftstoffe-und-antrieb/default.aspx?ComponentId=63539&SourcePageId=6729

ADAC Fahrzeugtechnik (2011): Elektroautos: Bestandsaufnahme/Kenndaten. Februar 2011. S. 2ff URL: http://www.adac.de/_mm/pdf/ElektroautosBestandsaufnahmeKenndaten_46583.pd

Alphabet (2011): http://www.alphabet.de/leistungen/fuhrparkverwaltung/alphacity

Alternative Kraftstoffe (o. J.): Wasserstoff Auto. URL: http://alternative-kraftstoffe.com/alternative-kraftstoffe/wasserstoff-auto/

Amann, S. (2006): Luxus boomt. In: Financial Times Online, siehe: http://www.ftd.de/unternehmen/handel-dienstleister/:luxus-boomt/111215.html, 13.06.2010

Arbeitskreis der Banken und Leasinggesellschaften der Automobilwirtschaft (2009): URL: http://www.autobanken.de/, Stand 28.04.2009

Arbeitskreis der Banken und Leasinggesellschaften der Automobilwirtschaft (2011): Mitglieder, URL: http://www.autobanken.de/

Arbeitskreis der Banken und Leasinggesellschaften der Automobilwirtschaft (2010b): Pressemitteilung; Banken der Automobilhersteller bauen ihren Marktanteil weiter aus, URL: http://www.autobanken.de/intern/download/presse/Pressemitteilung_110413_fin_51.pdf

Arbeitskreis der Banken und Leasinggesellschaften der Automobilwirtschaft (2010a): Kennzahlen, URL: http://www.autobanken.de/download/fakten/AKA_Kennzahlen_2010_gesamt_78.pdf; http://www.autobanken.de/download/fakten/AKA_Kennzahlen_2009_74.pdf

Arbeitskreis der Banken und Leasinggesellschaften der Automobilwirtschaft (2006): Prioritäten und Herausforderungen der herstellerverbundenen Autobanken, URL: http://www.autobanken.de/intern/download/presse/statements/Vortrag_Dr.Renkel_050406_4.pdf?PHPSESSID=a…af493a4bb07f7fbb53aa9b63e

Association Auxiliaire de l'Automobile (AAA) (2011a): New Registrations in Europe by Country 2010. URL: http://www.acea.be/images/uploads/files/20110221_03_PC_90-10_By_Country_Enlarged_Europe.xls

11 Bibliography

Association Auxiliaire de l'Automobile (AAA) (2011b): New Registrations in Europe (EU27 + EFTA) by Manufacturer – 2010. URL: http://www.acea.be/index.php/news/news_detail/new_vehicle_registrations_by_manufacturer/

Association des Constructeurs Européens d'Automobiles (ACEA) (2011): Provisional – New Passenger Car Registrations by Market – European Union. 17. Juni 2011.
URL: http://www.acea.be/images/uploads/files/20110617_PRPC-FINAL2-1105.xls

Association des Constructeurs Européens d'Automobiles (ACEA): New Passenger Car Registrations – Breakdown by Specification. URL: http://www.acea.be/images/uploads/files/20101003_All_Characteristics_1990-201008.pdf

Association des Constructeurs Européens d'Automobiles (ACEA), Association Auxiliaire de l'Automobile (AAA): New Passenger Car Registrations in Western Europe – Breakdown by segments. URL: http://www.acea.be/index.php/collection/statistics

ATZ online (2009): BMW gründet Joint Venture mit SGL Carbon [online], Verfügbar: http://www.atzonline.de/Aktuell/Nachrichten/1/10785/BMW-Group-gruendet-Joint-Venture-mit-SGL-Group.html

The Autochannel.com (2012): Cars and Computers – 2012 Car Reviews, 2011 Car Reviews, New Car: http://www.theautochannel.com/mania/computers/news.html

AutoEuropa Bank (2012): http://www.autoeuropabank.de

Auto motor und sport (2011): China-Boom: China überholt USA als größter Automarkt. 09.September 2009. URL: http://www.auto-motor-und-sport.de/news/china-boom-china-ueberholt-usa-als-groesster-automarkt-1407884.html

Bähr, J. (2008): Einführung in die Urbanisierung.[online] http://www.berlin-institut.org/online-handbuchdemografie/bevoelkerungsdynamik/auswirkungen/urbanisierung.html [Eingesehen am 13.06.2010]

Begley, J. (2008): The Russian Automotive Industry and Foreign Direct Investement, siehe: http://www.gerpisa.univ-evry.fr/rencontre/16.rencontre/GERPISAJune2008/Colloquium/Papers/P_Begleyjason_Collisclive_MorrisDavid.pdf, 13.06.2010

Better Place (2009): Strong Consumer Interest in Electric Vehicles Bodes Well for New Era of Sustainable Transportation. 13. Juli 2009. URL: http://www.betterplace.com/the-company-pressroom-pressreleases-detail/index/id/strong-consumer-interest-in-electric-vehicles-bodes-well-for-new-era-of-sus

Better Place (2010a): Homepage der Firma Better Place. [online] http://www.betterplace.com/ [Eingesehen am 26.06.2010]

Better Place (2010b): Homepage/Untergliederungspunkt ‚Opportunity' der Firma betterplace. [online] http://www.betterplace.com/opportunity/ [Eingesehen am 26.06.2010]

Better Place (2011): Battery Switch Stations, URL: http://www.betterplace.com/the-solution-switch-stations

BIBB Report 10/09 (2009): http://www.bibb.de/dokumente/pdf/a12_bibbreport_2009_10.pdf

Bimmer Today (2011): iPhone-App MyCityWay nun auch für BMW-Stadt München erhältlich [online], Verfügbar: http://www.bimmertoday.de/2011/04/07/iphone-app-mycityway-nun-auch-fur-bmw-stadt-munchen-erhaltlich/

Bloomberg (2010): www.bloomberg.com

BMW (2010a): Unternehmensprofil – Strategie, siehe: http://www.bmwgroup.com/d/nav/index.html?../0_0_www_bmwgroup_com/home/home.html&source=overview, 14.05.2010

BMW (2010b): Unternehmensprofil – Standorte, siehe: http://www.bmwgroup.com/d/nav/index.html?../0_0_www_bmwgroup_com/home/home.html&source=overview, 15.05.2010

BMW Bank (2011): www.bmwbank.de

BMW Deutschland (2011a): Der BMW X6. Preisliste. April 2011. S. 3. URL: http://www.bmw.de/de/de/newvehicles/x/x6_active_hybrid/2010/showroom/allfacts/index.html

BMW Deutschland (2011b): Der BMW 7er. Preisliste. März 2011. S. 3. URL: http://www.bmw.de/de/de/newvehicles/7series/sedan_active_hybrid/2010/showroom/allfacts/catalogue.html

BMW Deutschland: Der BMW Active Hybrid X6 und der BMW Active Hybrid 7. Die dynamischste Art, Hybrid zu fahren. S. 13. URL: http://www.bmw.de/de/de/newvehicles/7series/sedan_active_hybrid/2010/showroom/allfacts/catalogue.html

BMW Deutschland (o.J.b): Der neue BMW Active E. Entwickelt, um zu elektrisieren. S. 9. URL: http://www.bmw.de/de/de/newvehicles/1series/activee/2011/showroom/allfacts/catalogue.html

BMW Financial Services (2011): Vermögensmanagement & Kreditkarte, URL: http://www.bmwbank.de/vermoegensmanagement.html

BMW Group (2010): BMW Group und PSA bauen Zusammenarbeit aus. 18. Oktober 2010. URL: http://www.bmwgroup.com/d/nav/index.html?http://www.bmwgroup.com/d/0_0_www_bmwgroup_com/investor_relations/investor_relations.html

BMW Group (2011a): BMW Group und PSA Peugeot Citroen wollen 100 Millionen Euro in Joint Venutre zur Hybridtechnologie investieren. 28. Februar 2011. URL: http://www.bmwgroup.com/d/nav/index.html?http://www.bmwgroup.com/d/0_0_www_bmwgroup_com/investor_relations/investor_relations.html

BMW Group (2011b): BMW Group und PSA Peugeot Citroen gründen Joint Venture zum Ausbau der Zusammenarbeit bei Hybrid-Technologien. 02. Februar 2011. URL: http://www.bmwgroup.com/d/nav/index.html?http://www.bmwgroup.com/d/0_0_www_bmwgroup_com/investor_relations/investor_relations.html

BMW Group (2011c): Geschäftsbericht 2010. S. 3ff URL: http://geschaeftsbericht.bmwgroup.com/2010/gb/files/pdf/de/BMW_Group_GB2010.pdf

BMW Group (2011d): Number One. S. 6ff In: Geschäftsbericht 2010. URL: http://geschaeftsbericht.bmwgroup.com/2010/gb/files/pdf/de/BMW_Group_GB2010.pdf

BMW Group: Online im Internet: http://www.bmwgroup.com/d/0_0_www_bmwgroup_com/verantwortung/management_nachhaltigkeit/nachhaltigkeitsstrategie_content.html

BMW Group Firmen-Homepage: Online im Internet:http://www.bmwgroup.com/d/nav/index.html?../0_0_www_bmwgroup_com/home/home.html&source=overview

BMW i (2011): Mobility Services, URL: http://www.bmw-i.de/de_de/mobility-services/#mycityway

BMW i (a): BMW i3 – Das MegaCity Vehicle. URL: http://www.bmw-i.de/de_de/bmw-i3/

BMW I (b): BMW I8 – ein Symbol des Fortschritts. URL: http://www.bmw-i.de/de_de/bmw-i8/

BMW i (c): Die Geschichte der Elektro-Mobilität. URL: http://www.bmw-i.de/de_de/history/htm

Bode, S., Stiller, S., Wedemeier, J., Koller, C., Pflüger, W., Blohmke, J. (2007): Klimawandel. Studie der Berenberg Bank und des HWWI. (auch online einsehbar] http://www.hwwi.org/fileadmin/hwwi/Publikationen/Partnerpublikationen/Berenberg/Strategie_2030_Klimawandel.pdf

Börse Express (2011): BMW gründet Venture Capital-Gesellschaft [online], Verfügbar: http://www.boerse-express.com/pages/939991

Boston Consulting Group (2010): Batteries for Electric Cars, URL: http://www.bcg.com/documents/file36615.pdf

Breuer, W. et al.: Stichwort: Stakeholder Ansatz, Online im Internet: http://wirtschaftslexikon.gabler.de/Archiv/54861/stakeholder-ansatz-v3.html

11 Bibliography

Breuer, W., Breuer, C.: Stichwort: Finanzmanagement, Online im Internet: http://wirtschaftslexikon.gabler.de/Archiv/6779/finanzmanagement-v6.html

Buchmann, I. (2005a): Die Brennstoffzelle. URL: http://batteryuniversity.com/parttwo-52-german

Buchmann, I. (2005b): Wie weit sind neuere Batteriechemien noch entfernt?. URL: http://batteryuniversity.com/parttwo-53-german.htm

Buerkle, T. (1998): BMW Wrests Rolls-Royce Name Away From VW, http://www.nytimes.com/1998/07/29/news/29iht-rolls.t.html?pagewanted=all

Buerkle, T. (1998): New York Times, BMW Wrests Rolls-Royce Name Away From VW, URL: http://www.nytimes.com/1998/07/29/news/29iht-rolls.t.html?pagewanted=all

Bundesanstalt für Finanzdienstleistungsaufsicht (2009): Merkblatt – Hinweise zum Tatbestand des Finanzierungsleasings (§ 1 Abs. 1a Satz 2 Nr. 10 KWG)

Bundesinstitut für Bau-, Stadt- und Raumforschung (2011): PKW-Dichte – Laufende Raumbeobachtung. URL: http://www.bbsr.bund.de/nn_23744/BBSR/DE/Raumbeobachtung/GlossarIndikatoren/indikatoren__dyncatalog,lv2=104780,lv3=105246.html

Bundesministerium für Umwelt, Naturschutz und Reaktorsicherheit (2009): Was Investoren wollen – Nachhaltigkeit in der Lageberichterstattung, Online im Internet: http://www.bmu.de/files/pdfs/allgemein/application/pdf/broschuere_investoren_bf.pdf

Bundesministerium für Wirtschaft und Technologie (Bmwi) (2011): Regierungsprogramm: Elektromobilität. S. 13ff. URL: http://www.bmwi.de/BMWi/Redaktion/PDF/Publikationen/regierungsprogramm-elektromobilitaet,property=pdf,bereich=bmwi,sprache=de,rwb=true.pdf

Bundesverband Carsharing e.V. (2010): Carsharing für gewerbliche Kunden; Gute Beispiele der Carsharing-Nutzung in Unternehmen, Verwaltung, Organisationen und Vereinen, URL: http://www.carsharing.de/images/ stories/pdf_dateien/broschre_business-carsharing_endversion_mailfhig.pdf

Bundesverband Carsharing e.V. (2011a): Für wen bzw. für welche Zwecke eignet sich Carsharing, URL: http://www.carsharing.de/index.php?option=com_content&task=view&id=111&Itemid=154#Eignung1 (zit. als Bundesverband Carsharing e.V. (2011a))

Bundesverband Carsharing e.V. (2011b): Über Carsharing, URL: http://www.carsharing.de/index.php?option=com_content&task=view&id=202&Itemid=176#ueber1

Bundesverband deutscher Leasinggesellschaften e.V. (2010): Top 5 Leasing Märkte in Europa, URL: http://www.leasing-verband.de/markt.php?y=2&z=38

Bundesverband deutscher Leasinggesellschaften e.V. (2011): Verzeichnis der Mitglieder, URL: http://www.bdl-leasing-verband.de/download/mitgliederverzeichnis_mit_international_6-2011.pdf

Bundesverband deutscher Leasinggesellschaften e.V. (2011): Verzeichnis der Mitglieder, URL: http://bdl.leasingverband.de/zahlen-fakten/leasing-in-deutschland/jahres-und-strukturdaten

Bundeszentrale für politische Bildung (2011), http://www.bpb.de/wissen/1KNBKW,0,0,Bev%F6lkerungsentwicklung_und_Altersstruktur.html

Busse, N. (2006): Freude am Fahren zwischen Gorki Park und Kreml. In: Russland.RU – Die Internetzeitung, siehe: http://www.russland.ru/auto/morenews.php?iditem=144, 13.06.2010

Butler, R. A. (2005): Carbon Dioxide Emissions Charts. URL: http://rainforests.mongabay.com/09-carbon_emissions.htm

BYD: F3DM Parameters. URL: http://www.byd.com/showroom.php?car=f3dm&index=6

BYD: Green Tech for Tomorrow. S. 7f. URL: http://www.byd.com/downloads/broucher/2.pdf

Canzler W., Hunsicker F., Knie A., Peters J. (2009): Blockierte Moderne? Die Auswirkungen des demografischen und wirtschaftsstrukturellen Wandels auf die Verkehrsinfrastruktur in Deutschland bis zum Jahre 2030. InnoZ GmbH – Baustein 6. [auch online einsehbar] http://www.innoz.de/fileadmin/INNOZ/pdf/Bausteine/innoz-baustein-06.pdf [Eingesehen am 12.06.2010]

Car2go (2012): Das Mobilitätskonzept, URL: http://www.car2go.com/

Car2go Blog (2009): Car2go bewegt Ulm, URL: http://blog.car2go.com/2009/04/01/car2go-bewegt-ulm/

Car2go Blog (2010): Das Unternehmen; Erfolgreich, einfach, gut und günstig, URL: http://blog.car2go.com/kategorien/corporate/

Caradvice (2010): Brazil leapfrogs Germany to become fourth-largest new car market. 22.12.2010. URL: http://www.caradvice.com.au/96087/brazil-leapfrogs-germany-to-become-fourth-largest-new-car-market/

Carbon Disclosure Project: Online im Internet: https://www.cdproject.net/en-US/Pages/HomePage.aspx

Chevrolet (2011): Der Chevrolet Volt startet in Deutschland mit einem Einstiegspreis von 41.950 Euro. 01. März 2011. URL: http://www.chevrolet.de/chevrolet-erleben/neuigkeiten/2011/neuigkeiten-2011-overview-news/news-details-2011-13.html

Chevrolet: Cruze. URL: http://www.chevrolet.de/modelle/cruze/

China Association of Automobile Manufacturers (CAAM) (2011): China automobile sales decrease 0,25% in April 2011. 07. Juni 2011. URL: http://www.caam.org.cn/AutomotivesStatistics/20110607/1605056989.html

China Economic Net (2011): China leads 2010 auto market with record car sales. Feburary 2011. URL: http://en.ce.cn/Insight/201102/10/t20110210_22201313.shtml

Citroen (2010): Citroen C-Zero Airdream. Vorabpreisliste. 22. November 2010. S. 1ff. URL: http://www.citroen.de/Resources/Content/DE/10_pdf/07_preislisten/Preisliste_CZero.pdf

Computerwoche (2011): Mittelstandstudie nennen die Gründe für Personalengpässe. URL: http://www.computerwoche.de/bild-zoom/2486433/1/945558/EL_13073697395609813872567/

Concawe, EUCAR, European Commission JRC (2007): Well-To-Wheels Analysis of Future Automotive Fuels and Powertrains in the European Context. Well-to-Wheels Report. März 2007. URL: http://ies.jrc.ec.europa.eu/uploads/media/WTW_Report_010307.pdf

Continental AG (2010): Reifendruckkontrollsysteme von Continental, siehe: http://www.continentalreifen.de/generator/www/de/de/continental/reifen/themen/sicherheit/reifendruckkontrollsystem.html, 23.05.2010

Creditracer: http://www.mercedes-benz-bank.de

Credit Suisse (2011): Non-Deliverable Forwards, http://www.credit-suisse.com/ch/unternehmen/kmugrossunternehmen/doc/nondeliverable_forward_de.pdf

Czajka S., Mohr S. (2009): Internetnutzung in privaten Haushalten in Deutschland. In: Statistisches Bundesamt – Wirtschaft und Statistik 6/2009. [auch online einsehbar] http://www.destatis.de/jetspeed/portal/cms/Sites/destatis/Internet/DE/Content/Publikationen/Querschnittsveroeffentlichungen/WirtschaftStatistik/Informationsgesellschaft/InternetnutzungHaushalte,property=file.pdf

DailyGreen (2011): Kalifornien: Programm zur Förderung von E-Autos bald ausgeschöpft. 09. Juni 2011. URL: http://www.dailygreen.de/2011/06/09/kalifornien-programm-zur-forderung-von-elektromobilitat-bald-ausgeschopft-23798.html

Daimler Group AG (2009): Investor Relations, URL: http://www.daimler.com/dccom, Stand 08.06.2009

Daimler AG (2010): Renault-Nissan Allianz und Daimler AG vereinbaren weitreichende strategische Kooperation [online], Verfügbar: http://www.daimler.com/dccom/0-5-7153-49-1286402-1-0-0-0-0-0-8-7145-0-0-0-0-0-0.html

Dataforce news (2011): http://www.dataforce.de

11 Bibliography

Deck, S. (2009): Innovationsreport, siehe: http://www.innovationsreport.de/html/berichte/studien/kundenbeduerfnisse_anforderungen_gleichen_weltweit_133989.html, 13.06.2010

Der Natur-Blog (2011): EU plant Klimaziel bis 2050. 05. Mai 2011. URL: http://www.natur-blog.de/eu-plant-klimaziel-bis-2050/

Deutsche Bahn (2011): Flinkster, URL: http://www.flinkster.de/

Deutsche Börse AG (2008): General Standard und Prime Standard. Zugang zum europäischen Kapitalmarkt, Online im Internet: http://deutsche-boerse.com/dbag/dispatch/de/binary/gdb_content_pool/imported_files/public_files/10_downloads/33_going_being_public/40_stock_market_segmentation/sm_rcm_broschuere.pdf

Deutsche Börse AG (2010): 1585 – 2010. Die deutsche Börse feiert Jubiläum. Eine Chronologie effizienter Märkte, Online im Internet: http://deutsche-boerse.com/dbag/dispatch/de/binary/gdb_content_pool/imported_files/public_files/10_downloads/13_periodicals/40_1585/Jubilaeum425_1585.pdf

Deutsche Börse AG: Market Data & Analytics, Online im Internet: http://deutsche-boerse.com/dbag/dispatch/de/kir/gdb_navigation/about_us/10_Deutsche_Boerse_Group/20_Business_Areas/40_Market_Data_and_Information_Services

Deutsche Börse AG: Offenes Xetra-Orderbuch, Online im Internet: http://www.boerse-frankfurt.de/DE/index.aspx?pageID=201

Deutscher Bundestag 13. Wahlperiode (1998): Abschlußbericht der Enquete-Kommission „Schutz des Menschen und der Umwelt – Ziele und Rahmenbedingungen einer nachhaltig zukunftsverträglichen Entwicklung". Konzept Nachhaltigkeit. Vom Leitbild zur Umsetzung, Online im Internet: http://dipbt.bundestag.de/dip21/btd/13/112/1311200.pdf

Dow Jones Sustainability Index (2011): Online im Internet: http://www.sustainability-index.com/07_htmle/data/djsiworld.html

Drive-Carsharing (2011): Zeitgemäß mobil sein, URL: http://www.drive-carsharing.com/

DriveNow (2011): CarSharing von BMW i, Mini und Sixt, URL: https://www.drive-now.com/

DriveNow (2011): Tarife und Preise im Überblick [online], Verfügbar: https://www.drive-now.com/tarife/

Eichner, S. (2011): Aktuelle Entwicklungen auf dem russischen Automobilmarkt 2010 und 2011. 05. April 2011. URL: http://www.russland.ru/ruwir0010/morenews.php?iditem=19356

Electric Drive Org: Electric Drive Transportation Association: http://www.electricdrive.org/index.php?ht=display/Releases/archive/Y/view/

Elektroauto-Fahren (2011): Der Kampf um mehr Elektroauto Reichweite, URL: http://www.elektroauto-fahren.com/elektroauto-reichweite.html

Enzyklo (2010): Online Enzyklopadie, Konzept. [online] http://www.enzyklo.de/Begriff/Konzept [Eingesehen am 15.06.2010]

Europa (2011): Kommission stellt 24,2 Mio. EUR für Entwicklung der Elektromobilität in Europa bereit. 30. März 2011. URL: http://europa.eu/rapid/pressReleasesAction.do?reference=IP/11/381&format=HTML&aged=0&language=DE&guiLanguage=en

Eurostat (2011): Motorisierungsquote – Personenkraftwagen je 1000 Einwohner. URL: http://epp.eurostat.ec.europa.eu/tgm/table.do?tab=table&init=1&language=de&pcode=tsdpc340&plugin=1

Eurostat, Global Insight: Car Density in the World (car per 1,000 inhabitants) 2008. URL: http://www.acea.be/images/uploads/files/20100520_2010_KEY_FIGURES_4_Vehicles_in_Use.pdf

Export Development Canada (2011): Natural Hedging, http://www.edc.ca/english/docs/fx_managing_foreign_exchange_risk_e.pdf, 15.10.2011

Fiat S.p.A. (2011): From Genesis to Revelation and then there were two, Online im Internet. http://www.fiatspa.com/en-US/investor_relations/investors/presentazioni/FiatDocuments/2011/From_Genesis_to_Revelation_and_a_then_there_were_two_Flims_January_15_2011.pdf

Fiat S.p.A.: Investor Relations, Online im Internet: http://www.fiatspa.com/EN-US/INVESTOR_RELATIONS/FAQ/Pages/default.aspx

Fiat S.p.A.: Online im Internet: http://www.fiatspa.com/en-US/Pages/Home.aspx

Focus (2010): Automarkt China: Das gelobte Land des Lächelns, Online im Internet: http://www.focus.de/auto/automessen/peking2010/automarkt-china-das-gelobte-land-des-laechelns_aid_501113.html

Focus Online (2008): Ohne Strom fährt künftig gar nichts, URL: http://www.focus.de/auto/ratgeber/unterwegs/tid-11103/elektroautos-groesstes-problem-sind-die-hohe-kosten_aid_317323.html

Ford Motor Company: Online im Internet: http://corporate.ford.com/about-ford/sustainability

Fraunhofer ISI: Forschungsergebnisse_Elektromobilität_Batterieentwicklung. S. 3ff. URL: http://www.fraunhofer-isi-cms.de/elektromobilitaet/Batterieentwicklung

FTD (2011): Kampf um SGL Carbon eskaliert, URL: http://www.ftd.de/unternehmen/industrie/:rangelei-zwischen-bmw-und-vw-kampf-um-sgl-carbon-eskaliert/60116792.html

Geiger, T. (2008): Moskau ist die Hauptstadt des Maybach. In: Welt online, siehe: http://www.welt.de/motor/article1966183/Moskau_ist_die_Hauptstadt_des_Maybach.html, 14.06.2010.

General Motors: http://www.gm.com/company/aboutGM.html

German.China.Org.CN (2011): „VW erhöht erneut seine Investitionen in China", http://german.china.org.cn/business/txt/2011-09/28/content_23511804.htm

German Trade & Invest (2010a): Britische Regierung kürt förderfähige Elektroautos. 22. Dezember 2010. URL: http://www.gtai.de/DE/Content/__SharedDocs/Links-Einzeldokumente-Datenbanken/fachdokument.html?fIdent=MKT201012218004&suche=[suche][land]415[/land][sort]dat[/sort][kat]-Eua[/kat][ber]698[/ber][fachDb]matrixsuche[/fachDb][sicht]suche[/sicht][/suche]&snavi.page=0

German Trade & Invest (2010b): Indiens Makt für Elektrofahrzeuge soll Fahrt aufnehmen. 06. Oktober 2010. URL: http://www.gtai.de/MKT201010058005

German Trade & Invest (2010c): Viel Zuversicht bei Japans Elektroautoherstellern. 22. September 2010. URL: http://www.gtai.de/MKT201009218011

German Trade & Invest (2010d): E-Mobilität hält in den USA Einzug. 25. August 2010. URL: http://www.gtai.de/MKT201008248000

German Trade & Invest (2010e): Japan sorgt sich um Spitzenposition in der Elektromobilität. 17. Februar 2010. URL: http://www.gtai.de/MKT201002168011

German Trade & Invest (2011a): VR China will sich bei E-Mobilität an die Spitze setzen. 30. Mai 2011. URL: http://www.gtai.de/DE/Content/__SharedDocs/Links-Einzeldokumente-Datenbanken/fachdokument.html?fIdent=MKT201105278014&suche=%5Bsuche%5D%5Bland%5D42%5B/land%5D%5Bsort%5Ddat%5B/sort%5D%5Bkat%5D-Eua%5B/kat%5D%5Bsicht%5Dsuche%5B/sicht%5D%5Bber%5D698%5B/ber%5D%5BfachDb%5Dmatrixsuche%5B/fachDb%5D%5B/suche%5D&snavi.page=0

German Trade & Invest (2011b): US-Automobilmarkt steuert auf höhere Effizienz zu. 04. Mai 2011. S. 1. URL: http://www.gtai.de/DE/Content/__SharedDocs/Links-Einzeldokumente-Datenbanken/fachdokument.html?fIdent=MKT201105038015&suche=%5Bsuche%5D%5Bland%5D228%5B/land%5D%5Bsort%5Ddat%5B/sort%5D%5Bkat%5D-Eua%5B/kat%5D%5Bber%5D698%5B/ber%5D%5BfachDb%5Dmatrixsuche%5B/fachDb%5D%5Bsicht%5Dsuche%5B/sicht%5D%5B/suche%5D&snavi.page=0

German Trade & Invest (2011c): Branche Kompakt. Kfz-Industrie und Kfz-Teile – Indien. April 2011. S. 2f. URL: http://www.gtai.de/ext/anlagen/PubAnlage_9010.pdf?show=true

German Trade & Invest (2011d): Branche kompakt: Kfz-Industrie und Kfz-Teile – Japan. April 2011. S. 2ff. URL: http://www.gtai.de/ext/anlagen/PubAnlage_9000.pdf?show=true

German Trade & Invest (2011e): Erneut Rekordabsätze für Kfz in der VR China. 28. Februar 2011. S. 1. URL: http://www.gtai.de/DE/Content/__SharedDocs/Links-Einzeldokumente-Datenbanken/fachdokument.html?fIdent=MKT201102258007

Gesamtverband der deutschen Versicherungswirtschaft e.V. (2011): Statistisches Taschenbuch der Versicherungswirtschaft 2011 S. 15, http://www.gdv.de/wp-content/uploads/2011/11/Statistisches_TB_GDV_2011.pdf

Geschäftsberichte der Volkswagen Aktiengesellschaft: Geschäftsberichte. Online im Internet: http://www.volkswagenag.com/vwag/vwcorp/info_center/de/publications/publications.standard.acq/icr-2annual_reports/index.html

Green eMotion (2011a): About us. URL: http://www.greenemotion-project.eu/about-us/index.php

Green eMotion (2011b): Partners. URL: http://www.greenemotion-project.eu/partners/index.php

GreenTech (2011): BMW teams up with, invests $5 Million in MY City Way, URL: http://techcrunch.com/2011/02/25/bmw-teams-up-with-invests-5-million-in-mycityway/

Hartman R. (2010): Was ist Mobilität? In: mobileusability. [online] http://www.mobile-usability.info/2008/11/27/was-ist-mobilitat/

Haynes, P., Hale, P. (2010): European CO2 Emissions Continue To Fall, Online im Internet: http://www.jato.com/PressReleases/European%20CO2%20Emissions%20Continue%20to%20Fall.pdf

Hofielen, G. (2010): BMW – Bitte Mehr Wertebewusstsein bei der Nachhaltigkeit: Eine Konzernstudie des Dachverbands der Kritischen Aktionärinnen und Aktionäre, Dachverband der Kritischen Aktionärinnen und Aktionäre/Köln 2010, Online im Internet: http://www.kritischeaktionaere.de/fileadmin/Dokumente/Konzernstudien/BMW_Konzernstudie_2010-05-17.pdf

Hofmann, M. (2011): Rechnet sich der grüne Anstrich?, in: Die Welt, Online im Internet: http://www.welt.de/print/die_welt/wirtschaft/article13430330/Rechnet-sich-der-gruene-Anstrich.html

Honda (a): CR-Z. Daten & Preise. URL: http://www.honda.de/automobile/modelle_cr-z_technische_daten.php

Honda (b): Insight. Daten & Preise. URL: http://www.honda.de/automobile/modelle_insight_technische_daten.php

Honda (c): Jazz Hybrid. Daten & Preise. URL: http://www.honda.de/automobile/modelle_jazz_hybrid_technische_daten.php

Hones, B. (2010): Russische Automobilindustrie ist verhalten optimistisch. German Trade and Investement, siehe: https://www.gtai.de/DE/Content/__SharedDocs/Links-Einzeldokumente-Datenbanken/fachdokument.html?fIdent=MKT201003048005, 13.06.2010

Hucko, M. (2010): Schwierige Partnerschaft – Suzuki räumt Probleme mit VW ein [online], Verfügbar: http://www.ftd.de/unternehmen/industrie/:schwierige-partnerschaft-suzuki-raeumt-probleme-mit-vw-ein/50178049.html

I am Informed (2011): green energy – We Are Informed: http://iaminformed.wordpress.com/category/green-energy/

Institut für Automobilwirtschaft (2008): http://www.ifa-info.de/files/1486/Press

Interbrand (2010): Best Global Brands 2010, http://www.interbrand.com/de/best-global-brands/best-global-brands-2008/best-global-brands-2010.aspx

International Energy Agency (2010): CO2 Emissions from Fuel Combustion. IEA Statistics 2010. S. 9. URL: http://www.iea.org/co2highlights/co2highlights.pdf

ISDA: http://www2.isda.org/about-isda/

IT Wissen (2011): LBS (location based services), URL: http://www.itwissen.info/definition/lexikon/location-based-service-LBS-Ortsbezogener-Dienst.html

J.D. Power (2011): J.D. Power and Associates Reports: India Expected to Become the World's Third-Largest Light-Vehicle Market by 2020. However, Profits Not Likely to Match Two Largest Markets, China and the United States. 13. Juni 2011. S. 2. URL: http://businesscenter.jdpower.com/JDPAContent/CorpComm/News/content/Releases/pdf/2011081-indi.pdf

Japan Automobile Manufacturer Association (JAMA) (2011): JAMA – Active Matrix Database System. URL: Vgl. http://jamaserv.jama.or.jp/newdb/eng/index.html

Jünigk, T. (2009): Die Rolle und Bedeutung von Automobilbanken in Deutschland, In: Deutsches Institut für Bankwirtschaft – Schriftreihe, Band 3 (12/2009), URL: http://www.deutsches-institut-bankwirtschaft.de/Juenigk%20Automobilbanken%20Deutschland.pdf

Kauschke P., Reuter J. (2009): PWC-Studie: Megacities – eine logistische Herausforderung für Güter und Menschen. [online] http://www.pwc.de/portal/pub/!ut/p/c4/04_SB8K8xLLM9MSSzPy8xBz9CP0os3gDA2NPz5DgAF9nA0dPN3M_V0tnAwjQL8h2VAQAXrjpRg!!/?topNavNode=49c411a4006ba50c&siteArea=e52c1a4e810c53b&content=e52c1a4e810c53b [Eingesehen am 15.06.2010]

KB Investment & Securities (2010): 17. Februar 2010. S. 9. URL: http://www.kbsec.co.kr/index.jsp

Kilimann S. (2010): Mobilitätskonzept von Peugot – „Mu" mach mobil. In: autoplenum.de, Testberichte. [online] http://www.autoplenum.de/Auto/Testberichte/Mobilitaetskonzept-von-Peugeot----Mu--macht-mobil-id11064.html [Eingesehen am 23.06.2010]

Koch, R., Raible, K.-F., Stadtmann, G. (2011): Vorstandsvergütung in Deutschland – Ist eine Trendwende in Sicht?, European University Viadrina Frankfurt (Oder), Online im Internet: http://www.wiwi.europa-uni.de/de/forschung/publikationen-projekte/dp/_dokumente/299_Koch_Raible_Stadtmann.pdf

KPMG (2010b): Autobranche setzt Hoffnung auf Schwellenländer, siehe: http://www.kpmg.ch/WasWirTun/17063.htm, 11.06.2010

KPMG AG Wirtschaftsprüfungsgesellschaft (2011): BilMoG: Reform des Bilanzrechts, Online im Internet: http://www.kpmg.de/Themen/2631.htm?print=1

Krix, P. (2011): BMW und Sixt gründen Car Sharing-Konzept „DriveNow" [online], Verfügbar: http://www.automobilwoche.de/article/20110321/REPOSITORY/110329999/1056/REPOSITORY

Leaseurope (2010a): Annual Survey 2010, URL: http://www.leaseurope.org/uploads/documents/stats/European%20Leasing%20Market%202010.pdf

Leaseurope (2010b): Ranking, URL: http://www.leaseurope.org/uploads/documents/ranking/Leaseurope%20Ranking%20Survey%202010.pdf

Leonhard, R. (2009): Kraftfahrzeugtechnik. Vortrag zum 59. Internationalen Motorpressekolloquium [online] http://www.bosch-presse.de/TBWebDB/de-DE/Presstext.cfm?ID=4112 [Eingesehen am 24.06.2010]

Limbourg, M. (1999): Mobilität im Alter: Probleme und Perspektiven [online]: http://www.uni-due.de/~qpd402/alt/texte.ml/Senioren.html [Eingesehen am 14.06.2010]

London Stock Exchange: Our history, http://www.londonstockexchange.com/about-the-exchange/company-overview/our-history/our-history.htm

Manager Magazin (2007): Echter Volkswagen unter 8000 €. [online], URL: http://www.manager-magazin.de/unternehmen/artikel/0,2828,471065,00.html

11 Bibliography

Manager Magazin (2010): Kooperation – Suzuki will schnell bei VW einsteigen [online], Verfügbar: http://www.manager-magazin.de/unternehmen/artikel/0,2828,672229,00.html

Manager Magazin (2011): Einstieg beim SGL Carbon – VW überrascht BMW [online], Verfügbar: http://www.manager-magazin.de/unternehmen/autoindustrie/0,2828,748364,00.html

Mayer, S.; Rattey, F.; Pleines, R. (2007): Mega-Markt für Ultra-Low cost. In Schwellenländern wächst die Nachfrage nach Niedrigstpreis-Autos [online]. Düsseldorf: A. T. Kearny GmbH, 2007. URL: http://www.atkearney.de/content/veroeffentlichungen/executivebriefs_detail.php/id/50063/practice/automotive

Mein Elektroauto (2010): Vorerst keine Wechselakkus für deutsche Elektroautos, URL: http://www.mein-elektroauto.com/2010/08/vorerst-keine-wechselakkus-fur-deutsche-elektrautos/586/

Mein Elektroauto (2011): betterplace, URL: http://www.mein-elektroauto.com/tag/better-place/

Ministerium für Umwelt, Naturschutz und Verkehr Baden-Württemberg (2010): Themen Straße und Verkehr. [Online] http://www.uvm.baden-wuerttemberg.de/servlet/is/66210/

Mongabay (o. J.): Carbon Dioxide Emissions Charts. URL: http://rainforests.mongabay.com/09-carbon_emissions.htm

Mu by Peugeot (2011): Online im WWW unter URL: http://www.mu.peugeot.de/

Müller, V. (2010): Deutsche Autobauer kämpfen gegen Billigautos, siehe: http://www.wiwo.de/unternehmen-maerkte/indien-deutsche-autobauer-kaempfen-gegen-billigstautos-423403/2/, 13.06.2010

Newsclick (2009): Alte Fahrer lieben elektronische Helfer. 05.November 2009. URL: http://www.newsclick.de/index.jsp/menuid/2182/artid/11217701

New York Times (1998): BMW Wrests Rolls-Royce Name Away From VW. URL: www.nytimes.com/1998/07/29/news/29iht-rolls.t.html?pagewanted

NRI Community (2011): NRI Community for non resident Indians living as expats. URL: http://www.bricforum.com/brazil/the-world%E2%80%99s-fourth-largest-car-market-is-brazil

NYSE (a): Online im Internet: http://www.nyse.com/about/listed/f.html

NYSE (b): Online im Internet: http://www.nyse.com/about/listed/ttm.html

NYSE (c): Online im Internet: http://www.nyse.com/about/history/timeline_1960_1979_index.html

NYSE (d): Online im Internet: http://www.nyse.com/about/history/timeline_1980_1999_index.html

NYSE (e): Online im Internet: http://www.nyse.com/about/history/timeline_1940_1959_index.html

NYSE (f): Online im Internet: http://www.nyse.com/about/history/timeline_2000_Today_index.html

Oliver Wyman Studie (2010): Car Innovation 2015. Umfassende Studie und Ergebnisse online zu erhalten unter: http://www.car-innovation.de/studieninhalte.html

Organisation International des Constructeurs d'Automobiles (OICA) (o.J.a): Alternative Fuels. URL: http://oica.net/category/auto-and-fuels/alternative-fuels/

Organisation International des Constructeurs d'Automobiles (OICA) (o.J.b): CNG. URL: http://oica.net/category/auto-and-fuels/alternative-fuels/cng/

Organisation International des Constructeurs d'Automobiles (OICA) (o.J.c): Hybrid. URL: http://oica.net/category/auto-and-fuels/alternative-fuels/hybrid/

Organisation International des Constructeurs d'Automobiles (OICA) (o.J.d): LPG. URL: http://oica.net/category/auto-and-fuels/alternative-fuels/lpg/

Pehnt, M., Höpfner, U., Merten, F. (2007): Elektromobilität und erneuerbare Energien. Heidelberg: ifeu – Institut für Energie- und Umweltforschung Heidelberg. Wuppertal: Wuppertal-Institut für Klima, Umwelt, Energie. S. 4. URL: http://www.bmu.de/files/pdfs/allgemein/application/pdf/elektromobilitaet_ee_arbeitspapier.pdf

Peugeot (2010): Peugeot iOn. 100% elektrisch. November 2010. S.10f. URL: http://www2.peugeot.de/ion-auswahl/

Peugeot: Online im Internet: http://www.psa-peugeot-citroen.com/en/psa_group/strategy_b2.php

Porsche (2010a): Porsche Traction Management (PTM), siehe: http://www.porsche.com/microsite/technology/default.aspx?pool=germany&ShowSingleTechterm=PTPTM&Category=&Model=&SearchedString=&SelectedVariant=PMTCayenneAll, 22.05.2010.

Porsche (2010b): Porsche Active Suspension Management (PASM), siehe: http://www.porsche.com/microsite/technology/default.aspx?pool=germany&ShowSingleTechterm=PTPASM&Category=&Model=&SearchedString=&SelectedVariant=PMTCayenneAll, 22.05.2010.

Premium Financial Services (2012): http://alphera.de

PricewaterhouseCoopers (2010): Kapitalmarkt-Compliance signalisiert Vertrauenswürdigkeit börsennotierter Unternehmen, [online], Verfügbar: http://www.pwc.de/de/kapitalmarktorientierte-unternehmen/kapitalmarkt-compliance-signalisiert-vertrauenswuerdigkeit-boersennotierter-unternehmen.jhtml?preview=true

PricewaterhouseCoopers (2011): Eine Vielzahl strategischer Wachstumsoptionen: Die aktuelle Entwicklung in der Automobilbranche [online], Verfügbar: http://www.pwc.de/de/automobilindustrie/eine-vielzahl-strategischer-wachstumsoptionen-die_aktuellen-entwicklungen-in-der-automobilbranche.jhtml

PWC (2011): Automotive industry and summary, PWC/New York, [online], Verfügbar: http://www.pwc.com/gx/en/ceo-survey/industry/pdfs/CEO_Survey_Automotive.pdf

Razumovskaya, O. (2010): Volkswagen Introduces New Russian Budget Car. In: Moscow Times Online, siehe: http://www.themoscowtimes.com/business/article/volkswagen-introduces-new-russian-budget-car/407439.html, 13.06.2010

Reiche, L. (2010): Der Elefant jagt den Drachen. In: Manager Magazin, siehe: http://www.manager-magazin.de/finanzen/artikel/0,2828,679602,00.html

Reichenbacher, T. (2004), URL: http://tumb1.biblio.tu-muenchen.de/publ/diss/bv/2004/reichenbacher.pdf

Renault (a): Fluence Z.E. URL: http://www.renault-ze.com/de-de/gamme-voitures-electriques-renault-z.e./fluence-z.e./vorstellung-638.html

Renault (b): Twizy Urban. URL: http://www.renault-ze.com/de-de/gamme-voitures-electriques-renault-z.e./twizy-urban/vorstellung-652.html

Renault (c): Zoe PreVIEW. URL: http://www.renault-ze.com/de-de/gamme-voitures-electriques-renault-z.e./zoe-preview/vorstellung-647.html

Renault S.A. (d): Online im Internet: http://www.renault.com/en/groupe/Pages/groupe.aspx

Rettig, D. (2010): Arbeitgeberranking 2010: Vorsprung durch Image, 04.05.2010: http://www.wiwo.de/management-erfolg/arbeitgeberranking-2010-vorsprung-durch-image-428907/

Reuter, W. (2011): Partnerschaften in der Autobranche bergen Gefahren [online], Verfügbar: http://www.handelsblatt.com/unternehmen/industrie/partnerschaften-in-der-autobranche-bergen-gefahr/4054318.html

Reuters Deutschland (2009): US-Autobank GMAC wird Geschäftsbank – Zugriff auf Staatshilfen, URL: http://de.reuters.com/article/idDELO4061620081224, http://www.reuters.com/resources/archive/us/20090713.html

Renault.de (2012): Preisliste Kangoo Z.E. Stand 06.03.2012, http://renault-preislisten.de/fileadmin/user_upload/Preisliste_Kangoo_ZE_111202.pdf

11 Bibliography

Ribbeck, E. (2003): Megastädte. [online] http://www.bpb.de/themen/WY1EQV,0,St%E4dtischer_Transport.html

Roland Berger Strategy Consultants, VDMA (2011): Zukunftsfeld Elektromobilität – Chancen und Herausforderungen für den deutschen Maschinen- und Anlagenbau. S. 12. URL: http://www.rolandberger.com/media/pdf/Roland_Berger_DT_2_01_11_005_Komplett_06_20110511.pdf

Root, S. (2010): Prospects for the Russian automotive market, PricewaterhousCoopers, URL: http://www.pwc.ru/en/events/2010/autobriefing/automotive

Röpke W. (2009): Wer denkt für morgen? Wirtschaft mit Gefühl. In: Die Zeit Online. [Online] http://www.zeit.de/2009/15/PD-Shiller [Eingesehen am 16.06.2010]

Russland.RU (2011): Aktuelle Entwicklungen auf dem russischen Automobilmarkt 2010 und 2011. 05. April 2011. URL: http://www.russland.ru/ruwir0010/morenews.php?iditem=19356

Sandor, J. (2010): Runflat Reifen, siehe: http://www.reifensuchmaschine.de/runflat/michelin_pax.htm, 23.05.2010.

Santer, B. (2008): Automobilmarkt Russland – Aufbruch im Land der Extreme. In: Focus Online, siehe: http://www.focus.de/auto/automessen/automarkt-russland-aufbruch-im-land-der-extreme_aid_328474.html, 13.06.2010

SAP (2010): help SAP – Konzept. [online] http://help.sap.com/saphelp_xpd10/helpdata/de/9a/0d39dc5bdd41eb967b9240f5a6108c/content.htm [Eingesehen am 26.06.2010]

Scheider, W.-H. (2007): Bosch Homepage: Kraftfahrzeugtechnik – Bosch-Konzepte für den weltweit wachsenden Markt der Low Price Vehicles, siehe: http://www.bosch-presse.de/TBWebDB/de-DE/PressText.cfm?CFID=1354040&CFTOKEN=&ID=3186, 22.05.2010

Schmitt, T. (2009): Forscher erwarten mehr Katastrophen. In: Handelsblatt [online] http://www.handelsblatt.com/unternehmen/banken-versicherungen/rueckversicherer-forscher-erwarten-mehr-katastrophen;2505918 [Eingesehen am 14.06.2010]

Schneider M. (2010): Der Autokult kommt unter die Räder. In: Handelsblatt vom 03.03.2009. [Online] http://www.handelsblatt.com/unternehmen/industrie/der-autokult-kommt-unter-die-raeder;2183599 [Eingesehen am 27.05.2010]

Scotiabank (2012): Global Auto Report, URL: http://www.gbm.scotiabank.com/English/bns_econ/bns_auto.pdf

SGL Group (2009): SGL Group und BMW Group gründen Carbonfaser-Joint Venture. 29. Oktober 2009. URL: http://www.sglgroup.com/cms/international/press-lounge/news/2009/10/10292009_p.html?__locale=de

SGL Group (2010): SGL Group und BMW Group: Neues Carbonfaserwerk wird in Moses Lake/USA errichtet [online], Verfügbar: http://www.sglgroup.com/cms/international/press-lounge/news/2010/04/04062010_p.html?__locale=de

SGL Group (2010a): Leichtbau für Elektromobilität. Standorte Landshut und Wackersdorf in Vorbereitung für die Produktion des Megacity Vehicles. 19. Juli 2010. URL: http://www.sglgroup.com/cms/international/press-lounge/news/2010/07/07192010_p1.html?__locale=de

SGL Group (2010b): SGL Group und BMW Group: Neues Carbonfaserwerk wird in Moses Lake/USA errichtet. 06. April 2010. URL: http://www.sglgroup.com/cms/international/press-lounge/news/2010/04/04062010_p.html?__locale=de

SGL Group (2011): SGL Automotive Carbon Fibers: Neues Werk in Moses Lake fertig gestellt [online], Verfügbar: http://www.sglgroup.com/cms/international/press-lounge/news/2011/05/05232011_p.html?__locale=de

SGL Group (2011): SGL Automotive Carbon Fibers: Neues Werk in Moses Lake fertig gestellt. 23. Mai 2011. URL: http://www.sglgroup.com/cms/international/press-lounge/news/2011/05/05232011_p.html?_locale=de

Shell Deutschland Oil GmbH (2009): Shell PKW-Szenarien bis 2030 – Fakten, Trends und Handlungsoptionen für nachhaltige Auto-Mobilität. [auch online erreichbar] http://www.shell.de/home/content/deu/aboutshell/our_strategy/scenarios_2050/mobility_scenarios/ [Eingesehen am 12.06.2010]

Siemens AG (2011): Elektromobilität – Mit Energie in die mobile Zukunft, URL: http://www.siemens.de/elektromobilitaet/elektromobilitaet.html?stc=deccc020122

Society of Indian Automobile Manufacturers (SIAM) (2011): Automobile Domestic Sales Trends. URL: http://www.siamindia.com/scripts/domestic-sales-trend.aspx

Stadtteilauto (2011): Carsharing München, URL: http://www.stadtteilauto.de/

Statista (2010): Offliner in Deutschland. [online] http://de.statista.com/statistik/daten/studie/13078/umfrage/offliner-anteil-in-deutschland/#stat [Eingesehen am 12.06.2010]

Statistisches Bundesamt (2009): Bevölkerung Deutschlands bis 2060. Statistisches Bundesamt, Wiesbaden. [auch online Einsehbar] http://www.destatis.de/jetspeed/portal/cms/Sites/destatis/Internet/DE/Presse/pk/2009/Bevoelkerung/pressebroschuere__bevoelkerungsentwicklung2009,property=file.pdf

Stattauto München (2011): Carsharing, URL: http://stattauto-muenchen.de/

Stern (2009): Mangergehälter werden begrenzt, Online im Internet: http://www.stern.de/politik/deutschland/bundestag-managergehaelter-werden-begrenzt-704043.html

Süddeutsche Zeitung (2011): Carhsharing – Abgefahren, URL: http://www.sueddeutsche.de/auto/carsharing-abgefahren-1.1106986

Suzuki Motor Corporation (2010): Annual Report 2010 [online], Verfügbar: http://www.globalsuzuki.com/corp_info/financialinfo/pdf/2010/2010all.pdf

Tata: Online im Internet: http://www.tata.com/aboutus/articles/inside.aspx?artid=CKdRrD5ZDV4=

Techcrunch (2011): BMW Teams Up With, Invests $5 Million In MyCityWay, URL: http://techcrunch.com/2011/02/25/bmw-teams-up-with-invests-5-million-in-mycityway

Telebörse.de (2011): Sperminorität bei SGL Carbon. Klatten fährt VW in die Parade. 18. Mai 2011. URL: http://www.teleboerse.de/nachrichten/Klatten-faehrt-VW-in-die-Parade-article3360261.html

The Hindu Business Line (2011): Auto majors lose car market share to smaller firms. April 2010. URL: http://www.thehindubusinessline.com/industry-and-economy/marketing/article1684826.ece

Thieme, S. (2007): Gesellschaftliche Moral, Ethik und Regeln. [Online erreichbar] http://evoeco.forschungsseminar.de/k2s_thieme_pies.pdf

Toyota (a): Auris Das Leben kann so leicht sein. URL: http://www.toyota.de/cars/new_cars/auris/specs.aspx

Toyota (b): Der nächste Prius. Wegweisend. URL: http://www.toyota.de/cars/new_cars/prius/specs.aspx

Toyota Motor Corporation (2011): Form 20-F. Online im Internet: http://secfilings.nyse.com/filing.php?doc=1&attach=ON&ipage=7682594&rid=23#rom138060_29

Ueno, S. (2006): The impact of Customer Relationship Management, USJP Occasional Paper 06-13, Harvard University, URL: http://wcfia.harvard.edu/us-japan/research/pdf/06-13.ueno.pdf

Underwriters Laboratories Inc.: Electric vehicle infrastructure. Driving the Smart Grid. URL: http://www.ul.com/global/eng/pages/offerings/industries/powerandcontrols/electricvehicle/

United Nations – Department of Economic and Social Affairs (2009): World Urbanization Prospects: The 2009 Revision. URL: http://esa.un.org/unpd/wup/CD-ROM_2009/WUP2009-F02-Proportion_Urban.xls

United Nations – Department of Economic and Social Affairs (2011): World Population Prospects: The 2010 Revision. April 2011. URL: DESAhttp://esa.un.org/unpd/wpp/Excel-Data/DB02_Stock_Indicators/WPP2010_DB2_F01_TOTAL_POPULATION_BOTH_SEXES.XLS

United Nations Population Fund (2007): State of world population 2007 – Unleashing the Potential of Urban Growth. URL: http://www.unfpa.org/swp/2007/presskit/pdf/sowp2007_eng.pdf

US Department of Energy (2011): One Million Electric Vehicles by 2015. February 2011. S. 2. URL: http://www1.eere.energy.gov/vehiclesandfuels/pdfs/1_million_electric_vehicles_rpt.pdf

Verband der Automobilindustrie (a): Exportquote, http://www.vda.de/de/zahlen/jahreszahlen/export/, 26.10.2011

Verband der Automobilindustrie (b): Elektromobilität – Eine Alternative zum Öl. Mai 2011. S. 7ff. URL: http://www.vda.de/de/publikationen/publikationen_downloads/detail.php?id=969

Verordnung (EG) Nr. 1126/2008 der Kommission (2008): Online im Internet: http://www.ifrs-portal.com/Dokumente/IFRS%20IAS%20EU%20Deutsch.pdf

Verordnung (EG) Nr. 1606/2002 des Europäischen Parlaments und des Rates (2002): Online im Internet: http://eur-lex.europa.eu/LexUriServ/LexUriServ.do?uri=OJ:L:2002:243:0001:0004:de:PDF

Volkswagen (2010a): Produktionsstandorte, siehe: http://www.volkswagenag.com/vwag/vwcorp/content/de/the_group/production_plants.html, 15.05.2010

Volkswagen (2010b): Strategie, siehe: http://www.volkswagenag.com/vwag/vwcorp/content/de/the_group/strategy.html, 15.05.2010

WardsAuto (2011): U.S. Car and Truck Sales, 1931–2010.
URL: http://wardsauto.com/keydata/historical/UsaSa01summary/

Waschke T. (2007): Megastädte. In: Bundeszentrale für politische Bildung. [online] http://www.bpb.de/themen/ASUNB0,0,0,Wie_geht_es_weiter_mit_der_Stadt.html [Eingesehen am 18.06.2010]

Wauters, R. (2011): BMW Teams Up With, Invest $5 Million in MyCityWay [online], Verfügbar: http://techcrunch.com/2011/02/25/bmw-teams-up-with-invests-5-million-in-mycityway/

WCED (1987): Our Common Future, Online im Internet: http://www.bne-portal.de/coremedia/generator/unesco/de/Downloads/Hintergrundmaterial__international/Brundtlandbericht.pdf

Weitlaner, W. (2004): Brandrodung macht Brasilien zu Spitzen-Umweltsünder, siehe: http://www.innovations-report.de/html/berichte/umwelt_naturschutz/bericht-31475.html, 13.06.2010

Weltbank (2011): URL: http://web.worldbank.org/WBSITE/EXTERNAL/COUNTRIES/LACEXT/BRAZILEXTN/0,,menuPK:322351~pagePK:141132~piPK:141107~theSitePK:322341,00.html

Weltbank (2012): URL: http://data.worldbank.org/country/brazil

Weltonline (2010): Sicherheitsmängel: Defekte Bremsen zwingen Toyota zu neuem Rückrufaktionen, http://www.welt.de/wirtschaft/article10444275/Defekte-Bremsen-zwingen-Toyota-zu-neuem-Rueckruf.html

Werben und Verkaufen (2011): Facebook-Ranking – Deutsche Automarken belegen Spitzenplätze, vom 29.04.2011, http://www.wuv.de/layout/set/print/nachrichten/digital/facebook_ranking_deutsche_automarken_belegen_spitzenplaetze

WestLB, online: (2011): Exotenkurssicherung: http://www.westlb.de/cms/sitecontent/westlb/westlb_de/de/spk/prod/11/0/preisindikationen/devisenhandel/exotenkurssicherung.standard.gid-N2FkNDZmMzU4OWFmYTIyMWM3N2Q2N2Q0YmU1NmI0OGU_.html, 15.11.2011

Wiesinger, J. (2009): KFZTech – Reifen-Druck-Kontroll-Systeme, siehe: http://www.kfztech.de/kfztechnik/fahrwerk/reifen/runflat.htm, 23.05.2010

Willershausen, F. (2010): Wütende Bürger trotz Wirtschaftsaufschwung. In: Handelsblatt online, siehe: http://www.handelsblatt.com/politik/konjunktur-nachrichten/russland-nach-der-krise-wuetende-buerger-trotz-wirtschaftsaufschwung;2522836;2, 13.06.2010

Wirtschaftslexikon24 (2011): Definition Währungsmanagement, http://www.wirtschaftslexikon24.net/d/waehrungsmanagement/waehrungsmanagement.htm, 13.12.2011

Wirtschaftsministerium Baden-Württemberg, Fraunhofer IAO, WRS (2010): Strukturstudie BWe mobil. Baden-Württemberg auf dem Weg in die Elektromobilität. S. 7ff. URL: http://wrs.region-stuttgart.de/sixcms/media.php/923/Strukturstudie_BWe_Mobil.pdf

Wirtschaftswoche: Arbeitgeberranking 2010: Vorsprung durch Image. [online] URL: http://www.wiwo.de/management-erfolg/arbeitgeberranking-2010-vorsprung-durch-image-428907/. 04.05.2010.

Wirtschaftswoche (2011): http://www.wiwo.de/erfolg/jobsuche/ranking-die-beliebtesten-arbeitgeber-junger-ingenieure/5926240.html

WPP Brand Z (2011): BrandZ Top 100 Most valuable global brands, Online im Internet: http://c3232792.r92.cf0.rackcdn.com/WPP_BrandZ_2011.pdf

Xetra Deutsche Börse Group (2009): Xetra-Auktionsplan, Online im Internet: http://www.boerse-frankfurt.de/DE/index.aspx?pageID=44&NewsID=151

Xetra Deutsche Börse Group (a): Online im Internet: http://www.boerse-frankfurt.de/DE/index.aspx?pageID=201

Xetra Deutsche Börse Group (b): Online im Internet: http://www.boerse-frankfurt.de/DE/index.aspx?pageID=44&NewsID=5831

Zeit.de (2011): Bevölkerung: Deutschlands Einwohnerzahl steigt wieder, http://www.zeit.de/gesellschaft/zeitgeschehen/2012-01/einwohnerzahl-deutschland-zuwanderung

Zeit.de (2011): Leasing soll Elektroautos den Schrecken nehmen, URL: http://www.zeit.de/auto/2011-05/vertriebsmodelle-elektroauto

Ziesche, B. (2010): Interview mit Detlef Wittig über die Partnerschaft mit Suzuki [online], Verfügbar: http://autogramm.volkswagen.de/03_10/aktuell/aktuell_12.html

Zipcar (2011): Pressemitteilung: Zipcar's Second Annual Millennials Study Finds 18-34-Year-Olds Increasingly Embrace Collaborative Consumption and Access Over Ownership, http://ir.zipcar.com/releasedetail.cfm?releaseid=632391

11 Bibliography

Further internet sources:

„EconPapers: Energy Policy", zu finden unter: http://econpapers.repec.org/article/eeeenepol/

„C3 Handlungsfeld Verkehr | Klimaschutz in Kommunen – Praxisleitfaden", zu finden unter: http://www.leitfaden.kommunaler-klimaschutz.de/leitfaden/c3-handlungsfeld-verkehr.html

„Automotive News September 2010 Article Archives, page 2 | HighBeam ...", zu finden unter: http://www.highbeam.com/publications/automotive-news-p4309/September-2010/2

„Writers – Marc Rauch – 2012 Car Reviews, 2011 Car Reviews, New Car ...", zu finden unter: http://www.theautochannel.com/news/writers/mrauch/news.html

„Car – Pipl Directory", zu finden unter: http://pipl.com/directory/name/Car/5140/

„Nation-E Lauches the First Mobile Charging Station for Electric ...", zu finden unter: http://www.businesswire.com/news/home/20100912005119/en/Nation-E-Lauches-Mobile-Charging-Station-Electric-Cars

„Kommentare Geschichte WS 2011/12 – Home – Universität Regensburg", zu finden unter: http://www.uni-regensburg.de/Fakultaeten/phil_Fak_III/Geschichte/Kommentare/komgw2011.html

„UZH – Wirtschafts- und Sozialgeschichte online – Geld, Banken ...", zu finden unter: http://www.eso.uzh.ch/modul2/GeldBank.html?lesson.section=bibliography

„Innovation, learning, and exporting in China Does R&D or a ...", zu finden unter: http://wenku.baidu.com/view/326dc487ec3a87c24028c466.html

„Automotive market in Russia and the CIS Industry overview February ...", zu finden unter: http://www.ey.com/Publication/vwLUAssets/Automotive-2010-EN/$FILE/Automotive-2010-EN.pdf

„Rusya Federasyonu hakkında genel bilgiler", zu finden unter: http://www.oibrussia.org/tr/genel/

„Russia Automotive Market and the CIS 2010", zu finden unter: http://www.scribd.com/doc/46305240/Russia-Automotive-Market-and-the-CIS-2010

„Kommentare Geschichte SS 2011", zu finden unter: http://www.uni-regensburg.de/Fakultaeten/phil_Fak_III/Geschichte/Kommentare/komgs2011.html

„論文リスト（中国） – Hiroshima University", zu finden unter: http://home.hiroshima-u.ac.jp/er/ZR20.html

„Publikationen – Portal E-Campus Wirtschaft der JLU Gießen", zu finden unter: http://wiwi.uni-giessen.de/ma/pub/E-Campus/

„Die Europäische Wirtschafts- und Währungsunion", zu finden unter: http://www.uni-kassel.de/fb7/ivwl/michaelis/downloads/ewwu-debus-ws0708.pdf

„Exploring alternative theories of economic regionalism: from trade ...", zu finden unter: http://wrap.warwick.ac.uk/2029/

„Publikationsverzeichnis – Portal Fachbereich ...", zu finden unter: http://wiwi.uni-giessen.de/ma/pubvz/fb02/

„Automotive Publikationen – Ernst & Young – Deutschland", zu finden unter: http://www.ey.com/DE/de/Industries/Automotive/Publikationen

„Internationale Unternehmensfinanzierung – FinanceWiki", zu finden unter: http://finance.wiwi.tu-dresden.de/Wiki-fi/index.php/Internationale_Unternehmensfinanzierung

„Fahrgemeinschaft volksvan.de: März 2008", zu finden unter: http://fahrgemeinschaft.blogspot.com/2008_03_01_archive.html

„IDEAS: Energy Policy, Elsevier", zu finden unter: http://ideas.repec.org/s/eee/enepol1.html

„Business News", zu finden unter: http://change.ch/aktuell/news/index.html?page=34

„Bedürfnis | bpb", zu finden unter: http://www.bpb.de/wissen/5I3WZJ

„Amt für Statistik Berlin Brandenburg – Homepage", zu finden unter: http://www.statistik-berlin-brandenburg.de/Statistiken/statistik_Pm.asp?Ptyp=100&Sageb=820&creg=BBB&anzwer=0

„Wert haben und Wert sein. IBZ&L 04200700 für externe Die …", zu finden unter: http://www.markenlexikon.com/d_texte/verfahren_interbrand_ansatz.pdf

„Marken-Rangliste: Coca-Cola schlägt Microsoft – Marken-Rangliste …", zu finden unter: http://www.focus.de/finanzen/news/tid-6973/marken-rangliste_aid_67983.html

„Welcome – Automotive News Europe Congress 2012", zu finden unter: http://www.ane-congress.com/agenda http://www.ane-congress.com/speakers

„Interkulturelle Orientierung und Öffnung: Ein neues Paradigma …", zu finden unter: http://www.i-iqm.de/dokus/Interkulturelle_Orientierung%20_oeffnung.pdf

„Amazon.de: Means-End-Theorie – Bücher", zu finden unter: http://www.amazon.de/means-end-theorie-B%C3%BCcher/s?ie=UTF8&page=1&rh=n%3A186606%2Ck%3AMeans-End-Theorie

„Leseprobe – Marke und Identität im B2B-Geschäft – B2B-Handbuch …", zu finden unter: http://www.symposion.de/?cmslesen/q0002060_25920102

„baukosten-vergleich.de – Vergleichen sie effektiv ihre Baukosten", zu finden unter: http://www.baukosten-vergleich.de/

„Mobilityacademy/Home/Altersmobilität", zu finden unter: http://www.mobilityacademy.ch/home/altersmobilitaet.html

„Allterrain-Personentransporter – Jedipedia", zu finden unter: http://www.jedipedia.de/wiki/Allterrain-Personentransporter

„Währung – Private Webseite von Robert Bankwitz", zu finden unter: http://www.robawi.de/wik/themenreihe.p?c=W%C3%A4hrung

„Numismatik – Private Webseite von Robert Bankwitz", zu finden unter: http://www.robawi.de/wik/themenreihe.p?c=Numismatik

„Eurodollar – Wikipedia", zu finden unter: http://de.wikipedia.org/wiki/Eurodollar

„Electric Circuit: Free Encyclopedia Articles at Questia.com Online …", zu finden unter: http://www.questia.com/library/encyclopedia/electric-circuit.jsp?l=E&p=1

„Fisher-Effekt – Wikipedia", zu finden unter: http://de.wikipedia.org/wiki/Fisher-Effekt

„Bandbreitenoption – Wirtschaftslexikon", zu finden unter: http://www.wirtschaftslexikon24.net/d/bandbreitenoption/bandbreitenoption.htm

„Diplomarbeit/Kovacs_Diplomarbeit.pdf", zu finden unter: http://germanistik.univie.ac.at/fileadmin/user_upload/inst_germanistik/projekte/janke/Diplomarbeiten-PDF/Kovacs_Diplomarbeit.pdf

„Informelle Bewegungs-, Spiel- und Sportaktivitäten und …", zu finden unter: http://www.diplom.de/Informelle-Bewegungs---Spiel--Sportaktivitaeten-Bewegungsraeume-Kindern/14296.html

„Semantic Media Wiki – Winfwiki", zu finden unter: http://winfwiki.wi-fom.de/index.php/Semantic_Media_Wiki

„Soll-/Ist-Abgleich der Reporting-Werkzeuge im Personalcontrolling …", zu finden unter: http://www.hausarbeiten.de/faecher/vorschau/68100.html

„Rückfall und Rückfallprävention bei Alkoholabhängigen", zu finden unter: http://www.hausarbeiten.de/faecher/vorschau/147281.html

„Ideologien/Ideologie-Ideologien-Politische-Soziologie.pdf", zu finden unter: http://www.kai-arzheimer.com/Ideologie-Ideologien-Politische-Soziologie.pdf

„Vergleichende Analyse der Ansatz- und Bewertungskonzeptionen nach …", zu finden unter: http://www.uni-hamburg.de/fachbereiche-einrichtungen/fb03/iwp/rut/Arbeit810910.pdf

„Enterprise Management with SAP SEM Business Analytics", zu finden unter: http://www.docstoc.com/docs/520023/Enterprise-Management-with-SAP-SEM-Business-Analytics

„Investment Weekly News (2011-07-02) | VerticalNews", zu finden unter: http://www.verticalnews.com/premium_newsletters/Investment-Weekly-News/2011-07-02.html

„Marketing Business Weekly (2011-07-03) | VerticalNews", zu finden unter: http://www.verticalnews.com/premium_newsletters/Marketing-Business-Weekly-/2011-07-03.html

„India 2020, free PDF download", zu finden unter: http://printfu.org/india+2020

„Archive News & Video for Monday, 13 Jun 2011 | Reuters.com", zu finden unter: http://www.reuters.com/resources/archive/us/20110613.html

„(Page 1 of 4) – India's Auto Market Will Not Reach Its Full …", zu finden unter: http://www.jdpower.co.jp/press/pdf2011/India%20Automotive%202020_E.pdf

„LBS – location based service – Ortsbezogener Dienst – ITWissen.info", zu finden unter: http://www.itwissen.info/definition/lexikon/location-based-service-LBS-Ortsbezogener-Dienst.html

„Honda | Insight | Technische Daten | Daten & Preise", zu finden unter: http://honda.de/automobile/modelle_insight_technische_daten.php

„Freihandel als Chance zur Entwicklung im Zeitalter der …", zu finden unter: http://www.patrick-schunn.de/downloads/Freihandel.pdf

„Alle Neuheiten 2011, Teil 1: Neue Autos von Audi bis Lotus …", zu finden unter: http://www.autobild.de/artikel/alle-neuen-autos-2011-teil-1-1326041.html

„Honda | CR-Z | Technische Daten | Daten & Preise", zu finden unter: http://www.honda.de/automobile/modelle_cr-z_technische_daten.php

„★ホンダ インサイト終了葬式スレ 15★", zu finden unter: http://unkar.org/r/auto/1324511452, http://logsoku.com/thread/kohada.2ch.net/auto/1324511452/

„'Insight Elégance – Hybrid mit vielen Extras" Testbericht für …', zu finden unter: http://www.dooyoo.de/auto/honda-insight-1-3-hybrid/1501723/

„J.D. Power and Associates Reports: India Expected to Become the …", zu finden unter: http://www.prnewswire.com/news-releases/jd-power-and-associates-reports-india-expected-to-become-the-worlds-third-largest-light-vehicle-market-by-2020-however-profits-not-likely-to-match-two-largest-markets-china-and-the-united-states-123741299.html

„Rückstellungen 2010 | Jahresabschluss, BilMoG | wer-weiss-was", zu finden unter: http://www.wer-weiss-was.de/Anfragen/www_de/archiv/382657/rueckstellungen-2010.html

„Mobilität der Zukunft: CFK – ein Werkstoff der Zukunft.", zu finden unter: http://www.7-forum.com/news/Mobilitaet-der-Zukunft-CFK-ein-Werkstoff-3420.html

„Twizy Urban – bi-place Electrique – Renault Z.E.", zu finden unter: http://www.renault-ze.com/de-de/modelle-z.e./twizy/twizy-urban-652.html

„BMW-Standorte Landshut und Wackersdorf in Vorbereitung für die …", zu finden unter: http://www.7-forum.com/news/BMW-Standorte-Landshut-Wackersdorf-in-V-3450.html

„News: SGL Group", zu finden unter: http://www.sglgroup.com/cms/international/investor-relations/news/index.html?__locale=de

„BMW Teams Up With, Invests $5 Million In MyCityWay | TechCrunch", zu finden unter: http://techcrunch.com/2011/02/25/bmw-teams-up-with-invests-5-million-in-mycityway/

„Renault Twizy Z.E. Concept – 2WiD", zu finden unter: http://www.2wid.net/Auto/Antriebsvarianten/Elektroautos/Modelle/Prototypen/Markenhersteller/KleinPKW/st44475/renault-ze.com-de-de-gamme-voitures-electriques-renault-z.e.-twi

„Velomobil als Elektroauto mit 60km/h??? GO-ONE??? ca. 3KW? [Archiv …", zu finden unter: http://www.pedelecforum.de/forum/archive/index.php/t-9966.html

„CARE Deutschland-Luxemburg – Wikipedia", zu finden unter: http://de.wikipedia.org/wiki/CARE_Deutschland-Luxemburg

„Fundsachen Buchbranche – Wirtschaftsbuch", zu finden unter: https://sites.google.com/site/wirtschaftsbuch/fundsachen-buchbranche

„A.T. Kearney – Veröffentlichungen – Automobil- und Zulieferindustrie", zu finden unter: http://www.atkearney.de/content/veroeffentlichungen/industriepractices_practice.php/practice/automotive

„BMW in Not – E-Mini gebastelt [Archiv] – Pedelec-Forum", zu finden unter: http://www.pedelecforum.de/forum/archive/index.php/t-518.html

„Volkswagen Introduces New Russian Budget Car | Business | The …", zu finden unter: http://www.themoscowtimes.com/business/article/volkswagen-introduces-new-russian-budget-car/407439.html

„Wirtschaftsdaten Dänemark – Arbeitsgemeinschaft der Industrie …", zu finden unter: http://www.ihk-schleswig-holstein.de/international/laenderschwerpunkt_dk/735616/wirtschaftsdaten_daenemark.html

„Luxusautos: Moskau ist die Hauptstadt des Maybach – Nachrichten …", zu finden unter: http://www.welt.de/motor/article1966183/Moskau-ist-die-Hauptstadt-des-Maybach.html

„Controlling-Konzeptionen revisited: Definition von …", zu finden unter: http://mpra.ub.uni-muenchen.de/10503/

„Kapitalflussrechnung/Kapitalflussrechnung.pdf", zu finden unter: http://cms.uni-kassel.de/unicms/fileadmin/groups/w_030117/HGB-IFRS/Kapitalflussrechnung.pdf

„Model Development of Logistical and Economic Performance …", zu finden unter: http://www.grin.com/en/e-book/123925/model-development-of-logistical-and-economic-performance-evaluation-as

„Der Tagesnews Thread [Archiv] – Seite 3 – Alfa Forum Schweiz", zu finden unter: http://www.alfisti.ch/forum/archive/index.php/t-6128-p-3.html

„Wie viele Mitarbeiter hat BMW in Deutschland und weltweit? (Autos)", zu finden unter: http://www.gutefrage.net/frage/wie-viele-mitarbeiter-hat-bmw-in-deutschland-und-weltweit

„project paper to SAP Riskmanagement functionality", zu finden unter: http://de.scribd.com/doc/23951044/project-paper-to-SAP-Riskmanagement-functionality

„Ökonomie mit Energie | Literatur", zu finden unter: http://www.oekonomie-mit-energie.de/index.php?id=29

„Corporate Social Responsibility und ihre Relevanz in der …", zu finden unter: http://www.munich-business-school.de/intercultural/index.php/Corporate_Social_Responsibility_und_ihre_Relevanz_in_der_Luftfahrtbranche

11 Bibliography

„Die Bewertung einer Genossenschaftsbank mittels Discounted Cash Flow", zu finden unter: http://www.docstoc.com/docs/42462177/Die-Bewertung-einer-Genossenschaftsbank-mittels-Discounted-Cash-Flow

„Unternehmensbewertung, Modul Unternehmensrechnung II, fachliches …", zu finden unter: http://www.wiwiss.fu-berlin.de/institute/pruefungs-steuerlehre/ruhnke/Dokumente/LV_Diplom_Bachelor/UB_SS08/Glied_UB_SS2008.pdf

„Soja, Faszination Regenwald", zu finden unter: http://www.faszination-regenwald.de/info-center/zerstoerung/soja.htm

„Erläuterung zum Arbeitsaufwand (work load)", zu finden unter: http://pflege.sw.fh-jena.de/downloads/Modulhandbuch_bachelor.pdf

„Drehscheibe Online Foren – 01 – News – Schienen weg in …", zu finden unter: http://www.drehscheibe-foren.de/foren/read.php?2,4368116,page=all

„Publications – Science Policy | WZB", zu finden unter: http://www.wzb.eu/en/research/society-and-economic-dynamics/science-policy/publications

„Folie 1", zu finden unter: http://www.christianeeichenberg.de/hieb.ppt

„Barrierefreiheit in HTML5 – Winfwiki", zu finden unter: http://winfwiki.wi-fom.de/index.php/Barrierefreiheit_in_HTML5

„Siim Kallas – Vizepräsident der Europäischen Kommission", zu finden unter: http://ec.europa.eu/commission_2010-2014/kallas/headlines/press-releases/2011/03/index_de.htm

„Elektroautos [Archiv] – forum.ksta.de", zu finden unter: http://forum.ksta.de/archive/index.php/t-5952.html

„Reise nach Moskau. was sollte ich dort sehen? (Russland)", zu finden unter: http://www.gutefrage.net/frage/reise-nach-moskau-was-sollte-ich-dort-sehen

„Deutsche Umwelthilfe e.V.: Kontrolle des Reifendrucks", zu finden unter: http://www.duh.de/2622.html

„Der neue Chevrolet Captiva: Ein Kompakt-SUV für alle Lebenslagen", zu finden unter: http://www.chevrolet.de/chevrolet-erleben/neuigkeiten/2011/neuigkeiten-2011-overview-news/news-details-2011-08.html

„Publikationen – Wissenschaftspolitik | WZB", zu finden unter: http://www.wzb.eu/de/forschung/gesellschaft-und-wirtschaftliche-dynamik/wissenschaftspolitik/publikationen

„BBSR Informationen zur Raumentwicklung", zu finden unter: http://www.bbsr.bund.de/nn_23470/BBSR/DE/Veroeffentlichungen/IzR/2010/7/autoren.html

„Charles Franklin Kettering — Infoplease.com", zu finden unter: http://www.infoplease.com/ipa/A0767162.html

„Innovationszentrum für Mobilität und gesellschaftlichen Wandel …", zu finden unter: http://www.innoz.de/fileadmin/INNOZ/pdf/Bausteine/innoz-baustein-06.pdf

„Fließheckmodell des Chevrolet Cruze feiert Weltpremiere in Genf", zu finden unter: http://www.chevrolet.de/chevrolet-erleben/neuigkeiten/2011/neuigkeiten-2011-overview-news/news-details-2011-07.html

Printed in Poland
by Amazon Fulfillment
Poland Sp. z o.o., Wrocław